SIBERIAN DAWN

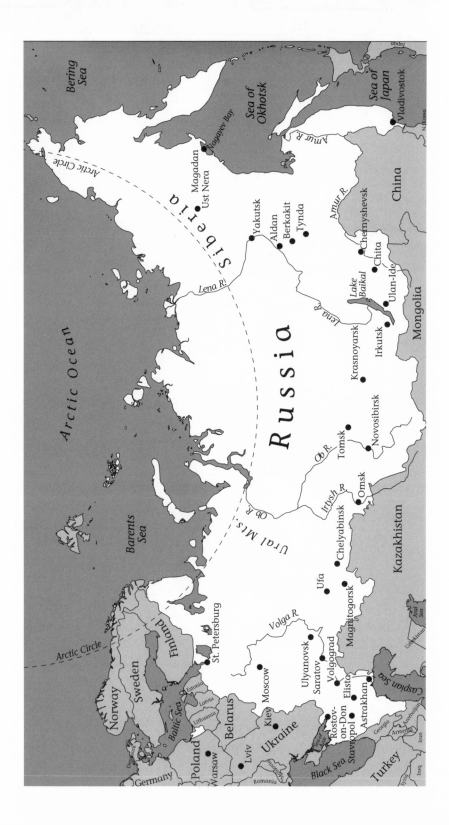

Siberian Dawn

A Journey across the New Russia

Jeffrey Tayler

RUMINATOR BOOKS

ST. PAUL · MINNESOTA

Published by Ruminator Books
1648 Grand Avenue
Saint Paul, MN 55105
www.ruminator.com

ISBN: 1-886913-40-4
Library of Congress Control Number: 00-131295

10   9   8   7   6   5   4   3   2   1
First paperback edition, 2000

Cover design by Krystyna Skalski
Cover photographs by Jeffrey Tayler
Book design by Will Powers and Wendy Holdman
Typesetting by Stanton Publication Services
St. Paul, Minnesota

AUTHOR'S NOTE:
To protect the privacy of the
people described herein,
I have changed some of their names.

Printed in the United States of America

"All places are distant from heaven alike."
ROBERT BURTON, *The Anatomy of Melancholy*

I would gratefully like to acknowledge the efforts of the following people who helped me in the preparation of this book: Elizabeth Houde for putting me up in Moscow at the journey's start and finish; Dr. Vanessa Van Ornam of Middlebury College for her careful reading of and comments on the first manuscript; Paul Hesse and Diana Derry for their suggestions and support; Tatyana V. Shchukina; Mary Dent Crisp; my mother, father, and sister for their encouragement; Brigitte Frase, my editor, for her inspirational whiplashing and scissoring; and my agent, Sonia Land, for sticking by the book through thick and thin and seeing it off to publication. My thanks to you all.

Contents

Prologue

My fascination with Russia began in America during my teen years, the 1970s. The magnitude of everything Russian enthralled me: the distance from one end of the country to the other, the extremes of temperatures that ranged from arctic to subtropical, the thousand-year history, the massive arsenals of nuclear weapons, the epochal threat the ideology of the Soviet state seemed to pose to the rest of the world. I imagined that a great drama was being played out daily across the land in cities and towns I knew only as points on a map. Indeed, for me, the Soviet Union (and Russia) were the very incarnation of human tragedy: strange as it may seem, reading chronicles of war, of famine, of expansion across inhospitable steppe and forest, and of near-satanic dictators infused me with a yearning to enmesh myself in the country's fate; if I made myself part of Russia, I felt, I would fill some void within myself, unite myself with something far greater, something, tragic or no, as timeless and boundless and grand as the Russian steppes.

There were, thus, no practical considerations at all involved in the genesis of my relationship with Russia, no utilitarian motives: it was a case of irrational infatuation. No lover of Russia is a practical person.

I took up Russian in 1982 while studying in Florence, Italy, in my senior year of college. During that year I began traveling to socialist Eastern Europe and felt energized by the very proximity of the Soviet border. In 1985, while a graduate student in Russian history at the University of Virginia, I spent two months touring the western part of the Soviet Union with a group; the restrictions imposed on our trip—preset itinerary, compulsory guides, KGB surveillance—only convinced me that the drama I had suspected was real and ongoing, and it was all the more intriguing because it was revealed to me in snatches and snippets. I left the country determined to get Soviet dirt under my nails, dreaming of a grand Russian adventure, of a crucible that would temper me and realize the romantic notions of my adolescence.

In September of 1992 I thought I had a chance to do this. I took the job of starting up a Peace Corps post in newly independent Uzbekistan (I had asked to be sent to Russia but Uzbekistan was as close as the Peace Corps would let me get). The experience in Tashkent, for reasons too complicated to warrant explanation here, proved disappointing professionally and devastating personally.

One day just after New Year's 1993 in Moscow, I stood gazing out of my window in the Radisson-Slavjanskaya Hotel by Kiev Station into the early-morning haze of snow and aqueous mist. CNN blared from the television. My suit hung pressed in the closet, crisp from the dry cleaners; the black leather of my shoes gleamed untouched by Moscow's slush. Beneath my window, Muscovites padded silently across the snowy streets leading to the station. Only the echoing calls of the stationmaster announcing trains reached my room; otherwise, I might as well have been watching a silent movie about Russia. I was not living Russia, or even Tashkent. The money and amenities of my job shielded me from the grit of the land, kept me above its life, and created a distance between me and its people, any one of whose entire monthly salary would have not covered, at that time, an evening of drinks at the hotel bar downstairs. I was inside a fishbowl looking out. I felt that I was betraying my dream and, in a way, my hosts, whom most visiting Westerners—especially those in the humanitarian aid community—viewed as children in need of Western wisdom and a stern, Western-style reeducation. I realized at that moment that I would never be able to know Russia as long as the country remained an exhibit I could exit by flashing a fistful of dollars at the doorman of an exclusive hotel.

So I quit my job. Two months later I was back in Moscow, planning to fly some forty-five hundred miles east to Magadan and cross the entire landmass of the former Soviet Union. This would entail traveling along an 8,325-mile route that would take me from the frozen reaches of the Russian Far East across Siberia, through the Urals, into the Black Earth zone and, finally, over the Ukrainian-Polish border to Warsaw by whatever means it took: hitchhiking with truckers, taking cars, buses, trains, and boats. At least such were my plans. Other Westerners had trained their way from Moscow to Vladivostok, but no one, as far as I knew, had set out to traverse Russia starting in Magadan. Through this trip I aimed to come to grips with Russia by submitting to a watershed ordeal that would tear down my own outlook on life and replace it with the Russian; I wanted to fuse my fate with the country's in a crucible of my own making.

I brought very little with me to Moscow. I carried only what I could stuff into an overnight bag, along with a satchel for my camera, four lenses, and some film. All of this, I figured, I could afford to lose or jettison if need be. My appearance was, at least, not distinctly un-Russian, and my Russian allowed me to pass, if not for a Russian, for a Soviet citizen from one of the Baltic republics. To cover expenses, I took about nine hundred dollars cash in small bills—a hefty wad—and carried it in a money belt around my waist. This would have to suffice for the three or four months I'd be on the road—it was all I had at the time. I had a year-long multiple-entry visa, but, distressingly, it was designated for Moscow only (Russian visas are city-specific). I asked in the American embassy if this would cause me trouble in the outback; they didn't know. No one could tell me or would even hazard a guess about how officials in remote reaches of the country would react to me; no one knew how well promulgated the U.S.-Russia Open Lands Agreement (jointly abolishing most restrictions on travel by foreigners in both countries) had been.

Russia was in turmoil in March 1993, when I began my trip. Boris Yeltsin had imposed presidential rule in his struggle with the reactionary Supreme Soviet, and confrontation was looming. Crime, especially violent crime, had increased tremendously, and much of it was directed at foreigners. Once-docile Soviet republics were declaring their independence and trying to find their way without Moscow. Local Soviet chieftains were setting up fiefdoms for themselves. Communists had renamed themselves as democrats but stifled reforms dictated by Moscow at every turn. Warnings issued from all quarters that a return to totalitarianism might be the outcome of the prevailing anarchy.

If the primum mobile of my trip was passion, there was indeed a stark political consideration to ponder, and one I believed justified my trip from a practical perspective: what was happening in Russia was critical for the future of the world. Despite the fall of communism, Russians and Westerners, especially Americans, knew and understood each other very little in 1993, and this has not really changed. If Russia is no longer the domain of Sovietologists, it is now, sadly, a land where no particular expertise serves to solve still-regnant riddles and enigmas. The volume of travel between the United States and Russia for average citizens of both lands has increased, but not as significantly as one might have expected, owing to the same bureaucratic hurdles that existed in the past on both sides. Americans and Russians, thus, have little *personal* knowledge of each other. This is distressing because both peoples are too powerful, too pivotal not to affect the rest of the world. I hoped my trip and the resulting book would in some way address this deficiency.

I chose as a starting point Magadan, on the shores of the frozen Sea of Okhotsk, because it was the gulag capital of the former Soviet Union, a ground zero of despair that symbolized the prison hell of the Stalin decades; if I could escape it, and succeed in crossing the entire country, I would have, I believed, played my own small role in the drama of the land, whether I made it all the way to Poland or not. These ideas did nothing to placate the fears of my Russian friends, who said that this was the wrong time to make such a trip. They cautioned that there was a risk of my simply disappearing along the way, that the odds were against me given the distances and terrain, both geographic and political, I would have to cover. And, they added, the route from Magadan was especially perilous. But I was determined to start from there: if Magadan was a city renowned for death and petrified gulag despair, it was also one of the first places where the shades of dawn warmed Russian soil.

SIBERIAN DAWN

ONE

Moscow and Russia's Unruly Elements

"This is a bad time here," said the driver, clenching a cigarette between his teeth, as we shot out of Sheremet'yevo Airport down Moscow's dark and empty causeways, rifling stray newspapers with drafts of displaced frigid air. "Our Supreme Soviet is about ready to force Yeltsin out. Who'll be the alternative? The speaker of the Parliament, Khasbulatov? He'd be worse than Stalin. He lies and looks you straight in the eye while doing so. And he *knows* you *know* he's lying. There'll be civil war if he takes over."

A banner fluttered over the road: RUSSIAN CINEMATOGRA-PHERS SUPPORT YELTSIN! We flew under it and ran a red light.

As the driver balanced his forearms on the wheel he lit another cigarette.

"Don't worry. The police have other things besides red lights to worry about these days. Say, where did you say you were from?"

We had already agreed on the fare, so I told him I was from the States.

"American! You should have told me so! I get fifty dollars from foreigners for this ride into town. That's what you should be paying!"

"We've already agreed on the price. Why should I have told you where I'm from if I'd have to pay ten times more for the same ride?"

"You earn ten times more, that's why. But no matter—this time, I'll let it go."

We pulled up in front of the building of my American friend Betsy. Three police cars flew past us, shouting through their loud-speakers into the March gusts, heading toward demonstrations down at the Kremlin. Moscow was tense: people stepped lively around blinking police lights, hurried by their sirens.

Betsy put me up for the few days I was to stay in Moscow. She introduced me to her grim bodyguard-assistant, Sasha, a veteran commando from the war in Afghanistan, and told me I might ask him for pointers on my trip. Sasha thought it sounded like a bad idea ("It's dangerous outside the Moscow Oblast. There are un-ruly elements everywhere, and there's not even food in many places"). He suggested I take a gun, and so did Betsy. Both thought I should get more advice from Russians before starting out. To placate them, I decided to call two Russian friends I had in Kiev, Valya and Oleg, whom I had known since my 1985 trip. Both got on the line.

"This could all turn out very badly," said Oleg. "Now is ab-solutely the wrong time for such an adventure. As terrible as our system was under the Soviets, there was at least order in the streets. Now there is no more dangerous country than ours, and we have the Bolsheviks to thank for it. They destroyed our moral-ity and built in its place a system of repression that has made peo-ple vicious. Wait a couple of years, and then try it. Yeltsin may not last—you see what's happened in Moscow since he declared presi-dential rule—and without him we'll have civil war. If you're caught out there and things blow up—"

Valya jumped in.

"To put it mildly, this is an ill-conceived idea. You will be all alone out there in places we'd never go. You should thank the thug who decides to rob but not kill you! Take a gun, or at least a gas grenade."

"Or a knife!" shouted Oleg.

Although I had no intention of buying a gun and regarded myself as lucky, all the warnings and fears and objections voiced by my Russian friends and Sasha took their toll on me, and I slept very badly the next few nights. I did my best to keep in mind what drove me to undertake the trip, but an image haunted my mind's eye: I was racing toward an abyss, and all my assertions that I knew the risks and could handle them would be of no use when I hurtled over its edge.

But I fortified myself with a vignette from my past, a memory that sustained me during my most difficult moments. Nine years earlier, during a March just as gloomy and disconsolate, I had climbed a stony path to a small cemetery above Iráklion, on the island of Crete. The grave of the writer Nikos Kazantzakis had drawn me there. Thunderclouds brooded over the mountains beyond the town. A wind whirled dust around crosses standing crooked over the recumbent dead, but there, atop Kazantzakis's grave, inscribed in stone, were three simple lines that were to become like haiku or a mantra for me:

> I hope for nothing.
> I fear nothing.
> I am free.

It seemed to me then, in 1984, that such a state without fear, where no hopes for the future stole energy from living in the present, would signify the dawn of true liberation, a fierce bliss of *now* rendered more intense by knowing tomorrow might not come. In Moscow, I meditated on these lines and tried to conceive of the freedom this trip would offer: the opportunity to exist solely in the present, to shape it and be shaped by it, and to utterly renounce the notion that tomorrow mattered, that anything existed but a *now* that had to be both accommodated and conquered.

I also believed in fate, that something had tied my life to Russia and would continue to do so, and that what I experienced on Russian soil would be to my ultimate benefit. But this abstract conviction did not offer me protection—it could, in fact, lead me to my destruction, fate not being synonymous with the guardianship of Providence. But now, having resigned from my job with the Peace Corps, and having made my way to Moscow for the sole purpose of undertaking the trip, I was coming up against something truly destructive and disheartening: the well-meaning, but ominous, words of friends, their descriptions of what they "knew" I would find in the farthest reaches of Russia. I argued against them during the day, but at night, they dogged me, gave me nightmares, and wouldn't let me recover from jet lag. The only consolation I could see was to buy my plane ticket to Magadan and leave as soon as possible; better to hurl myself clear of the abyss's edge with bold momentum than to hesitate and risk crashing down its walls from crag to jagged crag.

Betsy had come to Moscow with her two teenage children, Joe and Stephanie. One afternoon in the apartment, Stephanie dropped into my room as I was making an entry in my journal and plopped herself into a chair, holding her nails out to dry. There was someone she thought I ought to meet, she said.

"You're going to Magadan, right? There's this guy I know from there. His name is Steve. I call him Steve although he doesn't speak English and his real name is Stanislav. He likes me, and always stands around in our stairwell waiting for me to come out. He's studying here in Moscow. I should introduce the two of you. He might as well be of use to someone, instead of standing around in the stairwell all day."

A few minutes later, as I was poring over my National Geographic map of Russia, Steve came in. He was tall and broad-shouldered, with black, short-cropped hair, and skin so white it appeared never to have seen the sun. He shivered, still cold from being out on the stairs. We shook hands. He was a bit awkward, as teenagers can be, but hearty and sober.

"Can I see your map?" he asked. "Oh, it's in English. Where's Magadan?"

I showed him. He squinted at it and sniffled.

"So what is it you are planning to do?"

"I'm going to Magadan. From there, I want to cross by land to Yakutsk, by this road here."

I drew my finger along the thin tentative red line wavering from Magadan inland. Its thinness worried me: the key defined such a scribble as "road or highway," leading me to consider that it could be anything from a dirt track to an asphalt throughway, although it was not nearly as substantial a line as those zigzagging over western Russia, which at best, I knew, represented two-lane highways in ill repair.

Steve squinted at the line, looked up at my face, and dropped his eyes to the map again.

"What they're showing here is not a road but the Kolyma Route, a sort of track built by gulag prisoners in the thirties. It goes only to Ust-Nera, about halfway. After that, there's nothing. Only a *zimnik* [winter track, passable only when frozen, from the Russian *zima*, or winter]. We don't go by land to Yakutsk from Magadan. We fly."

Magadan was a natural prison, walled by the Arctic Circle to the north, the Sea of Okhotsk to the south, and ice-bound mountains to the west and east. In the past, prisoners were ferried there by boat from Vladivostok. I had seen the line on my map and thought a road had been built since those days.

"Are you saying it's impossible to cross to Yakutsk from Magadan by land?"

"It's possible, but only during the winter. We never do it, but sometimes trucks make the run. The problem is that the *zimnik* may have thawed by now—you may be too late. And then there's the issue of your safety. Trucks are often robbed once they cross from Kolyma into Yakutia. Drivers carry guns now."

"I'll worry about my safety when I get there, but the possibility that I might fly all the way to Magadan and not be able to get out because of the mud bothers me."

Steve agreed to call his father in Magadan and ask him if the *zimnik* was still passable. The next day, Stephanie brought him up from the stairwell. He shivered on his way in and shook my hand.

"I've talked to my father. He's not sure about the *zimnik*—no one has made the run lately. But he's given me a name to give you. When you get to Magadan, go see Alexander. He runs a local newspaper. Don't try to do anything on your own, he says. It's dangerous these days. Two Russians who tried to hitch last year were killed on the route."

The next day I was to depart. Stephanie sat and watched me pack.

"Do think you'll make it?" she asked absentmindedly.

"Of course. I'm not traveling through a war zone. Russians love to tell people how bad things are now. I think they're exaggerating."

"Sasha thinks you'll be killed. But then what does he know?"

Betsy was flitting about the kitchen nervously, slicing ham, buttering bread, and slapping the two together into sandwiches.

"You remember what Sasha said—you may find that there's no food, so I'm making you some sandwiches." She stuffed them all into a plastic bag and threw in some mandarin oranges and cheese, all with hurried motions driven by nervous energy. "At least you can eat this on the plane. Sasha is downstairs with your car."

Down at the entrance, Betsy and I found Sasha, but no car.

I looked at Sasha, who leaned against the railing, arms folded on his chest. His sullen eyes were fixed on me.

There were put-puts and bursts of backfire. It sounded as

though the Beverly Hillbillies were rolling up in their jalopy; instead, a battered Zhiguli taxi, half brown and half orange, sputtered to a stop in front of us.

Sasha and the driver, Dima, exchanged greetings, and we all said good-bye. I tossed my bag in the back and jumped in. To my annoyance, I discovered sticky brown paint on my hands—I'd touched the brown patches on the yellow door getting in.

"I couldn't get yellow paint. Brown was all they had," griped Dima, as though my groan on seeing the paint had more to do with his sense of decor than the sticky blotches on my fingers. He handed me a rag and I set about trying to wipe it off. We sputtered out of Betsy's lot onto Novy Arbat Street toward Domodedovo Airport.

When we chugged past the city limits and the road split off into drab woods littered with dirty snow, the gearbox began puffing an acrid brown smoke. Dima waved his hand furiously to disperse it. I reached for the window latch but found it had been broken off. Dima said, "Open your door," and I did, holding it ajar the rest of the way to the airport.

TWO

Chasing the Dawn
to Magadan

I remember . . . how we ascended the gang-plank
and entered the cold and gloomy holds.
Embracing one another like brothers, the prisoners
Groaned from the rocking of the ship. . . .
Upon the morn, as the mists melted away . . .
Magadan arose ahead of us,
Capital of Kolyma Krai.

FROM A RUSSIAN GULAG SONG

My breath puffed ahead of me as I forced my bag down the narrow aisle. Snow was blowing in through the door and settling on the carpet; it didn't melt. The plane was cold, and the flight attendant, wearing a parka over her blue-and-white Aeroflot jacket, emerged from her cabin with only the tips of her fingers protruding from her cuffs. She stopped, took a predatory look at the passengers settling into their seats, and sniffled. There were some thirty of us for a hundred spaces, and it looked as though the extra space might compensate for the bony seats and swatches of carpet curling up at the edges of the aisle. Paying no attention to places assigned on our tickets, we dispersed down the cabin and stretched out in the deserted rows.

The attendant wasted no time.

"This is not your seat! This is not your seat!" She moved down the aisle, scrutinizing tickets, snorting puffs of frosty air, and drawing her parka tighter around her waist. "You'll have to move to your assigned seat!"

There was no sense in this. The plane was almost empty and would remain so for eight nonstop hours to Magadan. She went on badgering and bullying, and within a few minutes had set most of the passengers into motion; bags rustled, feet were stepped on, carpet tripped over, and the cabin buzzed with grumbling and grousing and rasping nylon parkas, but Aeroflot's seating plan was fulfilled. When the relocations were completed, all of the passengers ended up in the first seven rows, and many discovered that their seats either reclined permanently or were jammed upright. Mine had a rod running crosswise that poked me in the tailbone. The pilot's call to order came, and we took off into the flurries and dull evening light.

After some fourteen flights around the former Soviet Union, I considered myself an Aeroflot veteran, but there was something especially disquieting about this one, or rather, about those around me. Green parkas bulged bizarrely, hair was scraggly and frizzled, hands were cracked and raw, faces were dazed with resignation. It occurred to me that had I been asked to identify this group elsewhere, I might have taken them for newly released prisoners, or survivors of a failed Arctic expedition; they were not going somewhere that permitted the luxury of a smile.

When we gained altitude and leveled out, the craft warmed, and the passengers again dispersed down the aisle. The stewardess appeared with dinner, trays of chicken gristle and grease. I declined and gratefully munched on Betsy's sandwiches. The man next to me prodded the bones with his fork, tapped at the stale bread crust, and raised his eyes to the stewardess.

"What *is* this?

"I know, I know. Don't complain to me about it. We are obliged to serve it to you. You are not obliged to eat it."

I finished my sandwiches and pulled out a book, but found it impossible to concentrate and soon put it down. As the plane shot into the night I thought about all I had left behind to make this trip—my American friends in the Peace Corps, the Russians I had met in Tashkent, my family in the States. I suddenly realized how alone I was. A numbness crept over me—I dared not compare it to the numbness of the prisoners shipped to Magadan in Stalin's day, but there seemed to be some similarity: our destination was unknown and unknowable from the world of western Russia. I dozed off, having wrapped myself into a bundle with my coat and scarf and curled up by the window.

My sleep was sporadic and interspersed with fitful wakefulness. We coursed east through a hurried night and emerged into an auroral half-light, dawn somewhere over Siberia. Our altitude was low enough that the landscape beneath us was visible. A featureless plain of white, gray-veined with frozen waterways, spread in oblique expanses beyond the realm of the discernible. Nothing caught my eye, and the monotony of the snowy void lulled me back into interludes of slumber still infused with the anxiety I had felt about my trip just before leaving. Dreams haunted me with vignettes of my childhood, of my mother and father and sister at our house at the beach, of Christmas mornings long since past and grandparents long since dead. My life seemed to be passing before my eyes, then vanishing into somnolent mist.

Hours later, I awoke with a start—as if from a nightmare—a steely glint striking me in the eye. We had banked in almost imperceptible descent, and I drew myself up to the window. A sterilizing arctic radiance rebounded off the whiteness below, playing upon the snow-bound *sopki* (low hills of eastern Siberia), some of which were rolling, some angular and harsh, but all stood bleak and battered by hoary gales that intensified as we neared the ground and hammered at our craft with such velocity that its wings wobbled and its flaps trembled. I drew down the polarized glass panel on the window, replacing glare with a shimmer that tinctured the desolate *sopki* with an unearthly copper sheen.

As we descended, the tops of needleless pines emerged suppliant from the snow, like the outstretched bony hands of starving prisoners. A fury of side winds lashed us in the final stretch, but we continued a long, low descent. No banks, no turns; a thud and a skid and we were on the ice in Magadan.

As we taxied down the runway, everyone grabbed at handbags and suitcases and pushed into the aisle. The plane lurched to a halt, leaving us listening to gusts of wind outside, some blustery, others sibilant and plaintive. A gangplank was driven up, and the attendant struggled to release the hatch lock. It sprang free and the door flew open.

As I approached the hatch, I was seized by the impression that we were all walking toward a freezer door opened to reveal an interior of blinding white, above which hovered a huge helicopter, whose propeller blades broke frost free from the freezer's crevices and drove it into a white maelstrom. I emerged with the others onto the mobile stairs, gripping my bag, and began to make my way down. An icy blast hurled us all against the railing, and the man ahead of me nearly lost his footing on the steps.

The airport building was a deserted Quonset hut. No stranded passengers, no gauntlet of cabbies, no flight announcements echoed within. Only two high-cheekboned, blond, young Russian women in fur hats sat behind the kiosk near the exit. Their skin was creamy, the fur on their hats lustrous.

I asked them about hotels in town.

"Hotel? Yes, there is a hotel, but it's in Magadan," said one, peering at me with puzzled sympathy. I wondered what sort of sight I must be presenting to them.

"Well, I'm in Magadan, right?"

She smiled and leaned forward, pointing toward the exit to the street.

"You're in the settlement of Uptar. Magadan is some thirty-five kilometers to the east. The bus will let you off by the Hotel Magadan."

There was one bus on the icy lot. The other passengers' faces looked like masks of deep ruts and raw furrows. Alcoholics who slept on the streets in Moscow looked like this.

Our bus creaked down the Kolyma Route, never topping twenty miles per hour. The road was cracked in places, iced over in others, and often chopped into bits for stretches. Steve's words about this being the "good part" echoed in my mind. Now and then, we stopped to discharge passengers at barrack-like settlements on opposing folds of *sopki*. No people in sight, no trees higher than a man scraggled through the ice. Kolyma's frosts had killed all color, leaving only the sterile white of snow and grays of pine trunks and rocks.

"Do you have a room?"

The lobby was cavernous, the windows cracked in places, encrusted in rime in others. The administrator sat impassively filling out forms. Like the women at the airport, she was young and her skin was exquisite porcelain.

"Yes, we do. Passport!"

I thought of my Moscow-only visa.

She glanced at it and handed it back to me.

"I can't read this," she said perfunctorily. "Please read me the details in Russian."

She had not even looked at the visa, but gave up on seeing Latin letters on the passport. I read her everything but the "Moscow" part of the visa, and she asked no more questions.

As I was filling out my registration form, a wizened man

barged up to the counter in a coat so bulky and rasping it almost drowned out his voice as he moved his arms.

"*Devushka* [Girl]! Where can I plug in my telephone!"

"Our rooms have no phones."

"*Devushka,* I know that! That's why I've brought my own."

"Then hook it up!"

"*Devushka,* there's no outlet!"

"That's because our rooms have no phones," she said, and handed me my key. The man and his parka rasped away.

After settling into my room, I decided to stay awake until nine that evening to beat the jet lag. That gave me six hours to kill. Just enough for a good look around town, I figured.

Huge, grimy shards of ice covered Magadan's roads and sidewalks. People trod carefully, taking tiny steps and looking down a lot. Cars were few. A wind gusted from atop Lenin Street—Magadan's main road—and it was clear from its wrenching chill that it came from the Sea of Okhotsk. The grit on the main streets permitted a foothold, but the ice was as slick as glass in the back alleys. I dropped into stores now and again to get an idea of the progress the free market had made, but shelves were nearly bare. I noticed, though, that I was invisible; no one stared or even looked my way. It was comforting to know I was not so obviously foreign. Then again, who would be inclined to look? The icy wind kept everyone's head down and focused gazes inward.

Prisoners built Magadan during the early years of Stalin's reign. It was originally a gulag town, known popularly as Maglag, or Magadan Camp. Its buildings looked like barracks and were pockmarked, as if pustules of ice had festered on their surfaces and burst. Over one such barrack hung several newspaper logos, and it occurred to me that I might come across Alexander there. Inside, most of the offices were closed up, but I found one woman at her desk going through papers. Her head nodded rapidly, almost as a sparrow's might. She sat erect with the plainness and exactitude of a grade school librarian and appeared to be in her mid-forties. I told her I was looking for the editorial office.

"May I ask where you're from?"

She and her friend, a woman sitting in a lethargic lump behind some poetry anthologies, were astonished to find an American wandering around in their workplace. They sold books for the publishing house and had never come across non-Russians in Magadan.

The schoolmarmish one began fidgeting to and fro, tidying up her book selections.

"Oh, no. It can't be! You are our first foreigner! My name is Klara," she said, "and this is Lyudmila! May I give you a present?" She was blushing. She handed me a book of poems by a Kolyma author. "I proofread this edition. See? Here's my name next to 'proofread by.' And *what* are you doing here in Magadan?"

I began to thank her for the book when Lyudmila interrupted.

"May I give you a present, too? Take this book on Vadim Kozin. Be seated. I will bring you tea."

Klara objected.

"Perhaps the American would like coffee."

"He won't like our coffee."

"Or perhaps he would like tea, then, but with milk and pie!"

As they argued, a little blond boy came in, whom Klara introduced as her nephew, Yura. She whispered something to him, and he ran to the phone and dialed.

"Mama, we've got an American here and we're about to feed him pie!" he shouted. We all laughed. Klara raced out and reappeared with tea and pie. Yura continued, "Now the American is eating our pie!"

Klara asked my name.

"*Dzheff?*" Klara repeated after me, Russifying the *J*. "How do you like Magadan?"

"Well, I've only just—"

"Eat your pie, please! You were saying—"

"Thank you. I've only just—"

"And drink your tea!"

She fidgeted with her book selections.

"You don't like it here, do you?" she asked.

"Actually," I said, "I've only just—"

"Lyuba! Lara!" Klara shouted to two women passing by.

"We have an American here!"

The two giggled and ran off. Klara was unperturbed.

"So how is Magadan for you?"

"I've only just arrived. I haven't seen much yet."

"Admit it—it's a hole, isn't it? Our weather is terrible. Only in July can we really go outside."

A large blond woman stepped in wearing an enormous baby-blue overcoat and fur hat resembling a raccoon perched atop her head. Klara introduced us.

"Dzheff, this is . . . a customer!"

We both smiled a bit awkwardly, I especially so, since my mouth was full of pie. "Customer" listened to us banter for a few moments, then turned to me.

"If you're interested in learning about Magadan, read this!" She pointed to Evgeniia Ginzburg's *A Precipitous Journey* on the book table. Klara and Lyudmila agreed with her.

"Eat more pie . . . These are more customers . . . Your tea is getting cold . . . Perhaps you need more milk," Klara continued nonstop. When she thought I wasn't looking, she set about frantically stuffing her graying temple hairs under her hair bow, doing all this as a little bird would, with precise pecking motions. Lyudmila sat immobile as a log and stared at me in a vaguely maternal way. I felt touched by their attention. I was still disoriented from jet lag and the shock of the trip, and I could think of no way to express it to them.

The large woman in the overcoat paid Klara some money and turned to me, grabbing Ginzburg's *A Precipitous Journey* and pushing it into my hands, saying, "American, I'm giving you this book. It's a woman's account of her seventeen years as a prisoner in a labor camp here in Kolyma. My mother was also imprisoned here. Good-bye."

She walked out before I could respond.

"Yes, it's true . . . Eat more pie . . . Most people here are descended from these prisoners. Who else would come to this place?" said Klara. "Well, I'm not, actually. A prisoner, that is, or a former prisoner, or even descended from one. I had the misfortune of marrying a man in Vologda, north of Moscow, who moved here during the sixties for the high salary. Now, these salaries have evaporated, and we're stuck. We can't even afford to visit our relatives on the continent."

"The 'continent'?"

"That's how we refer to the rest of Russia. You see, we're stranded. You can only get out of Magadan by air, and a one-way ticket to Moscow is now three times what I make in a month. The boat to Vladivostok doesn't run anymore."

"So it's impossible to drive out?"

I got a bit nervous, suddenly remembering my plans to go west by road.

"Impossible!" Klara answered.

Lyudmila corrected her.

"It's not impossible. Sometimes trucks go to Ust-Nera. But who wants to go there? When you leave you will fly out."

I didn't pursue the subject of transportation any further—although it was the most crucial matter I had to attend to here, I felt too tired to think through my questions.

Neither these women nor their customers had anything good to say about their city, but Klara admitted it would be hard to adjust to living anywhere else.

At closing time we parted, and I returned to the hotel, where I opened the first chapter of Ginzburg's book and dozed off right away.

That evening, I walked into the hotel restaurant from the street and collapsed into a seat, suddenly sluggish with jet lag. The band was on break. The usual Russian *zakuski* (hors d'oeuvres) spread had been reduced to some sickly cucumbers and old sausage. Men in parkas with weathered faces under fur hats silently peered between vodka bottles in my direction from around the low tables. It seemed that very few in the restaurant were guests of the hotel; this was a local hangout, and I was new on their turf. I felt like an alien.

After a few moments my novelty wore off, and the men returned to their grim discourse, their jowls heavy and voices gritty, often leaning into one another's space and speaking in hushed tones, as though hatching a plot. When the band returned and started up, several young women, all with porcelain-white skin and lips painted blood red, arose and took to dancing listlessly by themselves. Two of the conspiratorial revelers steeled their resolve with shots of vodka and joined them, plodding about the floor in muddy boots, their eyes locked on the girls' hips, their arms wooden and straight in their parkas.

I ate my cucumber salad and meat cutlet quickly and retired to my room.

At four in the morning it began, piercing everything with a low, mournful howl. I awoke shivering, Ginzburg's book on my chest, my breath puffing white before me in the glare of the bare bulb I had fallen asleep under the evening before. It was the arctic wind, and it droned on and on, wailing and crying out, rending the air with octaves plangent and chilling, one more grievous than the next. I switched off my light and tried to settle under the blanket, but it was curiously square, and, as a result, came up short whichever way it was positioned. With the light off, the luminous haze of dawn filtered into the room, tinting it a boreal blue, then pink, then pale orange. I had the distinct impression that I was not alone, that some polar presence haunted my room.

The frigid air dogged me. Unable to sleep, I got up and went to the window; a gaunt stray dog shivered and slipped on the ice as it rummaged through the garbage in the alley behind the hotel.

The solitude was too much for me, and I dressed hurriedly and went out to walk the town.

Ice in broad gritty layers covered the lot in front of the newspaper building. It was eight-thirty in the morning, and the cold stung my nostrils and congealed my trachea. I asked at the front desk where Alexander was, and was directed to the third floor, to a woman of forty-five or so sitting under a mop of disheveled hair with sleep in her eyes. EDITOR read the sign over her room.

"Is Alexander in?" I asked.

"Who wants him?" She adjusted her glasses and set her eyes on me.

"I'm an American. I was given his name as someone who could arrange a trip for me overland to Yakutsk."

She peered at me suspiciously through her bifocals.

"An American, you say? Can I see your passport?" I showed it to her.

"You will excuse me. Just a formality. Alexander Stepanovich is at his other office. Please sit. Let me call him."

Her walls were barren except for a black-and-white print showing the moonscape around Magadan, which only made the emptiness of her office even starker.

"Alexander Stepanovich! This is Nina Andreyevna. You have an American here to see you . . . Yes . . . I'll put him on the line."

She handed me the phone. I introduced myself. A gruff voice with a heavy south Russian accent responded, "Don't go anywhere! I'll be right over!"

Nina Andreyevna offered me coffee and I asked about life in Magadan.

"Life in *Magadan*? How is life in Russia? you should ask. It is clear to all of us what is happening. Do you think the Soviet Union collapsed by chance? No, this happened according to a very definite plot. You are now witnessing a redivision of the world's natural resources, a realignment of forces, carried out by the major powers against Russia. What happened to us could only be the work of certain elements. It was no accident."

She went on and on in this vein. My thoughts drifted to the Kolyma Route and how long it would take me to cross it to Yakutsk.

Alexander's panting preceded him. In rushed the cold with this large man in a black fur hat and big black boots.

"Zdrasst'ye!" he bellowed, his voice resonating as if through a barrel. He pulled off his hat and revealed a massive bald head. "Excuse me. I'm busy today, but please come with me. We can talk while I run my errands."

We went downstairs to his jeep and driver, a sinewy twenty-two-year-old Buryat named Vlad glared quietly at Alexander as though he was about to mutter something under his breath each time his boss barked an order at him.

Alexander told me he had come to the Russian Far East (which he often called "the North") when he graduated from college. He had worked for twenty years as a journalist in Anadyr, a settlement just south of the Arctic Circle in Chukotka, but moved to Magadan after suffering a heart attack. In his opinion, Magadan was an improvement over Anadyr.

We jolted to and fro over nameless icy backstreets. A jeep was clearly a necessity just to negotiate the roads in Magadan, hacked as they were out of erratic *sopki* and coated in ice. After much bouncing and bobbing, we arrived at his other office. Alexander had two jobs: he edited the paper and he ran a local publishing house. I explained that I wanted to travel by land over the Kolyma Route and asked if he could find me a ride to Yakutsk.

"We don't drive to Yakutsk—we fly."

"I've heard as much. That's why my trip will be so interesting to people. I'm writing a book on it. I'll be doing something not usually done."

Alexander shook his head, incredulous.

"My advice to you is to forget about this trip. There are plenty of interesting things to do right here in Magadan, or on the route between here and Susuman. Going farther than that is dangerous. Even getting to Susuman is risky. Beyond, there are bands of robbers. Drivers have been carrying guns. And you picked the wrong time of year. If you had come in July, we could have gone out to the camps, the ruins of the gulags. But they're snowed in right now. Why don't you come back this summer?"

I politely insisted that since I was here, I might as well try to get to Yakutsk. He cut me off and told me trying was not the issue— my life and safety were. He changed the subject by inviting me to eat in the newspaper cafeteria.

As we drove there, Alexander began explaining a project he had for me if I returned the next summer.

"There is this camp, Butugychan. You've never heard of it. No one has. It's two days' drive off the route here. That's where the uranium was mined for the first Soviet atomic bomb. It's my secret, my discovery. Actually, maybe 'secret' isn't the right word for it now, since I have taken some journalists, Americans and Danes, up there to see it. Twice now. Both times, the same thing happened."

Vlad slammed on the brakes. Alexander grabbed his hat. We had arrived at the cafeteria. "We'll discuss this after lunch, when we're alone."

Alexander continued.

"The journalists had brought Geiger counters. Naturally, there's some radiation."

"Some?"

"Well, the needles on their Geiger counters went haywire. These journalists, even after the two-day ride out there, got angry and demanded we leave at once. Those that had gotten out jumped back in the car pretty fast. Didn't they, Vlad?"

Vlad said nothing, but he tightened his grip on the steering wheel.

"Vlad and I have spent a lot of time up there, and it hasn't affected our health. I told them this, but they made us leave at once. Too much radiation, they said. They were even angry with me.

After I took the Americans up there, I wrote an article describing their reaction. It was telling. Their reaction, that is."

"What do you mean?"

"I mean, Vlad and I are used to the radiation. The Americans valued their lives too highly to take the risk we took. That shows a difference in the way we relate to the concept of our life and death. So my idea is this: you and I and Vlad would go up there and spend a week or two this summer. I could show you everything: the barrels of uranium oozing radiation, the mine shafts themselves, how the prisoners worked unprotected and died. Yes, of course, they all died of radiation poisoning."

"They didn't get used to it, like you have?"

"No, not at all! Of course, they were exposed over months. They just got sick and died. Some died when their lungs filled with dust from the drilling."

"Let me think about it."

I had no intention of spending a week next summer being irradiated. But I didn't want to offend Alexander by refusing his offer.

Back at his office, I brought up the subject of my trip again. Alexander was adamant.

"Listen, you don't seem to understand where you are. You are in Kolyma! We Russians call it 'the White Hell.' You don't come here and tell me what you're going to do. I'm responsible for you now that you've been referred to me by a friend. This is the law of the North."

"I understand. But I *must* get to Yakutsk by land, or at least try! This is my only reason for coming to Magadan. I know the risks."

"What can you, an American, know about our life here in Kolyma? Do you know that the Kolyma Route was built by prisoners of Stalin's gulags who died in the cold and ballasted the road with their bones? They started from Magadan and worked inland in temperatures that can hit ninety below zero. Their tools shattered in their hands. They froze to death and could not be buried because of the icy earth here. They were tossed dead into the snow like logs. The Kolyma Route passes within a hundred and twenty-five miles of the Arctic Circle, north of the coldest inhabited place in the world, Oymyakan, where it reaches ninety-five below zero! Dressed as you are, you will freeze to death, or at best, lose your legs to frostbite!"

His words and tone were humbling. Of the roughly three million sentenced to the camps around Magadan, only five hundred thousand survived, the highest mortality rate of the Soviet gulag system. My idea of driving out suddenly sounded ridiculous. And I admitted that I had thought that by waiting until April, it would be warmer, and the cold would not be such a problem.

"It *is* warmer, but you can still freeze to death in thirty or forty below. Your American clothes are no good here. Let me see your boots."

I showed him my mid-calf Timberlands. He laughed.

"You will lose your feet to frostbite in those. I'm responsible for you here in Magadan. I won't send you off into Kolyma dressed like this."

I was humbled but felt that unless I showed bravado he would give up on me entirely.

Alexander took me around on more errands. When introducing me to friends of his in various offices in town, he would tell them that I want to go to Yakutsk by land—what did they think? "Dressed like that?" was their response.

He did seem to have a point.

"Maybe I can buy some better clothes here."

"*Buy* clothes? There's nothing in our stores—remember where you are. Come back this summer. Fly to Yakutsk for now. In fact, don't take my word. Tomorrow I have to head out to Palatka, a settlement on the route. Come with me—you'll have seen enough of Kolyma after that."

Alexander and Vlad picked me up, along with some others bound for Palatka. Asking how long the trip out would take elicited a stream of mockery from Alexander.

"Ah, see, what did I tell you? You do not know the ways of Kolyma! You ask such questions as 'How long?' but in Kolyma, we have no such vocabulary! Your Americanness is showing through!"

This pomposity was beginning to annoy me. Clearly he had to have some idea of how long—a day, an hour, three hours—a trip to a nearby settlement would take, the "ways of Kolyma" or "law of the North" notwithstanding.

"So you've got absolutely no idea?"

"Listen to him," Alexander chided, turning to Vlad. "In Kolyma, an hour-long trip may take a day, and a day-long trip may take a week. We don't plan or even think along those lines here."

When Alexander was out of the car, I turned to Vlad.

"So is the phrase 'how long' not even in your vocabulary?"

He smirked and looked away.

"It'll take three hours there and three back. What he says applies more to long trips."

"Is it really so dangerous to go to Yakutsk?"

"Well, I've never gone the whole way, and neither has he. We've been as far as Ust-Nera. Beyond, into Yakutia, is a different story. It's tough. And dangerous. But it can be done. Truckers do make the run occasionally. It's two thousand kilometers. If the *zimnik* hasn't spoiled, and you have no serious problems, it should take you between four and six days."

Palatka turned out to be a row of pockmarked barracks in the mud. It had thawed there and was always warmer than anywhere else in Kolyma, according to Alexander. Puddles the size of parking lots lay everywhere; even a minor thaw produced muddy pools it seemed a small boat could sail. Alexander explained that Palatka's climate had made it the gulag-warden resort area for the region. But just a few miles outside of Palatka it was frigid again. The unpredictability of the climate was a characteristic of Kolyma. A cold front could drop temperatures sixty degrees in an hour during the unstable fall and spring months.

That evening, Konstantin, a typesetter with a red nose who had been among Alexander's buddies on our Palatka expedition, invited us home for dinner.

Konstantin had a warm, homey flat in one of Magadan's dull concrete blocks. We arrived as his wife, Lara, an attractive Ukrainian woman in her early forties, was coming home from the movies.

Konstantin was dishing out heaps of pickled cabbage. I have always had the habit of eating what I don't like first and fastest; I tried to force the cabbage down painlessly and quickly so that I could enjoy the rest of the meal. The cabbage had a sour, tongue-shriveling taste, and its smell cleared my sinuses.

"Ahh, you're finishing your cabbage! Here, allow me!"

Konstantin plopped another mound of the slop in front of me. Pickling solution splattered on my sweater.

"Konstantin, just because you love cabbage doesn't mean everyone does," said Lara, endearing herself to me beyond words.

"But look at how he's putting it away! He'll be interested to know that I pickle it myself. I know a pickled cabbage lover when I see one, don't I, Jeff?"

When I walked into Alexander's office the next morning, I found him pacing up and down. He had given his wife three hundred-dollar bills as a birthday present that morning, but she, in opening the envelope, had torn them all down the middle. We set out for the various banks in town, but none would accept the torn bills for exchange. Later, back in the office, I decided to bring up my trip again.

"Alexander, I'll be leaving tomorrow."

"What is that supposed to mean?" he said, fretting and fingering the torn bills in his hand. "Are you flying out? You saw enough of the route yesterday, didn't you?"

"No, I'm leaving by car. I've imposed enough on you. I'm planning to go to the edge of town and hitchhike."

"Hitchhike?! You're crazy! This is Kolyma—we don't do such things here! This past winter, two Russians trying to hitch up the route were robbed and murdered. That's a certain way to get killed!"

I persisted. He grabbed his phone and began dialing.

Alexander was now doing his best to locate a ride for me, but another problem arose: either drivers and truck-station bosses were reluctant to take on a traveler, or they simply had no trucks heading to Yakutsk; it sounded suspicious, and in the event of trouble on the road, the traveler would simply be one more mouth to feed or one more body to keep warm. But Alexander's practical side emerged, and for this I was grateful.

"You see, the driver of a truck here in Kolyma is like the captain of a ship—he's fully responsible for his passengers. This is a law of the North no one here can ignore. I'm in the same position, having to answer for your safety. I'm naturally concerned that you arrive alive at the other end of the route."

Alexander repeated that dressed as I was, I would freeze to death in an emergency, and there would be emergencies. I no longer doubted him. Nothing short of fur-lined *sapogi* (heavy traditional Russian boots), a fur hat, and a full-length *shuba* (sheepskin coat) would do. He took me home and produced a forty-pound *shuba* with hood. It felt as though the sheep was still attached. He also gave me a rabbit fur *shapka-ushanka*, or hat with ears. Boots he could give me for a price, and a high one—the ruble equivalent of about eighty dollars. This, he said, was only to cover what he paid for them. I somewhat doubted this, and I offered him forty; he accepted. I'd have to resell these *sapogi* once I left Siberia, to stay within my budget.

That afternoon, as he was calling truck garages, Alexander explained the conditions of my journey, enthusing about the logistics as though planning a military campaign.

"You must have experienced drivers who know the route and have made the run to Yakutsk before. They must not know you are American. Tell them you are from the Baltics. Don't tell them you have dollars, and don't discuss money with them—you will pay them with a bottle of pure spirits. Drivers drink this on the

road before turning in to help them sleep. *Spirt* is the hard currency of the North."

He dialed and dialed, but no one would accept me. It occurred
to me that hiding my identity might be creating an unnecessary
difficulty—what motivation would a trucking boss have to aid a
regular Russian in getting a free ride to a place he should be paying a month's salary worth of rubles for a plane ticket to? The
same thought must have occurred to Alexander when he got
Sergei Vasilyevich of the trucking firm Indigir-Zoloto on the line.

"You see, I have an American sitting with me who wants to
write a book on the Kolyma Route. He needs a ride to Yakutsk.
Yes, yes, I've told him of these dangers—perhaps you could repeat
them to him. He doesn't take me seriously. Yes, I will see that he's
dressed properly and has provisions. He's done some traveling, so
I don't foresee any problems. Right . . . Right. Tomorrow morning? That will be fine."

My ride was set. The thought of my departure elevated my mood
as I set about buying provisions for the trip. Everything in Magadan seemed more cheerful now that I was sure to be leaving it. I
started my search at the Mayak food store above town next to the
television tower, overlooking the port on the Sea of Okhotsk. The
sun was slanting in low over the frozen *sopki*, radiating outward
from the horizon a fan of pinks and magentas and reds, dousing
the drab concrete barracks in color and driving away their bleakness. When I was finished shopping, I had a sack full of Chinese
luncheon meats in cans, batons of blood-red Chinese salami, Vietnamese dried bananas, Syrian chocolate, and Russian bread.
Alexander said he would give me the *spirt* I was to pay my drivers
with, but he forgot, and I could find none around.

"This is a first for us—we've never had an American here at
Indigir-Zoloto. In fact, we've never had any foreigners here at all."

Sergei Vasilyevich was young, blondish, and sturdily built. To
his right, a large map spread the Magadan Oblast over the wall.

It was massive and starkly empty of human habitation, and stretched almost to Alaska.

"You must know that life for our drivers has become almost unbearably difficult, but they are tough guys," Sergei said. "All our roadside rest houses where they could spend the night and eat have closed since Moscow decided it would no longer keep funding our gold and coal mines. So people are abandoning the settlements—you know they were set up first as gulags during the twenties and thirties—and things have become unstable. We all are worried about our future. So, are you ready for all this? If I may ask, what drives an American from the comforts of the U.S. to Magadan? This doesn't seem normal to me. And frankly, I wonder if an American can handle the toughness of it. You are used to luxury."

"No, actually, I'm not."

"Well, I watch *Santa Barbara*. I see the way you live and the mentality that goes with it. But if you're ready, you're ready. I'll call in Sasha, your driver."

Sasha was a Tatar in his late twenties, of sinewy build with high Asiatic cheekbones and smiling eyes. His mustache ends drooped like walrus tusks, and they, along with his cheeks, gave him a Genghis Khan visage. When we shook hands, I thought he might burst out laughing

"You are American? And you think our life here is *interesting?* I don't know," he said. "I suppose everyone is allowed his quirks."

The high salaries paid in Kolyma had drawn Sasha from his native city of Ufa, in the Ural Mountains, to Magadan some ten years ago. He neither understood nor accepted any motivation other than financial for living in Magadan. He did not dramatize the North or romanticize it—he knew what he needed to know to survive and concerned himself with little else.

We said good-bye to Sergei Vasilyevich and went out into the lot and over to the shining military-green Kamaz trucks ("made by Tatars in Tatarstan," Sasha said), and met his *naparnik*, or work partner, Sergei, a lanky Russian of similar age. Sergei wore

a floppy-eared fur hat and picked at his mustache with thick, cal-
lused fingers. I stood with them as they discussed their load (beer
and wine bottle conveyers for a plant in Yakutsk) and details of
repairs that they had made to ready their trucks for this run, and
my mind wandered as I looked out over the expanse of *sopki* that
spread to infinity from Magadan's scraggly edge. Gusts of wind
picked up snow and drove it onward into the folds and valleys between the *sopki*. Desolate. Forlorn. Only these words came to
mind—the vista of emptiness ahead drove a stake of fear into my
heart.

In the truck lot, the wind did little more than stir dust into our
eyes and make us wince. We all shook hands and jumped aboard,
I with Sasha, Sergei alone.

The Kamaz was clumsy in town, oversized for the ruts Magadan had for streets. It seemed we might crack the pavement,
squash a Zhiguli, or run down a pedestrian, so bulky was the
truck. After Sasha picked up his map, he opened the throttle on
the road leading to the route. Only when we passed the city limit
sign did I realize we were alone.

"Sergei will be waiting for us at the edge of town. We've been
naparniki for years now. That's how we work. We never leave
Kolyma without each other. A driver needs a reliable *naparnik*
with a good head to survive here. There's no one else but your *naparnik* who can help you make a repair, give you spare food, or a
warm cabin when your heater breaks down. We owe our lives to
each other many times over."

We rumbled past the shacks and junk-strewn yards of Magadan's outer reaches out onto the route. Sergei was waiting as
planned, and we took off in the lead. No sooner had we cleared
the shacks than it seemed as though Magadan had never existed,
so insignificant was it amidst the desolate expanses of the North.

"People mean nothing out here, nothing," said Sasha. "Kolyma
gives you only one chance. I think in America, you can regulate
everything. Not here. It's a man's world, Kolyma. There's no reason to be here if you're not a gold prospector or coal miner. Are

these women's jobs? The few people who lived here before the Russians came were Chukchis, and they bred reindeer. The name Magadan means 'hut' in their language. That's all Magadan was meant to be—some Chukchi huts in the middle of nowhere. It's not a place for a woman."

Sasha had learned a lot about Kolyma. As we drove along, he would point out various settlements and give brief histories. Waving toward strange lumps on the ground, he told me, "That mound there is what's left after they dig for gold and displace earth. A mess, isn't it? They've ruined nature up here." They certainly had: huge, barren, snow-covered mounds popped up everywhere along river beds, disrupting the steady rolls of the *sopki*. Only occasionally would we see a derelict *draga* (a bulky, mobile gold-mining steamer that drags the river bottom and sifts it for gold) collapsing under its own weight; more often we came on the remains of miners' cabins buckling under heavy snows with their windows knocked out, like skulls with empty eye sockets. Kolyma's prisoners had disappeared and its mines withered, leaving it a skeleton abandoned to the Arctic wastes.

We seemed to be moving at a fair pace. During the first couple of hours we'd kept up a steady eighty or ninety kilometers an hour.

I studied my map. Traveling at just sixty-six kilometers an hour, we would cover, with ten hours of driving a day, the two thousand kilometers to Yakutsk in three days. Ust-Nera by tonight. Tomorrow night, Khandyga. And by the third night, Yakutsk.

Sasha smiled at my map.

"Maybe."

I had slept little the night before and my eyelids were heavy. But no matter how I positioned myself in the cabin—and there was more than enough room—the jarring grind of the Kamaz over the roadbed kept me awake and tickled my nose with vibrations. We were climbing, gears shifting, cabin rattling, and trailer trundling. Sleep eluded me. It seemed that after each rise we might see something, be it a flat stretch, a settlement, or another truck, but over and over again, we reached new points from which a fresh gear-grinding, nose-tickling ascent would be visible, and more desolation, more snow and ice and ragged runts of bare pines.

By the end of the first afternoon, we were well past the *sopki* guarding Magadan's periphery, and, without sunglasses, my eyes ached from the light bouncing off the snow. The sky turned from turquoise to a steely white, and at last I had to close my eyes to protect them from the glare.

THREE

The Kolyma Route and the *Zimnik* to Yakutsk: Close Calls

By evening we had left the relatively temperate coastal zone of the Sea of Okhotsk and begun our penetration into the subarctic wilderness that stretches west across the northern reaches of the Eurasian landmass all the way to the Norwegian Sea. It turned colder, much colder. The snow shimmered pale blue and luminescent as heaven dust, and the polar twilight cast crimson and rosy hues into the mist drifting over the frozen road. It had been four or five hours since we had passed another truck, and the solitude we felt in our cabin turned to melancholy as the sun disappeared behind the *sopki*. We were alone and heading north into Kolyma, into the frozen wastes where, until the mid-1950s, floodlights swept the boreal vapors drifting through barbed wire fences and watchtowers stood in silent sentry over the barracks of Stalin's condemned.

Ahead, at the base of a *sopka,* yellow lights glimmered in the mist.

"It's Orotukan, a mining settlement. It was founded as a concentration camp. Now it's being abandoned."

The lights shone from houses along the outer reaches of the settlement, and, rising above them, in the heart of the habitations, stood a black tower. Our headlights occasionally picked up shadowy hammers and sickles and sloganless exclamation points on the sides of buildings.

"We need water for the trucks," Sasha said, his eyes searching the shacks along the road. "Looks like there's no one left, though."

Dark shapes of barking dogs bounded clumsily across the snow toward us, gaunt and bare-fanged. They caught up with our truck, then dropped behind as we accelerated past the lights.

"People bring these dogs up here to guard the settlements, then leave them when they go home. They'll starve soon enough. Or wolves will get them." He paused. "No one will give us water up here if it gets much later. They'll be afraid to open their doors. There's been a lot of robbery lately. And right on the road. People have gotten desperate since the mines started closing."

I remembered Alexander's and Steve's words about bandits in Yakutia and drivers riding armed.

"Guns aren't allowed now," Sasha said. "The police took them away. This is a problem. But what isn't these days?"

Dusk drew on, with the sun now half below the horizon, bleeding streams of magenta and pink into the snow as it expired. We trundled over a bridge crossing the Kolyma River, a snowy ribbon winding between stubs of pines, and came upon another cluster of dilapidated houses, of which three or four bore waning lights. This was Debin. Sergei stopped up ahead, and so did we.

We jumped out. Ahead, a man in a floppy-eared fur hat, reeling and lurching about in search of his equilibrium, tossed a bucket of water on a truck parked in front of Sergei's Kamaz. Mist suffused the twilight and transformed Sergei and the man into penumbral specters illuminated now pink, now crimson, by the declining sun behind them. It was an unearthly scene of pastels and shifting shadows.

"Wash . . . wash my truck . . . I want to wash . . ."

The man stumbled and slopped water, missed his vehicle, grumbled and belched, and tottered away. His words were belligerent, and he swung his bucket like a weapon. Behind him stood another man, who spread his arms wide and pleaded with him to stop.

It was clear that the man with the bucket was drunk; no sober person would wash a truck when it was ten below zero. His friend shouted to Sasha, "Look at this idiot. He's sloshed! He's got to be taken to Yagodnoye. Would you take him? Please, he's my friend!"

The drunk had refilled his bucket from behind the cabin and was charging back toward the truck, water splashing out of his pail, feet plodding irregular steps across the snow. Sasha gave him wide berth.

Sergei and Sasha both set about getting water from the pump behind the cabin. They returned with two full metal canisters.

The drunk began to cry and grasp at Sasha, who pushed him away. His bucket spilled on the road. Sergei appeared from around the other side of his truck with a mallet in hand and waved it at the drunk, frightening him back several paces and causing him to slip and tumble on the ice. He whimpered and crawled to his feet and began beseeching Sasha to take him up the road, then he began begging the other man to let him spend the night at his cabin. Soon, figures were pushing and shoving at one another in the mist and there were drunken cries. Sasha broke free and jumped aboard.

"Son of a bitch!" exclaimed Sasha. "We're not taking any drunk up the road! He'll just piss all over my cabin! Let's go!"

We drove another hour, then pulled over into a clearing, ahead of which the final vestiges of evening light played in subtle beams on the sky above where the sun had set, teasing fleeces of clouds drifting into the darkness, and painting among them a mélange of pink and melancholy magenta. From just beneath the horizon emanated a fan of soft shifting rays that pierced the mist still haunting the folds between *sopki*. According to Sasha, this mist was brought on by the drop in temperature and could become so thick that driving was impossible when it reached seventy or eighty below, as it did regularly during the winter months. The pastels of the landscape here were entrancing; they derived from the northern latitude, from the obliquity of light hitting the earth. They spoke, in short, of the remoteness of where we were.

Sergei climbed into our truck next to Sasha. They lit a gas camp stove and poured a teapot full of water, then produced sausage, bread, cookies, and cheese from satchels stored behind the front seat. I took out my canned Chinese lunch meat and Vietnamese bananas.

Sasha told me to put it away. "There's plenty of time for that canned food! You'll eat our sausage and cheese until they run out."

We were a merry bunch in that cabin, having covered a lot of territory with no breakdowns during ten hours of driving. I listened to Sasha and Sergei talk animatedly about the road and passes ahead. Sausage was chewed, tea slurped, and cookies crunched. Then came *konfety*, or candies. Sergei had a weakness for them and chomped through half a kilo within minutes.

I switched to Sergei's truck after dinner. Dusk dissipated entirely during our meal, leaving in its stead a night of silence broken only by the whir of our Kamazy or the faintest whisper of wind.

Around midnight, our headlights fell upon houses, some boarded up, others with pale yellow lights in frosted windowpanes. Yagodnoye, Sergei said. The Kolyma Route bisected it. Somewhere in the middle of the settlement, we diverged from the road and rolled to a halt in a clearing next to a floodlit brick barrack.

"We're spending the night here," said Sergei. "Come with me."

Out of the blackness behind me a hand grabbed at my elbow. There was a reek of vodka and two swaying figures.

"Hey, take us down the road," said one. "We live just two kilometers from here! Come on, take us!"

I jerked my arm free of the drunk. Sergei stepped over and shoved him hard, sending him into the side of the truck with a thud. The drunks, who were about twenty years old, recoiled and hurled curses at him, but then apologized and turned to whining about the cold and their long walk home and the certainty of their freezing to death on the way.

"I'll be back in half an hour," said Sergei. "We'll talk then."

He grabbed my arm and led me toward the barracks.

"Our truck garage has a room here in this hostel for its drivers," he said, nodding at the grim concrete structure we were about to enter. "It may be open. We'll put you up here for the night if it is. We'll sleep in the trucks to guard them."

The hostel was open, though unlit. The drunken youths followed us in. We found a labyrinth of dark corners, halls of shadows, and people snoring under ragged blankets. A television cast a blue hue on the wall of the office where we startled the hotelier, a bulging, sleepy-eyed woman of about forty with peroxided hair.

"Are these drunks with you?" she groused, looking behind us. "Get them out of here if they are."

"No, ma'am," said Sergei. "We're with Indigir-Zoloto. We need a room for our guest. Our guest is from—"

One of the drunks grabbed at Sergei and began importuning him to take him home. Sergei shoved him away.

"I told you I'd speak to you in half an hour! Beat it!"

The drunk blathered to himself and fell silent, stepping back into the hallway. Sergei turned to me and said, "My God! What a mess our country is in! When will it all end?"

A strange question, the woman must have thought, coming from a Russian to a Russian, whom she took me for. I wanted to keep it that way.

A young female voice lilted in a melodious half-tune behind us, drawing our eyes toward the hallway. A girl in an oversized man's white shirt and floppy slippers leaned on the doorjamb and set her eyes on Sergei and me, twirling a braid of blond hair around her forefinger. She was alluring in the same way bored country girls stuck on farms with only their brothers are. Her eyes were a clear green, her nipples stood erect and pink through the white cotton of her camise.

"Zdrasst'ye!" she said absentmindedly to me. "Have you come to see us?"

I nodded hello but didn't answer. Sergei signed some papers and led me past her down the hall to a clean green room that had four mattresses around the walls.

"Lock yourself inside—at this hour there'll be no others coming. There's no reason for you to open this door for anyone—remember that. Good night!" He disappeared down the hall.

I unpacked my night clothes and my journal and set my alarm clock for seven. The room was chilly, but there were adequate blankets. I climbed under the covers, humming with contentment at sleeping in a bed and not a truck cabin. But soon after, wavering, inebriated cries of disorder followed by shouts of anger resounded from the bathroom next door. A tape player began blaring, a bottle hit the floor somewhere and shattered. More shouts, then the thuds of bodies hitting the wall and shoes scuffling and muffled squeals. I heard the hotelier come shuffling down the hall in flip-flops; she broke up the row and lectured the drunks about sobriety, and her monologue lasted an eternity. Somewhere during that eternity, I fell asleep.

The next morning, Sergei and Sasha were beaming and fresh. I had slept well, too, despite the racket.

"We've got a job, a little moonlighting. It shouldn't hold us up more than an hour or two. We're going to move this Yakut and his things from here to Yakutsk."

The two of them drove off in Sergei's truck, leaving me in Sasha's with my book.

Two hours went by, then three, then a fourth. It was almost

three in the afternoon, and we were still in Yagodnoye. I had been getting out of the cabin and walking around to break the boredom, but Yagodnoye was no help. The few people left there seemed to be vagrants who stared at the ground and grumbled to themselves as they trudged from one end of the clearing—perhaps a central square in summer—to the other. Stores were boarded up. Wind blew snow squalls through town every couple of hours.

Boredom was definitely the real killer in living in a place like Yagodnoye—it would drive anyone to drink. Add to that days only a couple of hours long in winter—it was tough to see how people could stand it. I got into the cabin and began an entry in my journal when Sasha and Sergei finally drove up with a third smaller figure in between them.

Sasha climbed in.

"We're off!" His eyes dropped to my notebook, then settled on my face in sudden suspicion.

"What are you writing there—a report on us for the CIA?"

I laughed. He didn't.

"We ought to turn you over to the KGB!"

I laughed again. Sasha stared at me, then smiled.

"Boy, that Yakut sure does stutter!" he said, switching into first gear.

The Yakut—our new passenger who would ride in Sergei's cabin—smiled at me and waved timidly from the other truck. He looked to be fortyish, his hair was combed and parted meticulously, and his dress—a gray suit and wing-tipped shoes—made him stand out as foppish among the miners and gulag survivors of Kolyma. I thought I'd like to talk to him and was sorry he was in Sergei's cabin.

"What's his name?"

"I didn't ask. I did learn from him that 'Yakut' in Yakutian is *Sakha-bin*. I like that—*Sakha-bin!* That's what we'll call him. Anyway, he's tough to talk to, with his stuttering and all."

We pulled out of Yagodnoye with our engine toiling and huffing and our tires slipping on the packed snow. Our truck was now heavy with the Yakut's effects and responded sluggishly on the road as we ascended the *sopki* west of the settlement. The cabin shook and rattled as though it would tear apart. Pass after pass lay ahead of us, the long acclivities stretching toward the elevated reaches of the white hills to the west.

"*Bozhe moy!* This is some road, huh?" said Sasha as we climbed the steep bends and looked over into the chasms now appearing along the side of the road, snow-filled and almost devoid of trees, reaching a depth of a couple of thousand feet. The air grew colder and a wind picked up, driving snow across the highway.

We made it to the top of the high pass before Susuman and stopped for a break. Sasha and I climbed out and marveled at the wilderness ahead of us. The sky shifted like a kaleidoscope, a revolving iron cauldron of gray clouds vented with holes of turquoise, churning out streams of snow and shafts of sunlight. Beneath it, wind drove snow across some *sopki* while leaving others untouched, and radiant beams piercing holes in the clouds played on scattered patches of the panorama, but did not tamper with others. This was how it looked when the Ice Age overtook the planet, I thought.

Both trucks, it was discovered, had flat tires that Sasha and Sergei set to fixing. After that, we were off again.

"These miners up here," I asked Sasha, "they worked for the state, right?"

"Of course. It was illegal to sell gold here to anyone but the state. If you mined a chunk, the state alone would buy it from you. You'd be risking your life to find a buyer anywhere else here. Whatever Moscow decreed was the law. Even up here. But no one really cared about getting rich. If you weren't exiled here to serve a sentence, you came to leave the world behind.

"They were paid many times more than what anyone in a city could earn, it's just that they didn't become millionaires as the gold miners did in your West. Even if they could have, what could they have bought in Soviet days? They gave their gold to the state collective for which they worked. Lately, Moscow has decided that it's too expensive to supply and pay the miners. So they're going home if they can. But many know only mining—what are they to do?"

"If the state would let people mine the gold on their own, then I'm sure people would remain here," I said. "There'd be incentive. Everyone would get a piece of the pie. Wasn't that what perestroika was all about?"

"Listen to the American try to get me into a political discussion! I think we ought to turn you over to the KGB at the first town!" He laughed. "I don't talk politics. It would do me no good. I've got my wife at home and a decent job. I don't need more than that."

Susuman. A raw, grimy settlement without trees, entirely sunk in slush. We sloshed through the mud to the one food store.

I wanted a soft drink, but all they had was Russkaya vodka and a twelve-thousand-ruble bottle of peach juice. The food side had nothing but dusty cookies and batons of gray sausage. The customers, raw-faced men with snarls carved into their faces by the frosts, counted out tattered, soggy rubles in the doorway and muttered about the new price of vodka.

Sasha and Sergei patched up more flat tires and knocked huge dangling shards of ice off the undersides of the trucks with mallets. A truck coasted through the puddles in the road, which were more like small seas, sending mini-tidal waves as far ashore as our Kamazy. The muddy water lapped at our tires.

Sasha looked around and wiped his nose on his sleeve, his hands black with mud.

"A foul place, Susuman is. The East Germans used to test military equipment up here along with our army. To see how it reacted to extreme cold. During winter, it's one of our coldest places."

The shacks along the roadside stood weathered and dilapidated, the paint on them chipped off by frost and snow. Garbage lay frozen under the slush. Beyond the settlement, *sopki* rose ashen and mutilated, as though they had been strip-mined for coal. They had not been; the severity of the climate eroded their surface and let scant vegetation take root.

"Miners," said Sasha. "What do they care? No one up here cares about what this place looks like. So it's a pit. All they do for fun is drink, and that makes it worse. Now they want to leave, but where can they go? And what kind of people are they now that they've lived a life up here in this *bardak* [utter mess; literally, brothel]?"

That evening, just north and east of Ust-Nera, some 125 miles south of the Arctic Circle, we pulled off the road to fix a flat tire. The snow glowed with the pale blue luminescence it acquired in Kolyma when the sun's rays skimmed it obliquely, and once again the serenity of the coming twilight settled over the *sopki*. I got out and took a deep breath; the frost pierced me, scraping my trachea and sending my heart skipping. Only here and there did animal tracks—mainly rabbit—cut through the snow. Everything was in miniature, stunted by the cold; trees stood only as high as a man, and brush, where it was free of the snow, reached my knee. I took out my camera and stepped back off the road a bit to compose a picture.

Downward I shot into the white powder. When it reached my waist I hit bottom and scrambled to climb out. My boots were filled to the brim with snow. When I started brushing it off my socks, some of it melted on my hand. My skin began to burn and a chill wrenched my body. It was cold, but in the absence of a breeze, I hadn't noticed *how* cold. I climbed aboard the truck and read the thermometer on the rearview mirror; it was thirty-two below zero.

A minute later, Sasha climbed in, cursing and holding out his hands. He'd been working in overalls, without gloves, and the skin on his hands had frozen to his tools and been torn off in

places. He laughed, "No driver in Kolyma has his original fingerprints left!"

Around ten that evening, as another polar dusk of crimson sub-
sumed the hills and snowy vales, we passed a single wooden white
pole jutting into a sky scintillating with stars. It marked the border between Kolyma and Yakutia. Tiny, shaggy-maned white-
and-brown Yakutian horses scraped the snow with their hooves
and foraged at the roadside.

Dawn broke sterile and frigid on our third day, finding us cramped
and in foul humor after a night spent sitting up, trying to sleep,
just outside of Svetlaya, the first settlement west of the Kolyma
border. Sasha ran his hand through his hair, stretched, and hoisted
himself to the wheel and switched into first gear. The truck,
having been left running all night for heat, was ready to go. I
looked ahead and discovered we had, under cover of last night's
darkness, passed into territory exceeding anything we had seen
before in barrenness. Snow blew over gravel-gray *sopki* whose
lower reaches were dotted only here and there with dead pines;
their summits were bald, too exposed for anything to live on.
The thin air bit at our skin, like a school of piranhas at a dangling
limb.

We drove into Ust-Nera around nine that morning. Sasha advised
me to set my watch back two hours. Ust-Nera, for whatever
reason, had its own time zone, which we would ignore. A second
hour back put us on Yakutsk time. This was one way I'd planned
to gauge my progress. I was eight hours ahead of Moscow in
Magadan. Warsaw was two hours behind Moscow. Therefore,
from Magadan, I had ten time zones to cross to get to my destination, and eight from here. If even to think of Warsaw in a place
such as Ust-Nera seemed absurd, setting my watch back helped
me feel that I was making progress, that I had a destination ahead
where friends awaited me. Then I remembered that between

Moscow and Washington, D.C., there were eight time zones, too, and Warsaw seemed even farther away than before. My sense of progress disappeared in these calculations, numbness returned. I looked at the frigid vista ahead.

"This is barren land here," said Sasha, in characteristic under-statement.

Only the sickliest of trees grew like giant scorched weeds on the hills around Ust-Nera.

Sasha's eye scavenged the approaching settlement for signs of life.

"People are hungry here. We shouldn't stay too long. It's not safe."

Wooden and aluminum shacks stood in decay, encased in ice. Most had been boarded up. Windows had been smashed in others. Here and there, across the flatness of the settlement, smoke-stacks puffed feebly in the thin air. Bony dogs converged on the road and followed us as we drove toward a truck stop, forming a pack of shivering beggars with pleading eyes, protruding ribs, and dangling tongues. When we stopped they stood by our doors, visi-bly trembling in the twenty-below cold, all the while moving in little circles to generate heat.

"This used to be a big town for mercury miners. Now it's dying. Everything's closing down. We're only here to wash up. This here is a flophouse."

Sasha pointed to what looked to be a boarded-up hotel. The thought of a shower or at least running water lifted my mood. I got out my soap and toothbrush.

Sergei came over to our cabin. No sign read HOTEL, he said, and the two argued about whether it was the right building. Sergei grabbed his bath towel and raced across the lot to the door. Minutes later, he returned and jumped into our cabin.

"The old bitch won't let us use the sink. Says she's sick of min-ers making a mess in there."

"I'll try!" I said, fixated on the idea of running water hitting my face. I passed the front desk—there was no one there—and

washed up in the back. Still, Sasha and Sergei wouldn't enter.
They had decided there was another flophouse farther into town
we should try.

There was. Sasha, Sergei, and the Yakut washed up there. I got
out and took a couple of pictures. While I was doing this, Sasha
and the Yakut returned to the truck. Sasha saw me. His face
screwed up in alarm.

"Spy! A camera! I knew it! We're stopping at the KGB before
we leave town and we're handing you over!"

The Yakut froze in his tracks, and so did a pair of miners
emerging from the flophouse. They all stared at me. Was he jok-
ing? He had been the other day. If he was, the joke was getting
stale. The Yakut scurried to board the truck, keeping his eyes
fixed on me, as though I might explode a bomb or draw a gun. I
briefly wondered if the miners might not tackle me to the ground
or smash my camera in a fit of blind patriotism.

Sasha laughed once we were inside the truck. The Yakut
didn't see him, though, and arched his neck to peer in trepidation at me from Sergei's cabin. The miners who had been staring
at me continued on their way, glancing back suspiciously every
few steps.

"You don't think I believe that story about a book on the
Kolyma Route, do you?" said Sasha in a steady voice. "Now, what
is there to take pictures of here? I think that's proof enough."

I laughed, wanting to dismiss the joke in good humor and avoid
creating the impression I had been flustered by it. I knew I wasn't
a spy, of course, but the thought of what might happen to me
should I be arrested on even the suspicion of espionage in a place
as removed from the world as Ust-Nera was disquieting.

"The problem is, even if we turn you in, we'll all be seen as your
accomplices. I guess we'd better just put up with you until
Yakutsk."

His eyes were grinning.

An hour outside of Ust-Nera, Sasha and Sergei consulted their
maps. They couldn't locate the *zimnik* they needed. My National

Geographic map showed Ust-Nera to be on a dead end. This puzzled me. How were we to get to Yakutsk?

Sergei grabbed my map. "Where are we?" I asked.

"Your map doesn't show our *zimnik*," he said. "We aren't traveling on a road until Khandyga."

"But my map shows a solid road all the way from Magadan to Yakutsk. This one, here, that doesn't go through Ust-Nera. What's wrong with that road?"

"That's a dirt track, and one a good deal rougher than the *zimnik*. Not a single bolt would be left on our trucks if we took it. Probably impassable now. We just need to find the *zimnik*."

They conferred. We drove on, wondering where the *zimnik* would appear.

An hour later a Kamaz met us coming from the west. Its beer-bellied driver pushed his mirrored sunglasses back on his nose and snorted, tugging his greased handlebar mustache. Sasha knew him from the garage and stuck his head out the window.

"You coming from Yakutsk?"

"Yeah! Damn! Just made it! It's rough going!"

"Where's the *zimnik?*"

"Past the fork. You won't miss it. But it's rough. Be careful in the Suntar Khayata!"

I pulled out my map. The Suntar Khayata was a nine-thousand-foot-high mountain range between us and Yakutsk. It was the "prison wall" that cut off Magadan from the rest of Siberia and made it an inescapable natural gulag.

"Don't pull over near a Yakut village—damn them!" he said, shaking his head and smoothing his mustache. "I did that last night. All these Yakuts started pounding on my truck, demanding vodka. They wouldn't let me sleep! I thought I'd have to shoot them!"

He pulled away. We drove on and a half hour later turned southeast onto the *zimnik,* which lay flat and icy and indistinguishable from the road we had traveled over so far. It led us first across level open fields, then into a sparse forest composed not so much of trees as of hoary light reflected from snow and crystalline ice latticework adorning the branches and boughs hanging

solemnly in dominion over the taiga. The kingdom of taiga, un-
stirring and frigid. My eyes burned from the light, and I wished I
had brought sunglasses.

An hour or so into the *zimnik* Sasha grew agitated.

"It's spoiled. Look at this mud ahead!"

We drew up on a brown shiny section of road, akin to a great
slushy trough, and plowed into it. Our wheels spun and spewed
broad wings of muck on either side, but we emerged onto solid
ground. Sasha took this as a bad omen.

"We better hope that this is just a midday thaw, or else we may
end up marooned out here. We've got about eight hundred kilometers of *zimnik* left."

During our first two hundred kilometers of winter track we
passed only one village, Kyubyuma; a jumble of stables and fresh
wooden dwellings indicated it was a recent settlement. As we approached, Yakut villagers in *unty* (wraparound fur boots), heavy
fur parkas, and clumsy mittens flocked across the snow fields to
the *zimnik* to gawk at us and wave with blank looks on their
pudgy, flat faces.

"*Sakha! Sakha-bin!*" shouted Sasha as we roared past them.
"Did you see them! Our first real Yakuts! Their faces were flat as
pies!"

We passed no other villages. The *zimnik* threw us curves so tortu-
ous we had to slow to a crawl to negotiate them and very nearly
found ourselves mired in the mud on the bends. Around us stood
a forest submerged in the silence of white powder, canopied by a
radiant azure sky; it seemed odd that such a pristine winter scene
should be befouled with such muck.

Early that afternoon, we stopped at a fork in the road.

"Why are we stopping?"

"I don't know which way to go."

"How's that? You and Sergei have made this run before."
Alexander's words about riding only with "experienced drivers
who've made the run before" rang in my head.

"Who told you that? We're following those old maps of ours!"

He jumped out, and Sergei pulled up behind us. Neither he nor the Yakut knew the way. One fork led southwest, one west. The western track had tire marks in it and, to me, seemed the better choice.

Sasha was skeptical.

"And if you're wrong? We'll be out of gas by the time we find out. We need to reach Khandyga to refuel."

"Well, then, let's wait for a passing truck and ask," I suggested.

"Oh, listen to the CIA agent try to lead us astray! *What* passing trucks? And who'd stop? They don't stop for strangers around here. There have been a lot of prison breaks the past few years. Drivers who've stopped have had their trucks stolen. No way! Maybe, though, you could take out your CIA-issue pistol and shoot holes in their tires—that'd stop them!"

The Yakut's head spun around on hearing this. He blinked at me timorously for a moment and took a cautious step back, his eyes searching me for a pistol.

Sergei pulled out his primus and heated up two bloated tins of pork. It smelled like dog food, and it was all I could do to keep from retching when Sasha slathered spoonfuls of it over a chunk of lard and gobbled it up. And so we waited, the four of us on a vast snowy clearing in the woods; Sasha and Sergei chomping through gobbets of lard and greasy pork, I examining the fork in the *zimnik* for a clue as to which might be the right way to Yakutsk, and the Yakut keeping out of my sight, or perhaps peering at me from behind the truck in suspicion that I might start sending coded messages through a spy ring.

The Yakut's distrust of me began to get on my nerves—making me feel vaguely guilty of something. I crunched through the snow and extended my hand in greeting. He shook it, his face buried to the nose in a brown woolen scarf. I asked his name.

"My n-n-name?" He hesitated long enough to convince me he was trying to decide whether to concoct an alias. "Name . . . S-S-Stal. My name is Stal."

If it was an alias, it didn't befit him. *Stal* meant "steel." Stalin was the last man to choose a false name on that theme.

"Stal? How did your parents choose that name?"

"My f-f-f-father was illiterate, but he understood something. He had sixteen children, most of whom died early, so he named me Stal. I survived. Tell me, you're not a s-s-spy, are you?"

Stal and I got along well, it turned out. He had been an accountant in a geological enterprise in Yagodnoye and spent twenty years there; he was educated and I felt an immediate connection, as though he were a kindred spirit. Life in Yagodnoye was "not sweet," in his words.

From Stal I learned that the Yakuts were a Turkic people driven north by the Mongols. They had never become Islamicized and had adopted Russian Orthodoxy during the preceding two centuries. They had largely settled as a result of Soviet modernization campaigns and had forsaken their felt yurts for plastic tents if they did still wander. Most just lived in Soviet-style villages and worked reindeer kolkhozy.

After eating, Sasha and Sergei decided to follow the more trodden route leading away from the fork in the *zimnik*. It was soon clear that this was the correct choice—we passed another truck coming from Yakutsk. He slowed down to pass us a message: all we could hear, as he rumbled past us, was, "Coming from Yakutsk . . . watch out . . . Suntar Khayata mountains . . . bad road!" I wondered how a driver here defined "bad road"—the good *zimnik* was so rough I feared it would reduce all my camera gear to a jangle of metal and glass fragments.

We pounded on. The land was flat, the midafternoon sun blinding, the cabin hot. I began to doze off.

I was floating. So was the overnight bag over which I was draped. My camera bag, too, was in the air, at face level. Suddenly, CRASH! Sasha shouted, "Hold on!"

We bounced to a halt, with everything not tied down in our cabin smacking us in our faces or landing on our laps.

"Damn it! Damn!" he cursed, and struck the wheel in frustration. He climbed out.

We had flown over a two-foot sheer drop in the road at full speed. Sergei slowed to crawl down the cut, pulled over, and jumped out to help Sasha reattach the crates on the trailer that had been jarred loose. It was warm, or at least above freezing there. The *zimnik* led straight as an arrow, across what Stal said was a swamp during the summer. With eyes squinted from the reflected light, the snowy flat swamp looked like a vista of the Sahara.

That evening, as the sun began to decline, the Suntar Khayata range rose to the west. The prison wall. Its peaks and treeless escarpments towered ahead of us, jagged and unsparing; its abysses, dropping down a thousand feet or more even at its base, yawned sterile and lifeless. Nothing was living; not a bird fluttered in the sparse branches piercing the powder ahead of us; not a single paw had imprinted the fine snow.

Sasha stopped the truck and pulled over.

"I've never seen anything like this. Let me see your map!"

He pored over it, saying he didn't need help, but without knowing how to read the Latin alphabet, he couldn't locate the range, and gave the map back to me. His map showed a solid line until the range, then it turned dotted, with the mountains omitted, and only an arrow pointed timidly in the direction of Khandyga.

I got out and looked at the road ahead of us, which had narrowed to a single lane and led off circuitously into the rocky, snowbound range. The air outside was motionless and twinkled with the frost as if studded with thousands of shimmering crystals. The silence was lunar, cavernous, echoing only with the chug and drag of Sergei's engine somewhere behind us.

We pulled out with Sergei and Stal trailing us, creeping from ascent to ascent along the edges of ravines that led away in snowy smoothness down into snowy emptiness, perhaps disrupted by a craggy outcropping or a solitary boulder along the way. Here and there, the river our road followed glinted up fluorescent blue—no snow covered its ice. Sasha told me this was evidence of a *naled,* or river in which the water flowed on top of the ice and froze from the bottom up. This gave it a glorious turquoise glow, offset by the powdery white of snow along its banks.

The road diminished to a packed swath of mountainside, forcing us to crawl with belabored engines along its irregularities. Sheer ravines dropped well over a couple of thousand feet down to the turquoise river.

Parts of the road ahead appeared to have collapsed. Sasha's grip tightened on the wheel.

We drew up to a sign saying DANGEROUS ROAD AHEAD that heralded what appeared to be a stretch of *zimnik* that had slid away into the chasm.

"We have no choice; we've got to try it. There's no way to turn around here," said Sasha, as though he were trying to convince himself more than me.

He cracked his door and swung his head back to look at our trailer. I glanced over him—his open door revealed the abyss below. Our engine began to rev as Sasha's foot drove the gas pedal closer to the floor. He changed gears quickly. The view from my side through the windshield told me we were moving not as much forward, but sideways, toward the ravine's edge.

"The trailer is dragging us, dragging us over the edge!" shouted Sasha.

He slammed his door and told me to hold on. Our overloaded trailer was turning L-shaped in relation to the truck body and moving downward. I looked out of Sasha's side—all I could see was the river peeking out from below. Within seconds, we would pass into a free fall down the collapsed road into the ravine.

"Hold on! We're going over!"

I gripped the handle above my door and thought of nothing. Sasha hit the gas hard. Our engine roared and choked.

We skidded, then there was a grinding sound and a jolt. At this, we shot ahead.

Somehow, our wheels gained traction on a firm section of road and pulled us and our trailer onto solid ground. I looked at Sasha—his face was ashen. We pulled over and stopped, and burst into laughter.

We waited while Sergei passed above the section where we had had trouble and avoided the collapsed stretch. Upon seeing Sergei in the clear, Sasha clapped and shouted, *"Sakha! Sakha-bin! Sakhaaaa-biiin!"* and accelerated. *Sakha-biiin!* A primal scream in harmony with the primeval wilderness of Yakutia that had threatened to snuff us out.

The bad stretches continued, though, one after another. We crawled our way over two hundred kilometers of ravines, partly collapsed roads, ice, and slippery snow. As we approached particularly treacherous stretches, the kind that convinced me my trip would end at the base of a ravine under mangled metal and tire rubber, Sasha would break into song:

> *Black raven, why do you circle above my head?*
> *You will not get your booty!*
> *Black raven, I'll not be yours!*
> *Why do you spread your claws above my head?*
> *Black raven, I'll not be yours!*

His melodies drowned out the worrisome whir of the engine and gave us something to peg our thoughts on. They also took me back to the drama of Russia, to my desire to be a part of it, to my reason for sitting in that truck cabin in the middle of nowhere just south of the Arctic Circle.

Around midnight, on some nameless curve under a towering crag, we pulled over to sleep, exhausted from the tension and depressed by the extra slow pace imposed on us by the road conditions. The peaks around us loomed as black splotches on the glittering vault of stars. Later on, clouds moved in, and the night turned smothering, draping over the Suntar Khayata like a shroud of indigo felt.

At six or so, Sasha woke and put up tea. Sergei and Stal came over and got aboard. The slow, nerveracking ride had dispirited everyone, and the three of them sat in a silent row waiting for the kettle to boil. I could no longer face the thought of another meal in the cabin, listening to everyone slurp tea and chomp on dog food and lard and *konfety,* so I jumped out, preferring to stretch my legs and breathe fresh air rather than sit inside with my gloomy thoughts and selfish irritations.

We pushed on. Three more hours got us clear of the mountains; we emerged onto flat land where the road shot absolutely straight between two dead-calm flanks of forest, now thick with pines, but still utterly creatureless. This was taiga, Siberian wilderness, deaf to the cries of those who venture into it, and for this reason, the involuntary abode of exiles and refuge, conversely, for the persecuted who could learn its ways and master enough of it to survive. The taiga of Siberia, for Russians, meant both exile and freedom, both banishment from civilization and escape from human evils. It differed from the subarctic terrain of Kolyma in that it *was* habitable, if severe and sparing in its comforts.

Five hours later the *zimnik* joined the main road and we came upon what we took to be Khandyga. It was only a few wooden hovels with boarded-up windows. No, it couldn't be. We had been hoping for a place where we could wash up, see some people, and break our isolation.

It wasn't. The real Khandyga appeared twenty minutes later, announced by a Mother Victory statue: a stern steel woman with arms outstretched over KHANDYGA 1939. We weren't sure what the date meant. The town itself was a hodgepodge of green and blue shacks with peeling white windowsills and six-foot-long icicles hanging from the roofs, dispersed haphazardly across a random break in the woods. Three smokestacks at its western end belched soot that, in the absence of a breeze, fell straight back on the houses. The snowless road through Khandyga was a dry dirt track; as we drove along we raised a hanging tail of dust twenty feet high and five truck-lengths long that drifted over the hovels and settled on them, or dropped onto the black, grit-encrusted snow piled by the road.

"God, what a pit!" said Sasha. "We need to gas up, though. We've still got three hundred kilometers ahead."

We drove a bit farther down to a diner, where we washed up. Above the sink hung a placard showing an evil man in a black hat with a cigar; it advertised a movie called *The Sober Spy at the Wedding*. Sergei burst into laughter when Sasha remarked, "They're announcing your arrival, Jeff!"

Past the sinks, three thirtyish blond women in white smocks and thick flesh-colored leggings slopped *pelmeni* (dumplings) into soup bowls and plopped potatoes onto dishes. They had seen us coming and were taking up battle stations behind their assigned dishes, ladles in hand, dispirited, even accusatory expressions already assumed. I took *pelmeni* and moved toward the cashier to pay.

One of the women broke rank and smiled at me.

"*Molodoy chelovek* [young man], wouldn't you like some compote? I made it myself."

I took a glass, not because I wanted compote, but because her offer touched me. It was something personal—and she was soft and feminine, a change from the gritty-fingered male company I had lived with all week. Then Sasha came in and struck up a conversation with her.

"And this here is an American spy!"

They laughed even more uproariously.

"Just tell us where the nearest KGB post is. We're turning him in!"

Stal followed this dialogue with sufficient interest to halt the stream of *pelmeni* he had been spooning into his mouth. He blinked timidly and kept his eyes on mine.

"Really, every hour this American opens a secret CIA file and writes down everything we do."

Stal put down his spoon. The women laughed but asked not a single question. I'm sure it was too preposterous for them to imagine that an American, spy or not, would be sitting in their cafeteria, in Khandyga, eating their *pelmeni*.

"It's our duty, women, to see that his writings reflect socialist reality! We should examine his diary!"

Stal abandoned his plate half-full and scurried out all ajitter to the truck and climbed in, peering at me from the safety of his cabin. I paid and walked out, tired of Sasha's humor and curiously paralyzed in response to it. I was guilty of nothing, but Sasha's harping on the spy theme struck some nerve deep within me—I was not Russian, I was a citizen of the Soviet Union's erstwhile enemy number one, and no Russian could be expected to forget this. The women seemed to find the "joke" dull at this point and stopped laughing. I jumped aboard and thought about how near we must be to Yakutsk. My mood picked up when we started moving again; with only a three-hundred-kilometer stretch remaining, our ordeal appeared to be coming to a close.

"The Aldan River!" shouted Sasha.

"Where? I can't see it!"

"We're driving on it!"

The snow here lay unusually flat. Only the absence of trees distinguished this stretch of "road" as a river. It consisted of a path plowed across the snow on the ice, but it was bumpy, and upon closer inspection, cracked. Such hairline fractures in eight-foot-thick ice could mean little.

"Do trucks ever fall through?" I asked, searching for confirmation that they did not. Thin cracks in thick ice would present no danger, I hoped.

"Every year."

"All the way through, driver and all?"

"Driver and all."

"But not at *this* time of year."

"*Only* at this time of year! It will thaw soon. It's already cracked. See?"

We drove off the river half an hour later onto a spoiled *zimnik* of mud swells. For the next six hours we bucked these mighty swells, which heaved us high upon their crests, then threw us low into their breaches. We plowed through lakes of mud, *seas* of mud, sending out spray as high as our truck and as far as thirty or forty feet to the sides. We passed two Kamazy abandoned in the muck at roadside, lying on their flanks.

Around eight that evening we hit hard ground and started an unending ascent over jarring rippled frozen earth, corroded into speed bumps that shook every bolt of our truck and made my nose itch constantly with the vibrations. We stopped talking. Sasha was exhausted. No moon lit the snow. There were only headlights and dust and frozen ground.

"Wake up, Jeff! We're here!" I poked my head up. Tall coniferous trees stood bathed in floodlights. Unsoiled, crystalline snow. And a concrete apartment block draped in icicles. Sasha opened his door and nearly fell to the ground, just barely catching himself on the handle. Ahead, Sergei and Stal struggled to regain their land legs after the mud-sea and speed-bump ordeal. Stal opened my door and grabbed my arm.

"Jeff, come with me! We are at my sister's house in Verkhni Bestyakh. Yakutsk is across the L-L-Lena a bit farther west. We'll go there t-t-tomorrow. You can sleep on our sofa bed tonight."

Sasha and Sergei stretched out as sentinels in their trucks, as was their habit.

It was after midnight. We awoke Stal's tiny silver-haired sister, who must have been seventy and who had the chiseled Yakut features of a china doll. She spoke only a bit of Russian and seemed to be reproaching him for something in Yakut. She readied the sofa bed in the living room and let me shower. It had been five days.

I peeled off the clothes I had been wearing since Magadan. Hot water shot forth from the shower head I held in my hands. Grit and mud and sweat and dead skin whirled down the drain.

I put on my bedclothes and climbed between the clean sheets, reveling in being able to stretch out, and lost consciousness as though the soft touch of the bedding sent an anesthetic coursing through my veins.

The next morning, after a breakfast of chicken and warm buns, we all drove the remaining twenty kilometers over the blue ice of the broad Lena into Yakutsk.

—— FOUR ——

Yakutsk

If God's fist were to descend from the heavens and tear a city from its foundations in the permafrost, the jagged concrete, torn sheets of steel, and twisted cables that remained would look like Yakutsk. The city we arrived in sat exposed on a plateau as if the earth were offering it as a sacrifice to the arctic sun waning above. Plots of land lay vacant everywhere, metal twistings rusted under ice, *izby* (wooden houses) grew crooked over precarious permafrost, and heating pipes three feet in diameter, partly covered by ragged insulating fiber that looked like mange, crisscrossed above ground at forehead-banging height. Most buildings were one or two stories; none was higher than four or five. It was an open wound of a city, a shantytown trapped in ice.

In contrast to this decrepitude, however, were the women of Yakutsk; they glided through the frozen slums in round fur hats with fluffy tails, overcoats of tailored wool, and black leather mittens and boots. Their skin was soft and dewy; their cheeks were reddened by frost, but their hands and necks remained swan-white. And as if to spite the drabness of their surroundings, they splashed their lips with purples and pinks and even orange, which glowed like neon in contrast to the grays of old snow and leaden skies. After almost a week of cramped discomfort and gritty male company on the Kolyma Route, the sight of these women restored me to life.

Stal paid them no attention. Grinning in embarrassment, he called the bleakness of Yakutsk "our Soviet reality," but it was easy to see that such "reality" had as its base more than just seventy-five years of communist rule. Located some 325 miles south of the Arctic Circle, and isolated amidst thousands of square miles of frozen tundra and bogs, Yakutsk has an average winter temperature of fifty below zero. Until the 1920s, it was little more than a remote fortress for Cossacks and Russian Orthodox missionaries and a place of exile for revolutionaries and other undesirables. It was the center of an oblast from the eighteenth century onward, but most Yakuts (and other peoples of the region, such as the Evenks) lived independently of any state structure, scattered across the flat, frigid territory and wandering with their herds of cattle, tiny horses, and reindeer. After the establishment of Soviet power, most of these peoples settled and suffered collectivization with the rest of rural Russia. But Yakutsk had escaped the worst of Soviet modernization. It was a bleak polar outpost, not so much befouled by bolshevism as bedeviled by frosts.

Stal was dismissive about the future of the Autonomous Republic of Yakutia-Sakha (still a part of the Russian Federation): "We have diamonds and gold but can never do without Russia for food." It appeared that roughly half of Yakutsk's population was Russian anyway. Nevertheless, I was anxious to get out and around and meet Yakuts and see the town.

Stal led me to the Hotel Lena on Lenin Prospect and I checked in. My room there was spartan but clean, and tended by a fleshy blond Siberian maid who brought me pitchers of water and did my laundry. My room's window—a complex contraption consisting of three separate panes of glass with latches—looked out over a jumble of snow-covered concrete buildings and received the evening sun splayed through a massive Aeroflot eagle insignia above Lenin Square.

It was a typical spring day in Yakutsk: a vicious wind whipped the few errant citizens outside to and fro; the temperature was to reach a high of zero; and even a few minutes without gloves, as I learned when I fumbled with my camera, turned fingers into useless stubs. The city looked abandoned. Streets lay frozen under ice, and snow blew in circles around tracts of empty land. Even in April most of its two hundred thousand or so inhabitants stayed indoors unless there was a need to venture out.

I walked gingerly about on the ice on Lenin Prospect, Yakutsk's main drag, and dropped into the first building I came across to escape the cold. A peeling sign hanging in the doorway announced it as a computer games room. A surly Russian popped up from behind the counter. Behind him, in the leatherette-walled game room, bundled-up Russian and Yakut youths in floppy-eared fur hats stared into Bulgarian computer screens, their faces bathed in luminescent green. The man grunted and pointed to a sign above him: ENTRANCE BY INVITATION OF OPERATOR ONLY.

Down the avenue stood the Beryozka store—no relation to the hard-currency shops by that name of the Soviet past—and a half-dozen other shops, but all bore the same haphazard selection of shoes, dresses on plastic hangers, hair dyes, candy bars (Mars or Snickers), and soft drinks ("No Coke—Fanta"). At the Anniversary store farther on, the weather provided the only entertainment for those sheltering themselves there; as soon as customers turned the door knobs to leave, the wind sucked them out into the maelstrom, and they hung onto the knob as though they were drowning sailors clutching at a life preserver. When they lost their grip they were whisked away into the white, and the door would slam and bang with the wind. Each time, the stolid saleswoman would get up, hands in a muff, to reshut the door.

Hypothermia had begun to set in when I stumbled through the double doors of the Trade House. Tourism and sport, men's clothing, televisions and tape recorders, and even photography divisions were spread out over three stories. There was a lot of stuff for sale—Turkish laundry soap, Chinese women's underwear, Polish vodka, Serbian skirts—but little of it was Russian. I thought back to the jarring ride along the route and decided to look for towels to sew into covers for my battered lenses. I found some next to Serbian women's wear and Vietnamese bath soaps.

The saleswoman wore the standard Soviet retail facial expression, doughy and irritated, which said, "Don't waste my time!"

I bought my towel and left to find a place for lunch.

Acronyms form an important part of former Soviet life and language. In addition to the standard ones (NEP, New Economic Policy; AES, Atomic Electric Station; GAI, State Automobile Inspection, or traffic police), there are others that express peculiarly Soviet concepts. BOMZH (pronounced *bomsh*) is among these, standing for a person "Without a Determined Place of Residence," or lacking the official document, the *propiska,* indicating legal registration in one or another locale. A *bomzh* is, simply put, a bum, and very often, an alcoholic one.

And so I dropped into the Café Volna on Lenin Square for *pelmeni* and discovered it to be an abode of *bomzhy.* The place was silent except for the front door and its incessant banging to gusts of wind, and an ever-so-faint sibilant whisper from this same wind's passage through the windows facing the street. Around one-legged, chest-high tables, big enough for two to slurp soup on, stood Yakut *bomzhy* in execrable *shuby* and fur hats with floppy ears, leering sullenly at me as their heads wagged and their bony knuckles clutched tea glasses of vodka. One extended his arm to me as I passed and emitted a whine, followed by a rasping belch, then dropped his head to the table, which it struck with a sound like a hollow gourd.

I ordered a double serving of *pelmeni* with compote, which

came with apricots still submerged in the bottom of the glass for authenticity, and took a free table by the window. Soon, one of the *bomzhy* started yelping like a seal and dancing backward on one leg, his floppy hat ears bobbing up and down. Across from him, seemingly spurred into motion by his yelps, another Yakut pounded his chest and snorted, much as a gorilla would before attacking. The dancing one hopped backward, hooked a table in the crook of his knee, expectorated something in Yakut, and with a deft twist of his leg, sent the table and all its glasses crashing to the floor. The other, stunned by the racket of the falling table, loosened his arm, spilling vodka in a stream down his leg.

The double doors to the kitchen burst open and a tall Russian woman in felt knee-high boots and a white Chef Boyardee hat marched straight up to the drunk by the overturned table.

"What have you done? Tell me!" she demanded, her nose an inch from his.

The *bomzh* whimpered and slavered wordless babble as he flapped his arms in alarm.

She planted her hands on her hips.

"Pick up that table!"

He whined and grabbed his crotch, as if protecting it from a kick.

"PICK UP THAT TABLE!"

He scrambled back, keeping his eyes on her, and managed to raise the table and set it upright. She towered over him, still glowering. His eyes were slits in a face wizened and raw with all the frost of Yakutia. The woman marched back into the kitchen and returned to her *pelmeni* stand.

The *pelmeni* were delicious, and I went back for more. As I was about to be served, another sloshed Yakut began shouting and grasping at his companion's parka. My *pelmeni* server, who had just disciplined the dancing drunkard, thumped my dumplings back into their vat, and with a gymnast's dexterity, balancing herself on one arm, hopped over the counter. She headed straight for the obstreperous one, threw her arm back, and slapped a meaty

hand around his collar. She flung open the door with the other
hand and sent him flying out into the snowy maelstrom. She returned to the counter, smiled, and served me my *pelmeni*.

"Will you be having compote with that, young man?"

Dusk sent streams of magenta-hued light through the Aeroflot Eagle on Lenin Square, casting a perfect aquiline shadow on my hotel room wall. The snow had stopped hours ago, but it had gotten
much colder ("A frost has struck us," warned the maid). A howl-
ing wind rattled my triple-paned windows. I had napped and was
finally overcoming the vestiges of fatigue left by my long trip from
Magadan. I was now ready for dinner at Stal's.

"Jeff! Oh, Jeff!"

Stal and his borzoi and I stood in the doorway of his apartment.
His daughter, Vika, was calling my name.

"Jeff! Come to me!"

She dropped to her knees in front of us and opened her arms
wide. I was nonplussed. Was this the way young Yakut women
greeted foreign guests? Such radiant hospitality, such unbridled
zeal to salve a soul so far from home!

"Jeff! Come to me!" Her tone grew a bit sterner.

From behind me the borzoi bounded toward Vika and leapt
straight into her arms. She stroked his head and murmured, "Jeff,
Jeff, have you been a good boy with Daddy?"

Stal led me in and introduced us. Vika, with her doll-like, high
Yakut cheekbones and petite nose, was adorable. She had with
her a plump friend whose name was Sardana and whose eyes
were arresting with their biting skepticism. Both laughed when
they heard my name.

Vika, all giggles, could barely control herself.

"But, 'Jeff' . . . 'Jeff' is a dog's name! Hee-hee-hee!"

"I understand that's the name of your dog, but—"

"No," she twittered. "I mean 'Jeff' is not a name for people
at all!"

I said I hadn't known too many dogs called Jeff and that, in fact, it was a name reserved for humans in English-speaking countries. Why had they decided to name the borzoi that?

"Well, we get names from your television shows and movies. 'Jeff,' 'Bruce,' 'Eddie'—only dogs have such names here!"

Vika continued to giggle. Sardana grew tired of her silliness and went in the other room.

Vika, short for Viktoria, was in medical school in Yakutsk; Sardana, also a Yakut, studied in Khabarovsk. They both sat with their tiny feet pulled up under them on the sofa.

Sardana was direct.

"*What* are you doing here?"

"I'm traveling. To see Russia."

"You *like* it here?"

"I'm finding it interesting."

"*Interesting?* Our life here kills all that is good in us, all that is human."

She glared at me, as if to say, "What is *interesting* to you as an outsider is sheer hell for us. We have to live here."

Stal and Sardana tried to outdo one another in convincing me that no one could live as badly as the peoples of the former USSR. Vika took no part in this and disappeared from the living room. Soon she called us into the kitchen for dinner. At table, I tried to explain my lifelong passion for Russia, but my words fell on uncomprehending ears: the three of them remained incredulous, and Sardana's smirk had spread to Stal and Vika.

Cats supposedly fall feetfirst, but roaches always land on their backs. This is what I learned from dinner at Stal's. Vika had served us borscht and chicken. Stal's periodic slurps were interrupted by an occasional curious "tap" from somewhere nearby. I heard it a couple of times but paid no attention. But then, as I drew my spoon to my lips, I heard it again and saw that a plump roach had dropped from the ceiling onto its back in front of Stal and me.

Stal beamed, his eyes darting from the roach to me and back.

"Ooooh!" he exclaimed. The roach confirmed Sardana's and his criticisms of Russia. "I b-b-b-bet you don't have that in America!"

Sardana stared at me with her smirky eyes. *Interesting,* isn't it?

I paid no attention to the roach until one landed on my arm and became entangled in my sweater fuzz.

Vika deftly plucked it away with a lacquered nail.

Sardana crossed her arms.

"'Our Soviet reality.' Tell me you could find such a *dump* in America! I wonder why an American would come here. I know their life—I watch *Santa Barbara.*"

"*Santa Barbara* is one thing, real life another," I said. "There are plenty of poor and dispossessed in the States. Roaches, rats, bad plumbing—you can find them all over the world, not just here."

I stopped, embarrassed. Had I just called Stal poor and dispossessed?

He smiled at me and blandly laughed the kind of laugh that fills uncomfortable moments of silence.

I tried to think of some way to change the subject. Stal returned to slurping his borscht. At that moment, a bulge in the wallpaper behind him moved. There was scratching and a squeak. A mouse popped out on the counter and sniffed the air. Sardana turned in her chair to look, and he scurried back into the wall.

"It's this house, J-J-Jeff." Stal was embarrassed. "Really, all the old p-p-p-places in Yakutsk are like this. I'm ashamed."

"I see no reason for shame. With the scarcity of housing—" A roach sailed past my nose. "With the scarcity, it's completely understandable . . ."

I'm not sure where I was going with that, but I felt terrible for him.

Sardana jumped to her feet, throwing her napkin on the table.

"No one in this country cares about anything! That's what the problem is. We've never had anything but *shit*. I'm sorry. It's not 'this house' or 'scarcity.' Our old people, all these thick-skulled

Communists, have led us into this mess! I see no reason to mince words. A person from the country of *Santa Barbara* should just say it straight out."

Stal walked me out to the bus stop and we agreed to meet the next day.

The grizzled Russian ahead of me stood dipping his fingers in his *pelmeni* bowl. He was incensed.

"What are you shoving these cold *pelmeni* at me for?!"

"Go eat them! You paid for them, after all!" snapped the cashier, a doughy women with a lisp.

"I don't like things shoved at me, and I demand a hot meal for my rubles!"

The strong-armed *pelmeni* boiler stepped into the dispute with livid eyes.

"Take your *pelmeni* and go! Or get out! Everyone here loves them! No one is complaining!"

I had come to respect the *pelmeni* boiler for her way with drunks. She pointed at me.

"Look at this young man! He's eating his *pelmeni* cold and loves them! He eats here all day long!"

I looked at my bowl. In fact, my *pelmeni* were steaming. I quickly stifled the steam with the palm of my hand, feeling it would somehow drag me into this squabble. The angry Russian, tall and strong and slightly drunk, pulled up beside me at the little table.

He was attempting to draw the dumplings out of his bowl by sheer suction, it seemed. The spoon played only a minimal role as he dished the *pelmeni* to the general proximity of his mouth, then inhaled vigorously as if to levitate them and their sauce from the spoon through lung power alone, until they were caught in this traction of sorts and his suction germinated a lusty *ssslu-u-u-rp!* He downed the last few, licked his spoon, and buttoned his *shuba,* as if ready to leave.

A teenage urchin with streaks of grime on her cheeks, the first female *bomzh* I had seen, accosted him. She had on a oily lamb-skin coat that looked as though it had been unearthed from a compost heap.

"Give me a smoke!"

He straightened up.

"No way! Who do you take me for, anyway?"

She leaned very close to him and bared yellowed teeth.

"I don't take you for anybody. Just give me a smoke!"

"Then who's that guy on the street out there?" he questioned, tossing his shoulders back triumphantly, as though he'd exposed her scheme. She said she didn't know. The two of them walked out.

I got in line for more dumplings. As bad as the company was, they were delicious.

"Hey, what are you doing here? Hey! I'm talking to *you*."

A Yakut youth in a torn *shuba* stood leaning against the pillar across from the cashier. There was a glint of malice in his eye and a glass of vodka in his fist.

"I'm waiting for my *pelmeni*."

He tossed back a gulp of vodka.

"You a local?"

"What's it to you?"

"Businessman from the Baltics?"

The *pelmeni* lady handed me my dish and told him to bother someone else. He was too drunk to hear. He sidled up next to me.

"Sakha-Sire [Yakutia in Yakut] is independent!" he sneered.

I didn't dispute this or point out that it was only autonomous within the Russian Federation or mention that Moscow still takes the revenue from the sale of most of its mineral wealth. It seemed natural that nationalism had sprung up; because of my skin color, this youth had taken me for just another Russian imperialist. I ate my *pelmeni* and returned to the hotel.

The next day, Stal was waiting for me in the lobby as we agreed. We were to see about my transportation south to the rail line, which began in the settlement of Berkakit. He had offered to help me with this when he heard how I managed to get a ride arranged from Magadan to Yakutsk.

"You used the old hairy-paw technique! Yes, there's no other way to accomplish anything here, given our Soviet reality. No one will help you without the hairy paw!"

The "hairy paw" meant using a person of influence to set up things. I was coming to see that this was how I would have to arrange my trip across Russia.

We jumped aboard the number eight bus to the *aftobaza,* or truck depot, on the edge of town. Once we arrived, there was confusion about which entrance we should use, then what type of truck I'd travel in, then whether, in fact, this was the *aftobaza* at all. It wasn't. The watchman pointed down the road to the next series of sheds, and we started walking.

We passed through some gates and were directed to an office in the compound.

Stal wasted no time.

"This is an American c-c-correspondent. He needs to g-g-go to B-b-b-Berkakit at once." Everyone in the jammed truck dispatcher's office turned around and stared.

"Wrong office. Next door!" said one.

Next door, Stal repeated his request. The dispatcher—a big, stalwart Siberian with an iron handshake—asked if I spoke Russian. When I explained that I had come overland from Magadan, he raised his eyebrows.

"Not bad, not bad. No foreigner has done that since two Czech geologists made the run in the early seventies."

"Is the road south is a tough one?"

"Not as bad as the Kolyma Route, but don't forget you're in Siberia. Let me see if I can find a driver headed to Berkakit tonight." He stepped out.

Stal shook my arm with glee—he was quite proud of himself. I thanked him and told him that without his help, I'd never have been able to get any of this arranged. This might not have been true, but I was touched by the way he did his best to help me.

Anatoly, my bandy-legged driver, walked in, his head topped by a Daniel Boone fur hat. He was unshaven and had a heavy mustache, and was swarthy for a Russian. I noticed his trousers seemed to be falling down—the cord he used for a belt was coming loose. We shook hands.

The dispatcher turned to Anatoly.

"I'll let you two work out the bottle arrangement, of course."

"Oh, no! You can fire me for drinking on the job! I don't drink. No, not me!"

His words trailed away into chuckles. He had a soft smile in his dark eyes.

"I take off at six. All you need is food. For three or four days."

Stal accompanied me to the *aftobaza* that evening. On the lot, trucks belched black smoke as they rumbled through lake-size pools of brown water, cutting deep tracks in the mud as they emerged. Coal, junk, mining vehicles: they were carrying everything. The drivers had the same grit-encrusted look they had in Magadan, but here there was much more mud. Mud on *sapogi,* mud on trousers, mud on faces, mud everywhere. Mud *was* Yakutia as soon as the mercury crept above the freezing mark.

Anatoly drove to the edge of one of these lakes and jumped out, plopping into the muck with a *thwack.*

Stal and I said good-bye, and we were off.

"Just have to stop by my *svalka* [hovel] for a minute. For some tea. Gotta have tea."

The word "tea" seemed to trail off in his mouth. The Kamaz trundled clumsily into Anatoly's neighborhood of wooden shacks and tar hovels.

We pulled up beside a plank cabin surrounded by a fence of boards. Anatoly led me into the yard, pointing out the outhouse "for your needs." He threw open the door.

The *svalka* was dim, like a tomb. A figure sat up in the gloom. Grunting and clearing its throat, it hawked up phlegm and expectorated onto the floor, and moved its tongue over its teeth as one dying of thirst might. The expectorations reverberated in the cave-like dankness of the hovel.

"Sasha!" shouted Anatoly. "Get up. I'm getting ready for the road. Put on some tea!"

Sasha was a skeleton sheathed in loose flaps of tattooed skin, tanned in places, sallow in others. He spat out something about tea through dark stubs of irregular teeth, and wiped his hair out of his eyes with a palsied motion. Above his bed was a tattered Samantha Fox poster—there she stood, arms raised over her head seductively, breasts pressing through her T-shirt, her hair light and fresh. Seeing that poster, I was reminded me of the world I had come from and how far I was from home.

"He's my brother-in-law," said Anatoly when Sasha stepped into the yard. "My wife divorced me long ago, but I can't get Sasha to move out. Nowhere for him to go."

Sasha put up tea, then sat on the bed and covered his face in his hands. He reminded me of an old picture I had seen in a newspaper of a prisoner waiting for execution; looking at him, I felt a numbness returning, a premonition. When he went out in the yard again, Anatoly told me Sasha had just been released from prison, where he did four years for theft. He was only twenty-four, but looked forty.

We finished tea and had scrambled eggs. Sasha lay down and faced the wall. As we were leaving, he pulled on an overcoat and followed us out to the truck like a dog begging for a scrap. Anatoly handed him a wad of rubles and jumped into the truck—Sasha nodded good-bye and slunk back into the house.

"He'll drink it all," said Anatoly. "I give him money for food, but when I return, I always find he's done nothing but drink it.

FIVE

Blizzard

"So how are the winters where you're from? I've heard snowy and damp, with the sea and all," asked Anatoly.

We were pulling beyond the raw shacks and squatters' huts that had melted their way into the permafrost on the vast empty tracts outside Yakutsk. Our Kamaz, with its load of coal, was as heavy as a battleship of iron.

"What sea? You mean the Atlantic Ocean?"

"The Atlantic what?"

"Washington, D.C., is about a hundred and fifty miles from the Atlantic Ocean," I said.

His swarthy face registered a sudden mute perplexity, but he said nothing more. He seemed to be on the point of letting the conversation drift away, but then his head jerked up.

"What is Vasheentoon, a river?"

"It's the capital of the U.S., where I'm from."

Anatoly's thin frame jumped, and he grabbed at his fur hat.

"You're from the UNITED STATES? I thought you were from the Baltics!"

The dispatcher at the garage had told him nothing about me. He squirmed in his seat.

"I've taken you home . . . my God, will the KGB come after me for this? I've shown an American my *svalka!* I'm so ashamed! Will they arrest me for this?!"

"I don't think so. I think things have changed."

Who was I to reassure him, though? I doubted there was a risk, but if there was, I thought he had accepted it willingly, out of interest in meeting a foreigner, of whom there were few in Yakutsk. It was upsetting that my nationality might change the way Anatoly related to me—immediately, the words *stydno* (shameful) and *svalka* popped into his vocabulary, and I worried that he might edit his thoughts and monitor himself out of fear of some future reprisal from the KGB. If I were just another Balt, he would have had nothing to worry about. No matter what affinity I felt with the Russians, the very history of conflict and drama that so intrigued me set me apart in their eyes.

We rumbled down to the banks of the Lena, which glowed white with snow in the moonless night. The only way to Yakutsk by road from the south was via the river; during the winter, the *zimnik* passed over it some for some five kilometers; in summer, a ferry took trucks along the same route over water. The absence of a bridge seriously disrupted transport, ice and ferries notwithstanding; with the thaw in May, all road traffic would cease for a month until the river became navigable by ship in June. It would freeze over in October, and the reverse process would paralyze traffic for another month.

Bezdorozhye, or roadlessness, isolates settlements all across the Russian north during the spring thaw and autumn rains. The term is somewhat inaccurate: there *are* roads, dirt roads, but they become impassable when wet and leave people dependent on air travel, if it is available. Asphalt is nonexistent until western Siberia; you can't keep the mud off your shoes in Yakutia any more than you could use an umbrella in a tsunami. Outside the city, the permafrost and endless bogs and tracts of muck are predatory and carnivorous: they suck children in and drown them, people vanish in them; they devour powerful beasts in one gulp. In fact, Yakuts boast that more prehistoric mammoth remains lay marooned in their muck than anywhere else in the world.

"Stalin sure knew where to build gulags. He picked Yakutia for a reason," Anatoly mused as we passed frozen swamps. "Try to escape from one—during the winter, you'll freeze to death. During the summer, the bogs will suck you under or the clouds of midges will devour you."

Yakutia's history in Soviet times was entirely intertwined with diamonds and death, prison labor and the extraction of precious minerals from beneath its permafrost. Once the former Soviet government had renounced Stalinism and at least reduced its dependence on the gulag work force, it turned to financial incentive to draw western Russians to labor in the cold and mud and midges.

Anatoly wore his fur hat high atop his head, and its subtle browns melted into the tints of his skin, a leathery bronze with a red patina in places.

"Looking at me now, you wouldn't know it, but I'm from Nizhni Tagil in the Ural Mountains," he said, as we pounded down the *zimnik* heading south, his skin turning into a net of golden wrinkles glowing faintly in the dashboard light.

"I never knew my father. The KGB arrested him after I was born in 1937 and he disappeared, and my mother earned too little to support us. I had three brothers. So she had to put me in an orphanage. Just to get by. Not because she didn't love me. I didn't ask that sort of question. There, we read in our books about our Great Father, Iosif Vissarionovich [Stalin], and ate American sausage. The war had begun by the time I started remembering things. Your government sent us sausage. Thank you, by the way. It was tasty. When I got out of there at eighteen, I took off to the north and wandered around the arctic settlements, doing odd jobs as a vagrant would, needed by no one and of use to no one. Just skin and bones without a reason to be. But there was always work in the north, and the pay was good, and no one cared about my *propiska* so I stayed on, and eventually ended up in Yakutsk, where I married. That's what a man does when he has nothing else, no place to go. He makes his own nest from what he finds around him."

"Was it a mistake?" I asked.

"Nothing went right between us. The wife drank and dumped me for another man. She left me her brother Sasha for company. But she did let my son stay with me."

"What's he doing now?"

"My son . . . huh . . . What business had those girls being down at the port at four in the morning?" His voice shook with a sudden rage. "It's obvious what they were. And now my son is in jail for attempted rape. Four years he'll be locked up. I'm sure he only meant to rob them, just rip off their earrings. But the militia arrested him and beat him up. There's no democracy here now, even with the Communists gone. They beat him. He had dropped out of school at sixteen. I don't know . . ."

As he finished each turn of his story, he waved his hand dismissively as if to say, "No use in getting upset," and turned his face to the numbing blackness outside the truck.

Somewhere north of Ulu, we pulled over that night under snow-laden boughs of pines petrified into stillness by the stony cold. Anatoly put up tea, muttering to himself, lost in tattered vignettes from his past. He was alone with his fate—I had ceased to exist for him. His mother, long since passed on, his wife, his son, his own death . . . He seemed to glimpse them all in the windshield glimmering with his reflection and the primus flame and the embers of his cigarette. If I was there for him, it was only in the capacity of stand-in for someone unknown to me, judging by the curious tones his mumbling adopted, as if he were confiding in a long-lost friend. He grumbled now and then in my direction, but I felt I should say nothing to his drifting thoughts and observe a silence, as at a deathbed.

After tea, he waved his hand and his voice lifted as he consoled himself with thoughts about Providence and fate and his having a job and brother-in-law—"blood all the same, if he does drink"—to look after him.

He let his words trail off and waved his hand dismissively again, as though he had finally exorcised himself of past griefs or gotten emotional over trifles.

I jumped out to stretch my legs. The taiga was deaf to Anatoly's fate: it was a forest thick and sunk in grasping snow, impassive and unresponsive, earless to the laments of those who lived in it or traversed it or died in it. There was no wind that night. No branches stirred. No moon. Just stolid pines, the lusterless dark, the feeble yellow light in our cabin, and the flame from Anatoly's primus. Still, I felt comfortable, much more at ease than on the Kolyma trip. From Yakutsk to Berkakit was, it appeared, going to be a cinch.

After Anatoly was done with his tea, I climbed into the *spalnik,* or sleeping shelf, behind the front seat, a luxury I did without on the run from Magadan to Yakutsk.

"Just remove the sack of corn and push the rags aside," he said. "And give me my hunting knife, if you can find it there."

I couldn't. I dug around in the junk he had accumulated during many long trips and cleared a space to stretch out in. Anatoly left the motor running for heat. Still in his hat, he stretched out on the seat, his small frame all at once losing its muscle tone with a cadaverous rattle from his lungs, and dropped into an instantaneous sleep.

Around three in the morning, dreams of heat and vertigo and airlessness had me sweating and tossing and gasping until I woke up with a start. The cabin was a rumbling furnace: exhaust fumes were pouring in through the window left open a crack, burning my eyes and choking me. Anatoly lay lifeless in the same position he had fallen asleep in. I reached over him and fumbled for a knob or key to turn off the engine, but could find nothing, though I did manage to shut the window. I stared at his chest. It was not moving.

"Anatoly! Anatoly!"

Death from pain and grief and lost chances, I thought; a suicide that nearly took me with him.

"Anatoly!"

I poked his shoulder.

"Anatoly!"

He started out of his sleep with a drool and a rasp.

"What's happened? What?"

His revival startled me.

"I just wanted to know how to shut off the engine," I said, relieved that he was alive, but light-headed from the fumes. "The exhaust is choking me. Don't you feel it?"

He punched a button under the wheel that silenced the motor and rolled over into his solitude and began to snore.

Just north of Ulu the next morning, we pulled into a deserted gas station sitting high on a rise and lashed at by snow flurries blowing in hectic circles. Anatoly asked me, as he grabbed a rag, "Now, in the States, wouldn't you have a black man jump out and wash your windows in such a station? You would. I don't need a black man. I'm black myself and wash my own windows."

The flurries thickened. We gassed up and moved on.

The snow poured from above, as if it were grain rushing free of a trapdoor in a silo, and blinded us to anything more than a few meters away. Now and then, shadows of trucks would take shape ahead of us and materialize fully only as we came upon them. The blizzard surprised me—there had been a thaw in Yakutsk when we left, and I thought the weather could only be warmer to the south. April in Siberia was a fickle month, said Anatoly.

He had recovered from last night and propped his fur hat on his ears.

"Madonna—the blond American. I've seen her. On TV. How old is she?"

"I'm not sure, but I think thirty-two."

"Well, she must be married then."

"No."

He couldn't understand why a woman so "old" would still be single, he said. Then an explanation occurred to him.

"She performs . . . *naked!*"

He averted his face, smiling bashfully at the word—he was ashamed to say it.

"I'd marry her, even so," he allowed, with palpable grace and magnanimity, raising his head high. "Then she could sit at home all day and not have to sing . . . *naked.*" He again averted his eyes.

"Sit at home in Yakutsk?"

"*Nyeeet!* I'd take her back to Nizhni Tagil!"

I guess to him that made a difference.

"Let's send her a telegram and let her know," I suggested.

"*You know her?* I guess you would, being an American and all." We both laughed.

We came upon a truck moving timidly out into the road's center and back to the side, over and over again. Anatoly tried to pass but failed. The blizzard thickened the air with white and muffled his honks.

"*Svoloch! Akh ty, svoloch!*" he muttered as we lumbered about in the snow behind the hesitant driver, waiting for a clear chance to pass. Bastard.

We emerged from the blizzard all of a sudden into thin air, with only a flurry or two drifting lazily to earth, and came immediately upon a militiaman waving a black-and-white baton at us. We stopped.

He jumped up to the cabin, jutting forward his perfectly

shaved square jaw, and shoved his face into Anatoly's, as though inclining his head for a kiss. He sniffed his breath.

"Are we drinking today?" he asked, backing down.

Anatoly laughed. *Nyet.*

"What about guns? Carrying any?"

Anatoly laughed in the same meek way all those laugh in countries where the police can lock you up for nothing, take away your license on a whim, or give you a thrashing just for the hell of it. *Nyet . . . Guns? . . . Ha ha ha . . . Who, me?*

The square-jaw ignored Anatoly's groveling chuckles.

"We know you're armed. Give up your guns."

The officer had dropped his chattiness and was drilling us both with his eyes.

Anatoly shrank in his seat.

"Give up your guns!" the officer repeated.

"Who told you we had guns?"

"Who? That fellow over there—we've just picked him up for drunk driving."

Down the road were the truck and driver we'd tried to pass earlier.

"Says you shot a deer up the road."

"We have no guns. We've shot no deer," said Anatoly with his hand over his heart, as though pledging allegiance to his flag. "No guns . . . Really."

The militiaman stared into Anatoly's eyes and cocked his head.

"Let's see your documents, then. Both of you."

I thought of my Moscow-only visa. I fumbled in my overnight bag to buy time. Anatoly twitched his eyes toward me—"No," he was saying to me. He handed the officer his license.

"Officer, just look at our cabin. No guns, nothing."

He did look, jumping up on the running board and poking his head in. I acted as though I was still searching for my passport. He jumped down and waved us on.

Anatoly accelerated and closed his window.

"*Svoloch.* He was no militiaman—he had no badge," said Anatoly with grit in his voice. "He was a *bandit*. Don't show any of them your American passport. They'll never let go of us if you do. Wouldn't let go of me or you."

"A *bandit?*"

It seemed to me that a "bandit" would just rob us or certainly not have let us go so easily. Maybe he just forgot to put on his badge. Being the militiaman for Ulu in Yakutia wouldn't be much to get worked up about. Then again, on a route with so much Yakutian gold passing north to south, maybe it would be.

The road became icy soon after. Anatoly decided we should stop for lunch in the hope that the sun would emerge and thaw it out.

"The Communists used to tell us," he remarked, pulling out his primus and striking a match to it, "that seaweed is so good for you! Eat seaweed for your health! Don't pass a day without a bowl of seaweed! Now I ask you, have you ever seen a Commie eat seaweed?"

I couldn't say that I had. But I did know people in the States who thought it salubrious. Anatoly dismissed this.

"No! You haven't seen a Communist eat seaweed! And they don't eat it in Vasheentoon. It's not fit for a human. Even a dog wouldn't eat it. And those Communists used to tell us, 'Exercise!' Ever seen a Commie doing push-ups? They all have round bellies!"

He poured water out of a steel canister into his cooking pot and swished it around with his fingers "to clean it," he said, though his hands bore a permanent patina of engine grit and motor oil. This done, he sliced potatoes and dropped them into the pot.

"No, Commies don't eat seaweed, no . . ."

His voice trailed away and he waved his hand dismissively. No use in getting upset. The meal he cooked up was a feast of potatoes, sausage, and greens. It tasted not of greasy fingers but of the unspoiled taiga in whose midst we were sitting.

After lunch, Anatoly forgot about the ice and we pulled out onto the road again, our bellies full. Within an hour, we left the clear

cold and entered drizzle and fog, our windshield steaming so
thickly Anatoly and I wiped it clean continuously with long
sweeps of his bandanna for some half an hour. The road at this
point disintegrated into swells of mud, stationary waves of muck.
It was incomprehensible—snow and cold, then muck and rain.
Belts of warm air cut by cold, not visibly prompted by geography.
The landscape, though, remained as bleak as ever in the warm
zones: dirty snow littered the taiga floor like spilled trash; trees,
scraggly and black against the mist, were sunk in an umber-
colored mire; and when we passed a truck, waves of mud splashed
over our front end with great force, as though shot from a fire
hose. Toward the end of the afternoon, a glutinous fog formed and
clung to our windshield, leaving us blind and groping along the
sides of the road, ever wondering if we might not be about to drive
over the edge into the mud.

That evening, we reached torn-up tracts of red-brown muck
hundreds of feet long, along with careful incisions into *sopki* flesh
that looked as though they had been made by a giant, zigzagging
scalpel. Strip mining. The gold mine north of the settlement of Aldan. Anatoly was to unload his coal there and proceed empty to
Berkakit. Belazy, giant excavating vehicles with tires as tall as a
man, raced about on errands in the fog. Floodlights poured over
tracks of mud. From work pits, steam rose in columns and drifted
through sheets of rain, and no one was visible above ground. Anatoly said he knew where to dump his coal: on top of the mist-
shrouded promontory above the main pit.

There we found coal lying in pyramids, surrounded by moats
of mire and wafts of fog. We backed up to one such mound,
lurched violently, then stopped. Our wheels spun and whirled
muck into the rainy gloom. Anatoly jumped out and sunk to his
knees in mud. We were stuck. He plugged around for a minute
and hauled himself back aboard. Wiping his nose on his sleeve, he
pulled back a lever by the steering column and dumped our coal
load with a roar and a lingering hiss.

"Stuck. Stuck in the mud. Time to put up tea. Gotta have tea. Strong tea."

More bread and sausage and black, tar-like tea boiled on his primus. We were shipwrecked for now. Anatoly said we would remain there until a Belaz or similar vehicle appeared tomorrow. Beneath us, floodlights illuminated clouds of drifting steam and sheets of insidious drizzle.

After dinner, I crawled into the *spalnik* and pulled out my map. We had covered only three hundred miles in two days. Two hundred remained to Berkakit. Sleep overcame me as I listened to the rain drum on the steel roof of the cabin.

Dawn never really came the next morning, but the clouds awoke with tints of gray blue. A cold snap had hardened the ground overnight. Mud swells were now like crusty moonscape. The air bit and chafed at my skin as soon as I stepped out of the cabin after breakfast.

The hard ground improved Anatoly's mood and sparked a new series of monologues.

"Russia is huge. And wealthy. You can bathe in any hole once the snow melts. Our water is pure. No one to fear. No snakes or crocodiles, like on your Canary Islands. I've seen your TV show about this. Snakes . . . America . . . Canary Islands . . . No, Russia is self-sufficient. A land where a man can feel free to bathe in the snow. And after that he can look at these larch trees. Queens of trees, the larches. You don't have them in Vasheentoon. I know. This is a land to be born in and die in."

The snow deepened at the side of the road. The sky turned into a descending pewter-tinted sheet and closed in on us. Not a truck met us coming north, and Anatoly muttered about weather changes. We were alone on the road. Trees thinned, more and more often struggling to breathe through the snow. Another cold belt.

Aldan, no more than half an hour south of the mine, had been struck hard by a hit-and-run blizzard. Trucks were pulled up by the filling station at the edge of the settlement, and Anatoly found his *naparnik* among them. This man, white-haired with thin skin and a belittling tone in his voice, told Anatoly he'd go no farther today and rolled up his window.

Anatoly pulled out his primus again to make tea. I sensed something was wrong.

"Anatoly, we just had tea an hour ago."

"That's right. But we've driven enough for today. We're going to drink tea and relax."

Driven enough for today? It was eight in the morning and Berkakit was less than two hundred miles south. What was the point of stopping so close?

"You mean we're going to sit here in this cabin all day?"

"What's a day, or two, or three out of our lives? My *naparnik* is staying put. So are we."

"You didn't even ask why he's staying! We've only got two hundred and seventy-five kilometers left!"

Anatoly muttered and peered into his tea sack, then clattered around in his satchel of tins and eating utensils. I was fading away for him again.

"Tea . . . Trucks stopped here . . . Ice ahead . . . After that, Vasilyevka . . . Bad . . . Ice . . . Strong tea."

"Ice? How do you know?"

A truck rumbled past us heading south. Then another.

I sat back and collected my thoughts. I knew I was being pushy by asking Anatoly to drive on, and I had no doubt that he knew his roads and weather conditions. But we were near our destination, and cabin life was starting to get to me again. It also seemed that he might be happier to sit and stay put; he was comfortable on the road and would be paid no more to hurry. Foul weather could be just an excuse for inveterate Soviet indolence.

He finished his tea and looked up.

"Okay. We'll take a look. Maybe we can go a bit farther."

South of Aldan, roads were built over *sopki,* not around them, and soon after the settlement disappeared from our rearview mir-

ror, a pass came into view, along with the sun, which shot metallic light earthward in searing shafts and burned our retinas. We
crept up the pass, our wheels spinning on ice, then catching on dry
patches and jerking us ahead. When we crested the rise, Anatoly
slowed and drew up on a lookout point above a roundabout curve
high on the *sopka*. A long, steep descent spread before us, at the
bottom of which the road veered right and then rose into another
grade.

Anatoly sucked in his stomach and we began the descent. Our
truck gained a threatening momentum and Anatoly touched the
brakes gently. We skidded, long and slow, our Kamaz moving
sideways down the slope. He let up on the brakes and we straightened out, then touched them again, and the same thing happened.
There seemed to be no way to slow down without skidding.

We hit the turn at the base of the descent and slugged through
plowed snow piled on its outer edge. This provided us with further traction, and so we drove, hugging the left shoulder, round
the curve to the next ascent. No trucks met us head-on, and we
continued to the top.

We reached a plateau rimmed on the south by *sopki*. Anatoly
drove a bit, then pulled over.

"I want to bathe."

"What?"

"I'm going to take a bath. I'll go no farther today. We'll have to
wait until the ice thaws. Bath . . . Tea . . . Gotta bathe."

Anatoly threw open the door. The air outside was frigid. He
walked along the road a few feet, then dropped into waist-deep
snow off its bank and floundered in it, like a swimmer moving
into the open past a choppy surf. He whipped his shirt over his
head and began snatching at snow and smearing it over his sallow
chest, under his arms, onto his face, into his hair. Wind drove
snow around him—he held his face to it as a sunbather would to
fresh beams of sunlight on a beach in June and opened his mouth
wide, then dove into the drift and wallowed around in it. When he
finished, he stretched and plodded back to the truck, lifting his

legs high and clumsily above the snow, as children do above knee-high waves when trying to run the last few yards to the beach.

"Aaaah! Bath . . . Good bath . . . Go no farther today. Ice . . . ice on the road. You want to take a bath?"

I couldn't bear the thought of sitting in that cabin another day. Or maybe more. Who knew? If there was risk involved in going forward, what about the danger in sitting still, waiting for some snowstorm to bury us? We had no access to weather reports, and neither of us had talked to anyone coming north, although we had seen several trucks moving south. Anatoly chortled to himself when I verbalized these thoughts. He was listening to me, but his mind was set on a long sleep- and tea-filled sojourn in the cabin on that plateau.

We sat in silence. A truck appeared in our rearview mirror.

"Anatoly, maybe I ought to stop that truck. He seems to be ignoring the weather. Do you understand?"

He did. He handed me a white metal cup.

"A souvenir. Drink tea and remember Anatoly!"

He jumped out and plodded through the snow, waving his blue bandanna at the approaching red Kamaz. It stopped. Anatoly talked to the driver and waved me over. I grabbed my bags.

"Drink tea! Remember Anatoly!"

Pavel, the driver, shifted into first and we drove off, leaving Anatoly, a tiny brown figure in the sheer whiteness behind us, waving a bandanna and moving through the snow on bandied legs.

Gripping the wheel as a cowboy does the reins of a bucking stallion, Pavel was big and strapping and blond and looked to be around twenty-five. He was originally from Blagoveshchensk, near China. I liked his clear head and complete sentences.

"You've been in a truck since Yakutsk with that old guy? Those old people can't restructure their thinking. I've got money to make—I'd never sit in a truck cabin for days hoping the weather will break. It may get worse!"

Kinship of age and spirit directed our conversation. Pavel

thought that I should have picked a young driver, that I wouldn't understand Russia's future by socializing with the old. I wasn't sorry to have ridden with Anatoly, though; rather, I was pleased with the chance I had to get to know a Yakutian old-timer, and glad that my ride with him introduced me to Pavel, with whom I felt I could talk freely.

We pounded ahead over the icy straight stretches of the plateau, as bumpy as corrugated steel, then began weaving downward in a slow descent through *sopki* under a sky of shifting beams of silver cast from a sun partly hidden behind the clouds. Pavel asked detailed questions about life in the States and the legal aspects of marriage. It seemed he'd had a marital problem ending with a divorce that turned out unfavorably for him; he had lost possession of his son to his ex-wife. He blamed "laws drafted by Communists" for this, and thought American judges would have been more inclined to let his son stay with him.

At the crest of the final *sopka,* a glimpse of the massive, rolling steppe below dissolved our discourse on family law and replaced our good humor with a sense of foreboding. The wind began to howl, weary undulations of steppe swathed in ceaseless rushing clouds of white stretched to the horizon, and the cabin grew perceptibly colder as we descended. Pavel shifted in his seat and threw away his cigarette.

"What's happening here?" I asked, awed by the sudden change in weather.

The wind, now screaming through the numerous slits and crevices in the cabin, lashed at our Kamaz and drove five-story-high clouds of snow across the road.

Pavel's voice cracked.

"This . . . this is bad. Maybe we should have waited it out."

The horizon had faded into white—the sky was white and the earth was white. A glare resulting from sunlight hitting flying snow struck our eyes from every angle. Trees had diminished to scarecrow-like burned twigs.

"This is bad. This is a bad place. Vasilyevka. There is radiation here. From the uranium gulag over there. Stalin had prisoners mining uranium here. The radiation is high."

To the west and south, about two hundred yards off the road, remnants of shacks and prison barracks peeked up through the snow, mirage-like in the blizzard, fading with the thickening waves of white, reemerging as they thinned. I was thankful to be in a moving truck.

We descended a gentle slope approaching the ruins of the gulag and stopped. Pavel's *naparnik,* a Yakut named Dima with a long, Genghis Khan mustache, had halted ahead of us, and ahead of him another two trucks had pulled over. Dima jumped out and slipped on the snow as he ran through the winds to our cabin.

Dima shivered, the wisps of his mustache hoary with frost.

"Something's happened ahead. I don't know what. We have to stay put."

Pavel suggested we eat. Food was the last thing on my mind in all this radiation and snow, but I kept this to myself and forced down some ham and tea. We fell silent. Within an hour, as we all chomped glumly on biscuits and stared at the road, the wind died with a death rattle, as if it were the final breath of an expiring elder, and the snow stopped blowing, dropping to the earth with a hiss.

The eye of the storm, Pavel said.

In the frigid, sterile stillness, the splinters of the gulag stabbed through the white powder to the west. Above us hung a sky of thin blue air, beneath which rolled sweeping expanses of lifeless white steppe dotted with black runts of trees. We sat in uneasy silence, the kind of silence one finds amidst those waiting for news of loved ones going under the knife.

One hour passed. Then two. Pavel and Dima dozed. I closed my eyes and wondered how much radiation we were being exposed to. When I'd asked the two of them about this, they'd answered, "We're used to it. We don't know. We know this is a bad place, but the authorities would never tell us the truth."

At the top of the third hour, the weather spoiled again with one wrenching boreal blast of gale and blowing snow, a blast so vicious it woke up Pavel and Dima and startled me out of my benumbed inertia, but at the same time the trucks ahead roared their engines and pulled away into the white. Dima cleared his throat and jumped down out the door. Pavel ran his hand through his hair and shifted into first gear. Dima's truck lurched ahead and was immediately lost in the snow cloud.

Ahead of us was a roll in the steppe, partly obscured by a maelstrom of white, where distance ceased to exist, where snow and earth and wind coalesced into a gaseous whirling mass. We entered it, groping for the road, and came upon a truck sunk sideways in the snow off the eastern bank.

"*That's* what held us up," shouted Pavel over the wailing wind. "He got off on the bank and had to abandon his truck."

The road lay on a raised bed; should a truck slip off its grade, it would simply disappear into the powder, as this truck had done. We passed it and drew up on another rise, beyond the crest of which we discovered wind driving snow in front of us like water rushing through a burst dam, burying what road we could still see as we crept along.

"*Zanosy.*" Snowdrifts.

Pavel pronounced the word as though it were a death sentence.

Ahead of us, in the drifts, a shadow resolved itself into a Zhiguli lodged sideways on the road, blocking our path.

"Son of a bitch! What kind of idiot drives a passenger car on these roads?!" shouted Pavel.

We crunched forward and halted. Pavel pulled a shovel out from behind the seat and jumped out to help the driver, a bundle of fur holding onto his hat flailing a shovel, dig himself free. Although they were no more than twenty feet ahead, their figures waned to white in the driving snow as they struggled to keep their balance in the gales.

They finished. The driver crawled into his car and lurched past our truck, stalling in the drift behind us. Pavel jumped aboard

and drove on anyway. We had covered no more than twenty yards
when we came upon the Zhiguli's *naparnik*.

"Goddamn!"

Pavel let loose a stream of curses, grabbed his shovel, and
started out again. I grabbed his arm.

"Let me do this one."

"No way. I'll just be a second."

He struggled through another brief, frantic ordeal of shoveling
with another fur-hatted driver faceless in the whirling white. As
before, the driver climbed in and hit the gas, trying to break free,
slipping back and grinding into the snow. But then Pavel dropped
to his knees, bracing himself on the shovel, and placed his forehead on the handle, fading to white in the hoary gale. He did not
get up, even when the Zhiguli lurched free. The wind drove snow
over him and screamed through the cabin. The thermometer on
the rearview mirror read forty-two below zero.

I jumped out and started through the snow. Pavel saw me and,
not wanting to appear weak, pulled himself up on his shovel and
started back toward the truck.

We climbed in. Pavel held his head in his hands for a moment
and winced, then pushed the heavy gearshift knob into first. A
whir followed, then a roll, then another whir, but we remained
stationary.

We were stranded in the drifts.

I reached for the door.

"I'll shovel now!"

"No, you won't. You can't shovel your way out of a drift. You'll
freeze to death if you try."

Pavel sniffled, his nose red and running as his body warmed.
He dropped his head to the steering wheel.

We sat in silence. I figured that if there were anything to be
done, Pavel would do it, or ask me to. But the cabin grew colder
and colder, and the wind continued to scream. I had wrapped myself in my coat and was still cold; Pavel never took off his parka.

Our silence stretched on and on, metastasizing into paralysis,

an inertia born of deathly white cold outside and the claustropho-
bia of the shrinking cabin. I wanted to do something, to say something, but couldn't. Pavel's face lost its expression, turning blank
and pallid. Snow rose about us, and we became part of the drift.
The truck dispatcher's warning came to mind: in Siberia, a man
had to be cleverer than nature to survive. Such cleverness might
be acquired with age—Anatoly's age. I wondered if my American
sense of time efficiency—my reluctance to sit tight in Aldan and
wait, as Anatoly had wanted to do—wouldn't now have the
gravest consequence of all.

An hour passed.

There was a rumble and the low whine of an engine. Something ahead of us broke the reign of the screaming winds. Gears
were changing, a motor was grunting. We looked up, and the
snow curtains parted to reveal a looming plow, which braked suddenly as its driver realized he'd come upon our truck. Pavel got
out and, without exchanging a word with the driver, hooked a
heavy cable from our front end to a claw on the plow. In one
wrenching spasm of creaking steel, it pulled us onto cleared road.
The plow driver disengaged our cable and disappeared into the
white behind us. Pavel hit the gas.

Dima was waiting for us at the high pass before Maly Nimnyr.
From the pass the Yakutian plateau free-falls to the low altitude
of the Siberian plateau. He left his truck and climbed into our
cabin.

"Look, we may want to wait this out. It's sheer ice on the descent ahead. I'm for tea and candy myself."

I wasn't, but I said nothing. Pavel was blunt.

"Tea and candy! Listen to you, lazy Yakut! I think we can make
it. I want to hit Berkakit by tonight."

So did I. It was already four in the afternoon, and the remaining 125 kilometers would take at least four hours to cover if we
maintained our same pace. Pavel prevailed.

Dima took a cautious lead. Although the ice had some gravel
sprinkled on it, traction was tenuous. We began to slip as soon as

we left the crest, and our trailer swung right, then left. Dima lost control within minutes and slid slowly into the snow bank; Pavel did some deft maneuvering and avoided his jutting trailer.

"We can't stop for him. Someone else will have to pull him out."

Down below, at the foot of the pass, stretched an expansive Siberian vista of low rumpled *sopki* covered with dark brown larches. The trees augured a return to life, an escape from steppe harshness and frigid sterility.

We pulled over in Khatymi and waited for Dima. The road from there to Chilman was violent and jarring, often little more than a rock-strewn clearing in the taiga. Pavel's shock absorbers were shot, but he bobbed up and down in comfort on a spring-mounted seat. I took it straight and whacked my head against the ceiling several times. The snow on the ground grew thin but the dust thickened—we were in Dima's dust trail and inhaled it unfiltered for five more hours.

At one in the morning, we pulled into Berkakit, all crime lights and glinting ice and restless wind, and collapsed into deep slumber, I on the seat, Pavel in the *spalnik*, with the road dust between our teeth.

SIX

Tynda:
Reprieve and White Fever

The Coke in the kiosk window caught my eye—I hadn't tasted a Western cola since Magadan. Yakutsk had had only Fanta, and the settlements south, nothing at all. Traveling through lands of deprivation breeds the strangest of fixations. I wanted that Coke.

Getting it wasn't going to be easy. Occupying the narrow pass leading between outdoor tables to the kiosk was a gaggle of *alka-shi* (street drunks), all in muck-splattered parkas that had been worn to a verdigris from incessant contact with their unwashed skin, and droopy trousers with hems frayed and flies unzipped. They swilled tea glasses topped off with a hundred grams of vodka After each belt, they let their heads drop and tugged tight the flaps of their parkas against the wind, awaiting the dull rise of Lethe.

A half-light filtered through the clouds and did not warm. It was only nine in the morning and the kiosk in Tynda had just opened. The faces of the *alkashi* were craggy, rutted raw with frost. And still sober, hostile. In every country there are drunks, but nowhere, I was coming to see, do they form an entire social class as they do in Russia. Russians implicitly recognize this by referring to them as *nashi alkashi*, or "our drunks," in much the same way they talk of "our former gentry" or even "our intelligentsia." *Alkashi* drink vodka when there is a choice, most commonly Russkaya vodka, produced by the state and dispensed in almost every conceivable establishment, from kiosks (where, at times, it is the *only* product for sale) to snack bars and even clothing stores. Vodka, as it is drunk in Russia, inebriates in sullen waves, bringing on a stupor that releases primal grief and hostility and often results in violence and crime. I watched that stupor descend over the faces of the drunks around the kiosk; no matter how enamored I was of Russia in the abstract, no matter how hard I tried to understand all the country had suffered under the Soviets, I found the *alkashi* disgusting.

A cold blast of wind whipped up dust around me and prompted me to hurry. I stepped forward. One of the *alkashi* expectorated with a threatening *thwack* and, as I approached, grabbed at my coat sleeve. I pushed past and asked for my Coke.

"Brother, give me some money! Hey, brother!"

Several of the drunks turned their heads at this; I was invading their hangout; I was not of their class; I was an opportunity for quick gain; I was alone. Even the kiosk man stared at me with some suspicion as he handed me my cola. I grabbed it and walked off.

"Brother! One minute! Hey!'

Tynda was not originally on my itinerary. In Berkakit, I failed to find a ride south to Never. No one was going that way, or even close. In fact, almost no one lived in Berkakit, as far as I could tell. I stood out on the road in the wind for five hours before giving up. Pavel had set me up at the Locomotive Team Rest House, where

I returned to spend the rest of the day sleeping and bringing my journal up to date. That evening, I bought a train ticket to Chernyshevsk, from where I hoped to hitch onward to Chita.

"Sir, would you accept a passenger?"

A head under a shock of black hair peered around the doorway into my compartment. I'd just taken my seat on the train and had been enjoying the solitude.

"If you have a ticket for a seat here, then come in," I answered.

"But I don't want to disturb you."

This courtesy was out of place and vaguely disquieting. He dragged in his bag and introduced himself with a vigorous extended handshake as Sasha. Under his forelocks were thick simian brows; his mouth bristled with pointy teeth. He looked like a clean-shaved ape, in Reeboks and prewashed jeans. Something in his civility clashed with his demeanor and alerted me to a dissonance of character.

When he took his seat opposite me, I smelled booze on his breath. His gaze was dull.

"Say, you need a job?" he asked.

"No."

"Let me tell you where you can work. I can help you."

Sasha's shoulders went limp and his sullenness evaporated. He rambled on about various positions he knew to be vacant in Tynda. He himself was a railroad station boss, he said.

"Can you weld? Ever worked a jackhammer before? Know anything about piping?"

"No."

"Then how am I supposed to help you get a job? You've got to have some skill! Every man does!"

He kneaded his knuckles. His upper-body musculature went taut. Another grunt escaped him. Somewhere in his brain, it seemed to me, neurons were misfiring. He stood up, looked at me, and walked out. Soon he was arguing with the group of workers drinking in the compartment next door.

Within the hour, he returned and sat down, pounding one fist into another and moving his head from side to side in a palsied fervor.

"You see, they screwed me at my old job." He leaned intrusively into my face. His voice rattled from somewhere deep inside him. "They screwed me. I'll prove it to you. You doubt me. I know you do. Look! Here's the document that shows it all!" He held out a yellowed sheet of paper covered with numbers. "See? And you doubted me!"

I kept my eyes on my book, trying to block him out by reading. It was no use.

"I see. I know your type. A man gets in trouble and you fire him. But I'm willing to drink with you." He pulled a Russkaya vodka bottle out of his sack. "You'll be drinking."

"No, thanks. I don't drink. Let me read my book."

"Don't drink? You mean, *with me* you *won't* drink! I knew it!"

He grabbed the neck of his bottle and squeezed it, as though he were strangling a snake. His eyes burned into my forehead. I resisted the urge to look up. He rushed out again, with his bottle. Ten minutes later, the compartment door flew open. He stumbled back in and collapsed on his seat.

"Shut it! Shut the door!" he panted. "They're coming, coming to beat me!"

I closed and locked the door. He was crying.

"They took my bottle!" He slapped his hands to his face and massaged it, smearing his tears and drawing his cheeks and eyes into ghoulish distortions. "My friend!" He sighed a vodka sigh. "My friend! He didn't do it! He was in the wrong place at the wrong time! She was forty, why would he want to?"

Lucidity seized him and he grabbed my forearm.

"Look, can you free him? You have money, power, you're from Moscow. HE DIDN'T RAPE HER! He didn't!"

I stayed silent. Sasha reclined again, spent and groggy, his head rotating in tremulous half-circles. After a minute, he rose, hanging on to the luggage rack, fortified himself with a deep breath, and stepped into the corridor.

It was dusk. Our passage over the rails was quiet, intoxicatingly rhythmic. We were drifting deeper and deeper into the nether regions of a taiga dim in subaqueous mist, glimmering in half-light; it was a land of forgetting, a realm where the colors of this world waned into the grays and ashen hues of the next, where shadows merged with shades, where beyond the edge of the forest extended realms of nepenthe, of penumbral vales and undulant *sopki* without end.

I stared into the dark and forgot myself and where I was. Dreams came to me; my mind floated images past my eyes in the gloom.

Sasha opened the door, slowly. I was drowsy, maybe even asleep, until the lock clicked. He stood at the threshold, swaying with the rocking of the train. His eyes were fixed on mine again, and his fists clenched.

"Get up! Get up! Fight! Let's have at it! And remember, next door I have all my buddies. Workers with bull necks. Tough as nails. Get up!"

His words rang with false bravado. Better not to take him seriously. But if he wasn't serious, he was on the brink of becoming so.

"Sit down, Sasha."

He kneaded his fists for a moment, shrugged, and sat down. His head was heavy, his neck rubbery. He threw his elbow up on the table between us, it landed with a bang that startled him.

"Arm wrestle?"

He's insane, I thought. We arm wrestled. I won.

His cheeks trembled, then twitched. He began to whimper.

"I'm nothing now. I was as strong as a whole bull."

We sat for a while. It was dark on the train. And quiet.

"Say, would you mind if I brought a girl in here?" His eyes were only half-open, the words only half-voiced.

"Not at all."

"The conductor . . . I like the conductor. We won't be disturbing you? No?"

"Be my guest."

"Just one thing: can you . . . talk to her for me? You know, persuade her? I'm out of form." He grabbed at the lapels of his denim jacket and straightened them.

"Nonsense," I responded. "With your charm, I'm sure you'll win her over."

I figured as soon as he approached her, he'd be thrown off the train. The conductor was a sturdy redhead who weighed more than he did.

He pounded his fist into his palm. A few minutes passed. He measured his words, which bubbled out of his larynx in groggy rage.

"You won't help me, you won't drink with me, you won't spring my innocent friend. I should throw you right out this window!"

"Try it." I kept my eyes on the taiga.

He looked away, snorted through his sinuses, then rubbed his crotch and groaned. "I've got to use the toilet," he said, and stumbled out.

It was entirely dark outside by now, and the absence of form passing by the window led my mind into wanderings again. I wondered what it was like a couple of hundred miles south, in China. I imagined teeming crowds, jammed buses, street vendors yakking over pots of noodles. And yet here, there was nothing! A few miles from the most populous country on earth! It made no sense. What kept the Chinese, throughout their long history, from expanding into Siberia? Was its gloom too oppressive? The cold too intense? What made Russians move east over Siberia from the sixteenth century on, when their motherland from Europe to the Volga was so much more habitable? Eastern Siberia remained an anti-world. Even those not in exile here seethed with a desperation as grievous as though they were.

"What is this? Urine?"

The conductor stood over a puddle by Sasha's legs in the corridor. I thought she was going to rub his face in it, as one would in toilet-training a puppy.

"That's urine! You are pigs, and I'm informing your workplaces."

Sasha swayed, almost ready to pass out. The conductor ordered him to clean up the mess and stomped away. I followed her, passing the compartment where Sasha had been drinking with his mates. Three men lay passed out in various positions. A puddle of urine slopped around the floor. That was it. I was changing compartments.

"Of course you will!" The conductor seemed as though she had been waiting for me. "Who could stay with such a pig? He's suffering from White Fever. I've seen it before. Those in that stage of alcoholism are goners. The mood changes, now happy, now sad, now violent. White Fever. There's nothing you can do about it."

Sasha had disappeared. I grabbed my bag and moved into compartment three. A slovenly fat fellow snored facedown until my turning on the light woke him. I apologized. He lay his head sideways on the pillow—he had big, goofy lips and his tongue protruded between them ever so slightly, as does a dog's in sleep. His eyes were closed.

I settled in. He let out a protracted yawn that dwindled into somnolent lip smacking. He looked to be about forty-five. I noticed his chinos and wool knit sweater—he did not seem to be a worker, he looked Western-dressed. He yawned again and babbled a bit in his half-sleep, like a little boy, and sat up with a start.

"We in Skovorodino yet?"

"No," I answered. He rubbed his face with both hands, squishing his lips together until his face looked like a reflection in an amusement park crazy mirror.

"Blaaah! Ooooh! Sooo tired!"

He had an endearing lisp and he chewed his words, spitting them out chomped to bits.

"You from around here?"

"Not exactly."

"It's peaceful here in eastern Siberia, that's true. And you can make money. Ooooh! So much money!"

He chomped on his tongue and hurriedly rubbed his fingers through his hair, which stood on end in the back in two spikes, almost forming the rabbit sign people make over a friend's head in photographs.

"Money you can make. But what can you buy? Only Chinese junk. Me, I buy West German clothes when I go home to Krasnodar."

"You work out here?"

"Oooh!" He slapped his blubbery face several times. "Work, yeah, you could say that. I'm in the military. Guard the Chinese border. I like it here. The climate's healthy."

"Healthy? How so?"

"You're not a Siberian, I can see. But neither am I. I've learned. These frosts we have out here—they stay at fifty to seventy below for three months. They kill all the microbes. Best thing for you. You dress for it; first the long underwear"—he drew on imaginary long underpants—"then the slacks of wool and cotton, then the *shuba*"—he buttoned his imaginary *shuba* to the neck—"then the hat with earflaps"—he tied these down uncomfortably tight, bunching up the flab of his double chin—"and finally the scarf around the face. What can you see now?"

He sat constricted in his imaginary winter gear.

"Only your nose and eyes."

"Right!"

I put down my book. It was nearly midnight. Conversation flowed smoothly with this gentle colonel. He had hoped to be assigned to hellish Novaya Zemlya in the Arctic Ocean, where one year of service counts as three and from where you can choose your next posting. But all he could get was Skovorodino. Pretty desolate, but not as bad as Novaya Zemlya, he said. He never asked where I was from. But he did comment on his home region, the Caucasus.

"Wars! All of them over land! Take your land, I say! And then what? We have war in Georgia, war in Armenia—for what? That war in Moldova cost ten billion dollars, but who paid? The Moldovans themselves! It's ridiculous. Now take America. No paradise, but they have the rule of law. A two-hundred-year-old country with a constitution that has only eighteen amendments! That's law! Russia's what, a thousand years old and she has no law!"

We stopped in Skovorodino. He wished me good-bye, grabbed his bag, and hurried out on his knock-knees.

Dawn as such never fully arrived. The same dreary *sopki* just rematerialized in my train window, cloaked in a pewter haze. The trees looked so colorless, so lifeless, that I asked the conductor about them.

"You don't like our *listvennitsy*?" she asked. "Larches. They're the queen of trees. You should judge them in the summer!"

Amazar, Mogocha, Sbega. Villages of mud, fog, tainted snow, and bundled-up old men with dirty net bags treading over planks laid down in place of sidewalks. The train would pull up and discharge a handful of passengers, with maybe one or two figures wrapped in rags wearily accosting them on the platform with bottles of milk or congealed pastries. I was hungry, but not that hungry. I found, though, that all the dining car had was candy, cucumbers, and vodka. I bought some candy, but it upset my empty stomach.

Later that afternoon, the *sopki* smoothed into dusty brown rolling hills. Mongolia looks like this. We were just north of there. The conductor stopped by my compartment.

"Now without the larches, see how depressing it is? They're the queen of trees. Remember that."

The next afternoon, we approached Chernyshevsk. I readied myself.

We were passing through a frozen bog. Here and there, wrecks of cabins and disabled vehicles littered the swamp.

"Look, just stay aboard until Chita. I'll cut you a ticket right now. There's absolutely no reason to go to Chernyshevsk." She sounded as though she were scolding a careless child.

"Well, maybe some other passengers going there can give me some information."

She shook her head.

"*What* other passengers going there? There's not *one!* There's no reason for you to get off here. If you do, you'll be the only one."

I was.

SEVEN

A Personal Guarantee
for My Safety
in Chernyshevsk

The train discharged me into the dusk and creaked away. I stood gripping my overnight bag, momentarily dazed from the sudden, comforting feeling of solid earth beneath my feet. Above me on the station wall hung bold placards with urgent warnings: PARENTS! DO NOT LEAVE YOUR CHILDREN UNATTENDED AT THE STATION! DO NOT ALLOW CHILDREN TO RUN ON PLATFORM! DO NOT LET YOUR CHILD PLAY UNDER RAILROAD CARS! There were no children or parents about. A crow cawed at me from atop a nearby shed.

I hustled my bag to my shoulder and turned to cross the tracks, very nearly stepping on a four-foot-high old lady who had crept up behind me unseen while I had been standing there reading the placards. The wind played with her frayed brown coattails and the loose ends of the scarf pulled around her cheeks. I was startled.

"Milk! Milk!" she bleated at me. "Buy my milk!"

"Where did you come from?"

"Milk? Buy my milk!" she bleated again, rocking back and forth on tiny feet beside me and holding out a bottle.

I hesitated and she moved directly in front of me, squinting her eyes at me and peering into the folds of my overcoat. I handed her a fifty-ruble note and grasped the neck of the bottle, but she wouldn't let go of it. At the same time, she tugged gently on the money.

"What's wrong? Are you selling me the milk or not?"

"It's . . . it's gone bad," she said, averting her eyes in shame.

I let her have the bill and the bottle and walked away.

The stationmaster told me to try the Trade House next door for trucks. It was deserted except for a cashier.

"I'm trying to get to Chita by truck," I said. "I've heard you have trucks leaving for Chita from here."

She scribbled "Solovyov" and a street address on a piece of paper.

"Only Solovyov can help you. In the morning."

She passed me the paper through the hole in her window and drew shut her curtain.

I returned to the station to ask the manager, a compact man in a trim blue uniform, if there was a hotel in town.

"Hotel?" He raised his eyebrows. "Why take the risk? You can stay right here in the railroad rest room."

"Risk? I just need a hotel room for the night."

"You are in *Chernyshevsk!*"

There was a certain puzzling gravity to the way he stressed the name, as though *Chernyshevsk* said it all.

"Please," I said, "just give me directions to the hotel, if there is one."

He did. Over the bridge, across the tracks, around the bog, between the shacks . . .

"What about the address? Does it have an address?"

"An address? In *Chernyshevsk?*"

As I was walking away, he called out to me.

"Young man! Our rest room is cheaper—only two hundred rubles! Why risk it?"

From atop the rickety steel overpass above the tracks, Chernyshevsk spread out before me. Near the station, pockmarked concrete apartment blocks lay in disorder over fields of dun-colored earth studded with rusting fenders, tire rims, and axles. Across the way, dark brown *izby* brooded behind larch fences, and still farther, past the edge of town, extended a barren steppe. From this steppe's most distant reaches originated a majestic wind that drove westward clouds of dust, one minute materializing into galloping dragons, the next, disintegrating into rolling swells as on an angry sea, but ever moving in on and sweeping over the town, then disappearing into the twilight emptiness that lay beyond. But what was *beyond* from here? From the overpass, it seemed that I was in the midst of *beyond,* that Chernyshevsk was lost in it, hunkered down against plangent gales blowing from nowhere to nowhere.

I descended. Somewhere below, as if sounding an alarm, wind banged metal against metal. Three rusted, abandoned railroad cars with yawning black maws for doors lay wheelless ahead of me on the lot, hissing with dust driven over their sides.

I rounded the corner. A rock whizzed past me at eye level and struck the wall with a crack. Ahead of me, a drunken youth with a bloodied eye tottered and swayed, surrounded by a circle of street boys taunting him and pelting him with stones. He swore and lunged at each in turn, but they were too fast for his groggy strikes. I crossed around them and tried to remember where I was to turn.

A woman with a child appeared from a gate across the street. I approached them to ask about the hotel, but the mother clutched the child and recoiled from me.

"Please! I'm only looking for the hotel."

She shook her head in mute alarm and hurried her child away.

The mess of scattered hovels confused me and disrupted my navigation. Stray dogs rooted in garbage heaps or growled at me in territorial jealousy from their mounds in the dusk, but there was no one about to ask for directions. I gave up my search and returned to the station.

"Okay, I'll take a room in the guest house," I said to the station manager.

"Ah, you've returned!" He leveled a gloating look at me and, with feet splayed, drew himself across the floor in his roller chair. "Who was it who told you to just stay in our rest room? That'll be two hundred rubles!"

I paid and went upstairs to the key lady.

In a cubbyhole at the top of the stairs I found her snoozing, ensconced in a bundle of shawls and hand-me-downs, her chin on her chest and her hands crossed over her belly.

"I'd like a room."

She started into grumpy wakefulness.

"Room!?" She rasped, hoisting herself out of the chair. "We have one common room. You'll get a bed!" She snorted and extended her arm. "Around the corner. No key. Go."

I looked around. Around the corner there was only a stench and what I took to be the bathroom door. I walked back to her cubbyhole and told her I couldn't find it. She got up and pointed at the bathroom with a bony finger.

As I approached the door, the stench grew stronger. I opened it and recoiled in disgust. On one bed a man lay snoring facedown, his arm hanging over the edge of the mattress, his hand clutching a vodka bottle lying on the floor. There was a puddle of urine next to the wall. On another bed, a man lay faceup, his eyes wide open and unblinking. He appeared dead. His pants were soiled with urine. On the bed in front of me reclined a huge fat man in his fifties with a shaved head and filthy bare feet, his toenails eaten away by fungus. He was reading a stained newspaper that looked rescued from the garbage.

"*Zdrasst'ye!* Come on in!"

He put down the paper. He must have read the expression on my face.

"Come on in! Don't mind the boys. They're a little depressed."

I took a deep breath and sidestepped the urine. Inside the room, the stench was rancid.

"We've been out of work for a year. We were miners in Ya-kutsk. Twenty years we worked there."

An ashen light suffused the room. The windows rattled with the wind.

"Don't be afraid! You have my word—I'll personally guarantee your safety. No need to even check your bags. Take that bed by the wall. It's the only free one, actually."

There were three wall beds—two occupied, one free. Eight bunks were shoved together into one large bed in the center, on the extreme edge of which lay the fat man.

I sat on the free bed and put down my bag. A gurgling sound emerged from the dead man. His arm began to twitch and jerk; his hand groped for the vodka bottle on the table next to him. He missed, and his arm dropped back to the floor.

The fat man queried me with a contrived offhandedness that aroused my suspicion.

"So, what have we got in our bags?"

He pointed at my camera bag and overnight bag and jiggled his eyebrows. I opened the latter, which I knew to be stuffed with books at the top, and tossed him the collection of stories by Valentin Rasputin I was reading.

"Books," I said. "I read a lot."

His eyebrows dropped.

"You don't like Rasputin?" I asked, going on the offensive.

"I'm a miner," he said, scratching the crotch of his gray, state-issue trousers that looked like the bottom half of a prison uniform.

"I don't have much time for books. I read the paper, when I have to read. Where are we from?"

If ever there was a time to dissemble, this was it, a voice inside told me.

"I'm from the Baltics."

"Ah, Riga, Tallinn, Vilnius. Yes. Worked up there in construction years ago. Where in the Baltics?"

My mind raced. Of all the luck—four thousand miles from the Baltics I run into someone who's been there. Estonia popped to mind.

"Estonia."

I thought I had anticipated his next move. It was unlikely he would have picked up any Estonian, a Finnic tongue with bizarre grammar and vowels unpronounceable for Russians, and it seemed even less likely that he would be able to test me on it. I was wrong. He blurted out something Finnic-sounding and watched for my response. I laughed knowingly, having no idea what he said, but guessing his words to have been a greeting of some sort.

"Sorry," he said. "It's been a long time. My pronunciation is off."

I assured him he sounded fine.

In stumbled a mean-eyed, broad-shouldered man in his thirties who collapsed on his bed in a stupor. The fat man shouted, "How rude of you, Kolya! We have a guest!" Kolya began to snore.

I got up to leave, without thinking, instinctively: my legs carried me toward the door without command. A sense of the un-savory, an intuitive inkling that some harm would come to me in that room, flickered within me.

The fat man sat up and spread his arms.

"Where are you going? Listen, I personally will guarantee your safety. No need to even check your bags!"

I thanked him and grabbed my bags and said I was just on my way out to get a bite to eat.

"In *Chernyshevsk?*"

"I'll find something," I said, and slipped out the door.

I walked down to the station waiting room, having nowhere else to go. The thought crossed my mind that the fat man might be an escaped prisoner. I was afraid to return to the rest room.

The crowd in the waiting room didn't look any better. An old man across from me stared at me as he dug his finger into his nose. Around the walls, vagabonds lay in heaps, collapsed over vodka bottles. One began coughing consumptively behind me, drawing up phlegm in protracted, convulsive spasms. I pulled out my journal and decided to distract myself with an entry.

There was a flip-flop of slippers on the station floor. It was the fat man. He'd thrown a wrinkled work shirt that resembled the top half of a prison uniform over his flabby chest and was padding toward me.

"Look, there's no need to come down here," he said with unseemly urgency. "Like I said, I'm ready to *personally* guarantee your safety. *Personally.*"

He stood over me, grinning expectantly, his arms outstretched.

"Come on, come back to the rest room. What do you say?"

He smiled, his lips drawing back over cracked shards of teeth, and rubbed his hands together, as though he were ready to enjoy a feast, but at my expense, I was sure.

"I'll be right up," I said. "I've just got to put away my book here."

"Grrreat!"

He jogged up the stairs on springy legs.

I grabbed my bag and walked over to the station manager.

"I've *got* to have directions to the hotel."

"But you've paid for the rest room! We don't give refunds here!"

He muttered on about the rest room and its advantages and seemed unable to focus on my request. I approached the baggage attendant, a sturdy, middle-aged, sensible-looking woman in horn-rimmed glasses and a neat blue uniform.

"The hotel?" she asked with alarm. "No one goes outside at this hour. We are scared even during the day. There are robberies and beatings and worse. I'm from here but I'll tell you, we have been cursed by God. Chernyshevsk is exile, the end of the road."

I asked for directions again. She put on her glasses and said we'd better call first, that maybe the hotel had closed up. No one answered.

"Their phone must be out of order. Or—"

Or maybe they're all dead! I thought, trying to cheer myself up with horror-flick humor.

"Or maybe they're closed."

"I'll risk it." I asked for detailed directions, got them, and headed out the door into the last traces of twilight.

The wind had died down. The crunch of my footsteps echoed through the shadows. I avoided the railroad cars and walked by a run-down apartment building. Three or four young men smoked in silence in the dimness of the entranceway, keeping their eyes on me as I walked past.

I followed the directions I had as best I could, but soon found myself uncertain of my path again. As before, there was no one to ask.

A black dog charged out of a garbage heap barking, fangs bared and saliva flying.

This will never end, I thought.

The dog seemed to be one second lunging at my heels, the next, backing away. I kept moving ahead and wondered whether he was rabid, whether he might sink his teeth into my leg, and how I would defend myself with my bag should he try. The rush of anxiety and adrenaline distracted me, and I lost track of the hotel again.

A man approached and asked for a smoke, and the dog took flight. I said I didn't smoke but asked for the hotel. He pointed to a square brick structure some four stories high across the lot.

I walked over to it. Then around it. No door. On the second floor, though, a dim light burned; above it, I finally made out a sign hanging sideways: HOTEL NORTH.

A huge plank of plywood lay against the side of the building. I circled the hotel once more, finding nothing, and came back to it. I pushed it aside. It covered an entrance. I could make out nothing inside at first, but as I stared inward, my eyes grew accustomed to the dark. Inside, against the back wall, three cigarettes glowed orange in the blackness. There was a cough.

"Is this the hotel?"

A low voice grumbled yes. A faint light emanated from a stairway. I stepped inside, unable to see the floor, onto a shard of glass. The cigarettes glowed, their embers infusing with oxygen, then dimming with exhaled smoke. My next step provoked an angry moan of pain—my foot had landed on someone's wrist. A stench of urine. I made it to the stairway, stepping over bodies and bottles, ascended, and emerged onto the second floor.

A television hissed with snow and hazy reception, bathing the lobby in cold blue light. Opposite it, three men sat with bowed heads on a couch, a spent vodka bottle in front of them. I asked for the proprietor. One of the men pointed to a room to the side.

The administrator, a thin woman in her fifties with her head in her hands, started at my voice.

"No single rooms," she rasped, clearing her throat. "Only beds in a common room."

At this, a young girl emerged from the back room and leaned on the doorway, her puffy cheeks smirched with streaks of rouge, her sepia hair stringy and smelling of smoke. She stared at me and plopped onto the couch, picking nervously at chipped nails of scarlet. She could have been no older than thirteen or fourteen.

"If you have a empty room, I'll take it. I'll pay for all the places."

"That will be very expensive. Two thousand rubles [almost two dollars]."

"I'll take it. Just give me the key."

"No keys. We have no locks."

The girl on the couch propped her head on her hand and stared vacantly at me, her eyes like waning gas lamps.

The administrator walked me to the room.

A window at the far end looked out into a gloom subtly textured with dark outlines of *izby,* and beyond, the looming vastness of the steppe.

"Here's your light," she said, drawing a bulb from her apron. "Plug it in where you like. Either over the sink or over your bed."

I screwed it in over the sink. Around the room, several mattresses lay scattered on the floor.

"Just take blankets from the other beds," she said. "Our heating is broken. And we don't have a bathroom. The uncultured men we get staying here just use the window as a toilet. I ask you to please use the street!"

I piled all the blankets I could find on my bed and slid under them dressed as I was, and fell asleep.

Drunken cries echoed from the thick night on the streets below and resolved themselves into a malevolent chanting, aggressive and wordless, like a slurred martial hymn. It came nearer, then stopped, stifled in asphyxiated gags. Then followed a scream and more screams, a frantic scuffling of boots on gravel, and a smashing of glass. Silence. I slept fitfully, wondering during the waking moments what would stop anyone from kicking open my nail-secured door and slitting my throat.

Snow had fallen during the night. The early morning sun shone feebly through tattered clouds, dabbing the steppes with tints of pale blue and frail yellow. I asked a woman on the street to direct me to Mr. Solovyov's address.

CHERNYSHEVSK DISTRICT — SOVIET OF PEOPLE'S DEPUTIES read the red-and-gold sign hanging by the entranceway. I walked in.

"You are going to see Mr. Solovyov?" said the old doorman, his lower lip dangling in dumbfounded trepidation. "Please, follow me!"

He led me up two flights of stairs, down corridors and around corners, shuffling with an urgency I could not understand. CHAIRMAN OF THE CHERNYSHEVSK DISTRICT — SOVIET OF PEOPLE'S DEPUTIES — V. A. SOLOVYOV read the doorplate of the office. I recoiled almost instinctively, realizing in a flash why the mention of Mr. Solovyov's name evoked so much apprehension: he was no mere functionary in the regional government, he was its head, the chief of the soviet, the district *president,* in a word. If once such figures did little more than enforce Bolshevik rule in concert with the KGB, the majority of them now were locked in a struggle against Yeltsin and the reformist central government in Moscow, and many had talked openly of returning the Communists to power. My gut feeling was that he would take no pleasure in an American traveler appearing in his region without his consent and without even a visa specifying permission to be outside Moscow.

Across a flowing carpet of red in a cavernous white-walled chamber, Chairman Solovyov sat under a glowering portrait of Lenin that reached to the ceiling, bellowing orders into one of the four phones on his desk, paying us no attention as we approached him. He looked to be about fifty, sturdy of build, with a high crop of dark hair. When he finished, his vice-deputy, who'd escorted me in with a self-effacing hunch to her shoulders and a meek grin, explained that I was an American just passing through Chernyshevsk looking to get a ride to Chita and hoped for Chairman Solovyov's most gracious assistance and could he possibly see fit to do something to help and . . . She seemed to sink into his carpet as she spoke, to grow smaller, to mute the veracity of her words, to undermine her credibility and mine.

When she ran out of things to say about me, she bowed and scurried out. He raised his brows in silent suspicion and his eyes, landed on my face like a two-by-four. The guileless story about being an American "just passing through" Chernyshevsk sounded implausible even to me. How could I be "just passing through"? She had understated this because, even to her, it must have seemed suspicious that I was there at all, and if I was, it had to be on some mission with an ulterior motive. I could think of nothing to say except that I hoped I would not be disturbing him, that perhaps this was too trivial a matter for a Soviet chairman.

"Excuse me, do you have *any* documents that prove you are who you *claim* to be?"

I pulled my passport from my shirt pocket. He took it and reached for the phone.

"Viktor, in front of me is a man claiming to be an American who claims to be here trying to get a ride to Chita, where he claims to be going. Step in here at once."

"I have asked the Chernyshevsk chief of internal affairs to verify your story. You claim to be an American. Do you speak English? Why do you speak Russian?"

I told him I had worked as a interpreter. His eyebrows remained elevated in suspicion.

The door flew open. In marched two uniformed police officers with a small, steely-eyed man in plain clothes.

"Documents!" commanded the small man.

Solovyov handed him my passport.

"You claim to be an American. What is this?" demanded the internal affairs chief, holding my passport in front of me.

"An American passport."

He put the passport down slowly, not taking his eyes off me. He began scrutinizing it, while the police pulled my visa free of the paper clip holding it to the cover. Solovyov stared at me with his hands clasped, his face assuming the contours of the Lenin portrait above his head.

The two policemen began hammering me with questions about the exact date and time of my arrival, the means of transportation by which I had come to Chernyshevsk, the purpose of my visit. These questions were easy enough to answer, but then followed a hostile interrogation about other places I had visited in Russia, who had authorized my sojourns there, who sponsored my trip, and what I was doing outside of Moscow, the only destination listed on my visa. Seeing no need to draw them into my plans to cross the entire country, I told them I had arrived in Yakutsk and would return to Moscow from Chita.

"So you will be going to Moscow from Chita? You are certain of this?" asked Chairman Solovyov from under V-shaped brows.

"That is my intention."

The internal affairs chief leaned forward in his chair across from me and drew my passport to his face.

"Are you married?"

"No."

"Then what is this?" he demanded, thrusting my passport in front of me, the page turned to an old Egyptian visa.

"This is a marriage certificate!" he declared.

"Actually, it's a visa for Egypt. I'm not married."

"Egypt? What were you doing in Egypt? You have traveled a lot for a simple private citizen."

He drew out the last three words and soaked them in cynicism, as if to say, "I know who you're *really* working for!"

Solovyov sat heavy as a mountain behind his oak desk, his eyes ever leveled at mine as though I might slip at any moment and reveal the "true" reason I had come to Chernyshevsk. He cleared his throat and the internal affairs chief shut up instantaneously.

"Enough! Mr. Tayler, I am a Communist. Before the recent changes we had no foreigners here in Chernyshevsk. And we have none now. But these days, there is anarchy in the central government in Moscow. Control is looser than it was. Foreigners do not come to Russia for vacation. They come with certain motives. It is entirely possible that these motives are inimical to the security and well-being of my citizens. It is my duty to protect them from such subversive elements."

"I am not an element. And I'm just trying to get to Chita."

"You will understand that our investigation is called for under the circumstances." He turned to the chief. "Viktor, I think it has gone far enough."

The chief handed me my passport, somewhat deflated. I was relieved but sat still, afraid I might somehow provoke Solovyov into continuing the interrogation, but he sat in silence, still staring into my eyes. Then the thought crossed my mind that perhaps I had misinterpreted his words: maybe he meant to say, "Our investigation has gone far enough. We have enough evidence to detain him."

"Mr. Jeffrey," said Viktor, leaning forward, "we have all heard of the world-famous Parker Pen Company." There was a change of tenor in his tone, a shift of intent in his glance. "Do you have such a pen with you?"

"No, I don't."

In fact, I did, but it was a memento from a previous trip, and I didn't want to part with it.

"But you could send us one. I realize they cost one hundred U.S. dollars, but with your country's high average salary, I think this is affordable for you."

Solovyov sniffed, indifferent to pens. I thought the police chief's begging made him look trivial, but it gave me a way out. I'd play the game. It was certainly better than arguing about visas.

"Yes, of course!" I said.

He beamed and sat back in his chair.

I asked if I could use the bathroom. Solovyov directed me down and around stairs, then outside. It took me several rounds through the halls to realize the only "toilet" the soviet had was an outhouse.

While I was on my way back up the stairs, Solovyov grabbed my shoulder.

"I thought you were lost! While you were out I took the liberty of calling a little meeting of my staff."

His tone was flat, inscrutable.

Back in his office some thirty former Soviet apparatchiks and functionaries sat around the wall, buzzing and twiddling their pens. We entered and Solovyov directed me to a seat behind a long table. He took a place next to me and cleared his throat.

"Ladies and gentlemen, the first American to visit Chernyshevsk!"

There was a subdued round of applause from the pale drawn faces and beehive hairdos and gray suits and thick, flesh-colored leggings. I played along and bowed slightly.

Solovyov's face was stony, his voice level.

"Mr. Tayler will be so kind as to answer a few questions you may have. You can think of the topics yourselves: workers and their rights, issues the simple American struggles with every day, even how much *Santa Barbara* reflects real life."

"Are you married?" asked a middle-aged woman.

"How does your family feel about you traveling to Russia? Are they worried?" asked another.

"Why are you not married? Can you not support a family?"

"What is your income?"

One man in a dark suit privileged to sit at the end of Solovyov's table leaned forward intently.

"Tell us about your pornography. From your films we know the West is synonymous with unadulterated sex!"

"That is correct," huffed Solovyov. "We know that in the West, you simply lay your dollar on the table and have your sex."

A woman objected: "Leave it to men to ask such questions!" Sex disappeared in the laughter, and we all bantered for some time. The America they wanted to hear about wasn't really the one I knew; I wasn't from the Wild West, I didn't know Michael Jackson, I hadn't even seen a single episode of *Santa Barbara*.

A while later, Solovyov looked at his watch. Ten-thirty.

"Enough! Enough! Back to work!" he commanded all of a sudden, as though he had grown bored with me and our meeting.

The audience immediately shut up and filed out.

I thanked him for arranging the little assembly, which was too short, as far as I was concerned. But his face remained stony and expressionless.

"You will be leaving now."

"I will be?"

The two police officers marched in from the outer office and took up positions on either side of me.

"Stand up!"

Was I under arrest? What for?

Solovyov turned away and walked back to his desk. The officers led me out the door, down the halls. Heads peered round doorjambs at me, as though I were an apprehended felon. We emerged into the empty lot in front of the building. Snow was dusting the frozen earth, and leaden-hued clouds unfolded over the steppe. The internal affairs chief stood by a blue-and-white squad car and grinned at me, his hair ruffling in the wind.

"Good-bye, Mr. Jeffrey! You will not forget the pen! Perhaps you will send two, one for Chairman Solovyov!"

I waved and got in the car. We pulled away.

"My orders are to take you to the city limits and place you in the first car heading for Chita," said the officer tersely. We drove out of the scattered deserted tracks of Chernyshevsk and picked up the dirt road leading out of town to the west. Not a vehicle was to be seen.

I sat with my bag on my lap, grateful to Solovyov for wanting to get rid of me as quickly as possible. We flew down the dirt road, bouncing over the undulations of steppe track, squinting from the light reflected by the snow spreading in blinding sheets on all sides of us. Not a tree stood anywhere. The officer took the rough patches deftly, decelerating with timely precision, accelerating as the road permitted, and it was clear he'd driven this road all his life. I tried to make conversation with him, but he seemed ill humored, so I gave up. Occasionally, a steppe hawk or mouse or brown eagle would appear. When I said, "Look, an eagle!" he barked *"Da,"* and stared at the road.

My officer blared his siren at the first truck that appeared and pulled it over. The driver, a peasant with leathery skin and thick knuckles, glanced nervously in his rearview mirror as we drew even with him.

"Take this foreigner to Chita!" ordered the officer. The driver shouted he was only going up the road. We drove on.

This went on for three hours. We pulled over some five or six trucks—the only type of vehicle on the road—with no luck, and even sat in ambush at a police checkpoint at a crossroads, but to no avail; those that we stopped were filled to capacity or not going anywhere near Chita. When we'd covered a third of the distance there, we pulled over a jeep with a pair of geologists in it; they accepted me and I got in. They asked me no questions, and I wondered if they were not annoyed at being ordered to take on a passenger they did not know.

We trundled across expanses of dun steppe so desolate it nurtured not a blade of healthy grass. Above us spread a vista of darkening mountainous clouds of iron that threatened us with some unnameable cataclysm, and the villages we passed, all weathered wooden shacks and decrepit cattle sties, seemed huddled and cowering on the denuded earth.

Six hours later, some thirty kilometers east of Chita, pines and larches replaced steppe in sudden groves, and a blizzard broke loose from the gray vaults above.

When at last we pulled into town, it was seven in the evening. Old stone buildings and scraggly black branches lay oppressed under masses of heavy snow. I saw a hotel and asked to be let off there. Without a word, the geologists stopped. I got out and thanked them. They nodded silently—without looking at me—and drove off into the blizzard.

— EIGHT —

Bad Vibes in Chita

I was *sure* I had seen HOTEL written in Russian on the building's sooty concrete facade. Or was I? Signs in Chinese characters hung over the stairs. Chinese men hurried in and out of the clattering steel-and-glass doors. Chinese massed and shoved and bartered in the lobby, jumbo-sized green-and-gold Chinese beer bottles stood on the tables or stuck out of trash cans, Chinese merchants dragged gimcrack suitcases on rollers that screeched their way across the linoleum. The thought crossed my mind that this might be some sort of Chinese trade representation, but if it wasn't, it was a Mongolian consulate: everyone in the lobby who wasn't from China was from Ulan Bator. There were very few Russians.

It was a hotel, though. If it hadn't been for the blizzard outside, I probably would have given up trying to get a room after seeing the crowd at the receptionist's desk; Chinese on the outside passed their passports over jostling heads to friends on the inside, some swilled beer and spat on the floor, others just spat for the hell of it, and nobody understood the Mongolians, despite their Cyrillic-lettered passports. I looked out at the snow, decided it would be a long hike to anywhere else, and dove into the crowd.

The Mongolians smiled at me and let me through. The Chinese forming the inner circle seemed to have locked elbows in a human barricade, but laughed and hawked up phlegm all the same, chattering to one another and grinning. I got no closer to the desk than one layer of Chinese bodies in leather jackets. Very thin leather, it seemed, sheer as paper and marred with stretch marks.

The receptionist, a sturdy female apparatchik behind fortified glasses, shouted in Russian at the Chinese, answered *"Nyet!"* before they finished stammering out sentences from their Russian phrase books, and pounded the NO ROOMS sign. But no one was leaving. There had to be something to this, some reason why people stood around long after they were refused a room. If language were a barrier, could they fail to understand gestures such as fist pounding and head shaking and fingers pointing to the exit sign? Maybe they knew something.

"Do you have a single?"

I felt silly asking the receptionist this with her fist still red from beating on the desk.

She did not look up from her scribbling. "Can you read the sign or not?"

"Then could you tell me where I might find another hotel?"

"All the hotels in Chita are full. Since they opened the border with China, every Chinaman coming to Russia stops here."

I found a phone and called around: *"Mest nyet* [No rooms]." I jumped back into the crowd and shoved my way to the front.

The receptionist tossed a Chinese man his passport.

"ARE YOU DEAF?" she bellowed at him. "I told you we have no rooms! NO ROOMS!"

He wasn't deaf; he just didn't understand. I loathed her at that moment for being so rude to a languageless guest in her country. But he just chuckled, his face screwing up in a pained frown, and emitted a nervous "Ahhh," the meaning of which seemed to be, "I have heard you. Please, can you do nothing at all?"

At this, she rolled her eyes, grabbed his passport, and wrote him out a room slip.

A tall, bulky Russian of twenty or twenty-five, with no small amount of muscle under his blubber, approached the crowd. He cocked his elbows to the side and extended his pinkies, looked both ways, then one by one, abruptly shoved every Chinese and Mongolian aside and emerged at the receptionist next to me. One Mongolian must have objected; fatso performed a perfect Russian-language version of Robert De Niro's *Taxi Driver* "You talkin' to me?" scene, thumping his chest like an ape and jutting his chin in the Mongolian's face. No, as it turned out, the Mongolian wasn't talkin' to him. Fatso handed the receptionist some sort of yellow card and left the way he came, extracting Mongolians from his path with deft flicks of his elbows.

"Still no rooms?" I asked. "All the hotels are full. I have nowhere to go and—"

"Dinner break!" she shouted, and thumped down an AT DINNER—HALF HOUR sign next to NO ROOMS and walked off into a chamber behind the reception area. We all froze, some in mid-sentence, others in midgesture—no one dared give up an inch of line. She sat down, in plain view of the crowd, and began gabbing and munching on a baton of bread with the other hotel apparatchiks.

No one said anything.

No one moved. I had thousands of miles and dozens of hotels ahead of me—numbing thoughts.

She didn't return to her chair until the last second of the last minute of her break had passed. When she put away her DINNER BREAK sign the crowd sprang into motion again, as though someone had pressed *play* on a VCR stuck on *still*.

"We have a bed in a room for four," she said to me. "Take it or leave it."

"I'll take it."

"Give me that Latvian passport of yours, then."

What? I handed her my passport. She scribbled out several forms and I paid at the cashier in accordance with those forms. For a single.

"I thought I was getting a bed in a room for four!" I said to the cashier. She knew nothing. The receptionist handed me my key. I walked off happy and decided not to question my good fortune. Later, I learned she had "canceled" someone's reservation to accommodate the American guest.

Chita was the nerve center of one of the world's formerly most militarized zones, the Chinese-Russian border. According to Russians, scores of intercontinental ballistic missiles trained on the United States surrounded Chita. All this meant that it was closed to foreigners until recently. Much is still behind walls, as I learned wandering around town the next day.

The Cossacks of Pyotr Beketov founded the city as a fortress and prison town on their way east in the seventeenth century. Chita was and still is a principal military outpost in the Zabaikalye (or "Beyond the Baikal") region of eastern Siberia. Now it also serves as an overnight shelter for the same Chinese the Russians once feared; the Chinese have invaded, but not with tanks. They've come bearing suitcases full of polyester blouses, "Rambo" leather jackets, second-rate jeans, and even cheap vodka. Yes, in the homeland of vodka, the Chinese were importing their own, and it was selling. They seemed friendly to me, and I wished I could have talked to them. My few attempts failed—very few knew any English, although some had survival Russian. Their smiles and laughter took the militaristic edge off Chita.

This invasion of sorts has had its consequences, though. There were fights around the hotel—Russians against Chinese, for the most part. Even as I waited for the floor maid to bring me my room key later the first evening, there was an incident: a Chinese man stood with two Russians counting money in the floor lobby.

He kept asking them to recount it, and the Russians grew annoyed and told him to keep his voice down. They concluded the deal by taking him into the stairwell and beating him up.

After settling into my room, I went down to the restaurant to have dinner. Tables were divided into camps of Chinese and Russians. The Chinese drank a lot of beer and stumbled around; the Russians held their vodka tight and grew saturnine and glowering. Fatso was there at the head of a table of Russians; he and his thick-browed buddies passed prostitutes among themselves, digging tongues in between their painted lips and holding their breasts up to the light to carry out on-the-rack comparisons. I sat on the opposite end of the hall from them and waited for my waitress.

Two bull-necked Russian youths with crewcuts and gold rings were sitting behind me and chatting over dinner.

One: "Sergei raised eighty thousand from the Chinese and didn't tell us."

The other: "We'll kill him then."

It made sense: big bucks were flowing through Chita, and the Russian mob was vying for its share. Russians had the muscle, Chinese the goods. Russian against Russian, Russian against Chinese. I ate quickly and left.

Chita's center boasted the usual array of private shops: Rus, Udacha, and Vsyo dlya Vas, to name a few. All had the same assortment of Chinese and Vietnamese trinkets, blouses, Russian and imported alcohol, and candy from everywhere. One shop—the Vesta—heralded by a sign almost entirely in Chinese, turned out to be a Chinese-Russian joint venture. When I asked there for toilet paper, I was told they had none and that there was none in Chita.

A massive statue of Lenin still dominates Chita's central square; gathered beneath it the next day, however, were not Communists but twenty youths singing gospel songs in Russian and accosting passersby with tracts urging them to convert.

Convert? Russians were already Orthodox Christian a thousand years ago, and quite a few had maintained their faith despite official discouragement during the Soviet years. Public singing and beatific smiles suggested foreign, maybe American, influence. This reminded me of a group I had seen in Tashkent called Ambassadors for God—Midwestern Americans "bringing God to the godless," as one of them told me. Never mind that Uzbeks were Muslims and Russians Orthodox; never mind that both religious traditions extend back in time to when the ancestors of these Americans were still pagans in bear skins running around the forests of Europe. There was something irritating and affected about this foreign religious influence in Tashkent, and it was equally irritating in Chita. Heavy-browed Russian mothers with bulging net bags and drooling children in tow wandered by these singers on the square and stared at them in suspicion. I caught myself doing the same.

As I stood watching the Russian kids sing, a young man with fervent eyes approached me with a tract.

"No, thanks," I said. "I'm just watching."

"The CIA is running Russia!"

"Excuse me?"

I took a good look at the evangelist. He held an armful of newspapers, not religious tracts. He shoved one into my hand.

"We are giving these out free because it's time people knew the truth. The CIA and its puppet, Yeltsin, have taken over Holy Russia. It's all in this paper. Read it!"

Russky Vostok ("The Russian East") was published in Irkutsk. The headline read, "The Plans according to Which Gorbachev and Yeltsin Are Operating Were Drawn Up by Hitler and the CIA." Other articles were "The CIA Is Governing Us," "Gays Support Yeltsin," and "Reform Yeltsin-Style—In the Interests of Everyone but the Russians." The headlines said it all—there seemed to be little reason to read further.

Two girls and a Saint Bernard passed by. One of them was blond with high cheekbones, and her eyes slanted enough that she could almost have been Chinese. I did something I rarely ever do: I stopped her and asked if I might photograph her with her friend and dog. She agreed. Afterward, we talked.

Angela, the blond, had a soft, lazy lilt to her voice, something like a southern drawl in Russian, that drew me into reverie as she spoke. Olya was swarthy and stark, and her assertive gaze and speech awakened me from the trance Angela's voice put me in.

"Chita is all army," said Olya. "My father is a soldier from Georgia—and it's a dead place with nothing to do. All young people have here is the park. Sitting around. And drinking."

They were both in their last year of high school, it turned out. This at first amazed me, then distressed me, as I realized how quickly they had matured. Olya was studying English. She tried a few phrases, but when I responded she decided she understood only British English, not American ("Listen to him! Was that the definite article he was using there? The British don't sound like this! The elongate their *o*'s"). Had they actually met British out here? I asked. All they had seen by way of foreigners in Chita were Chinese, Olya said, and they were not shy about voicing their opinions of them.

"They are disgusting the way they come here and sell junk and spit in the streets and walk around in big groups, as if they own this place," said Olya. "We wanted to go to China when the border was closed, but now, never! Do you drink?"

"Not really," I said.

"We know from your films that Americans drink only symbolically, unlike us Russians," said Angela. "You all sip and chat. We drink vodka. Vodka is not a drink for sipping. But we here in Chita have enough problems with our health—we shouldn't drink at all! Our radiation level here is very high. Our average age at death is only fifty-three. We're young—I don't think it will affect us. We're used to it already."

"Do you think you can get used to radiation?"

"We have—we are still alive."

"But you're not yet fifty-three! How do you know about this radiation?"

"Everyone knows," Angela said. "It's not published, of course. No truth ever is here."

Such cynicism, even from the young, and after seven years of perestroika! I had been hoping things might be different. Both smiled when I said this.

"Nothing will ever change in Russia," said Angela, examining her red nails. "The powers in Moscow will forever ride the people in the provinces to exhaustion. They will never let us know the truth. There will never be democracy here."

They had to return home, they said. We got up to say good-bye.

"Are you really an American?" Angela asked.

I showed them my passport.

"Oh, we believe you. It's just that people say a lot of things these days."

I had been undecided about how I'd get to my next destination, Ulan-Ude, the capital of the Republic of Buryatia, some four hundred kilometers west. A few hours of questioning hotel staff left me doubtful that I could hitch. They seemed to think few trucks went to Ulan-Ude; most freight was shipped via rail. Finding a private car on these roads was next to impossible. It was back to trains.

Chita's train station confused me. It was nothing like the clean and orderly (and empty) whistle stops in Berkakit and Tynda. Chinese tugged at suitcases bound with lengths of unraveling hemp, Russians in parkas dragged around sacks of cattle feed, a thin, wan woman in a scarf with black veins on her legs tended thousands of chicks chirping in cardboard crates, children skateboarded around tottering drunks. And there were lines, endless lines, immobile formations of sour-faced Russians, some standing passive and baggy-eyed, others chiding violators of line etiquette in strident tones that grated on my ears like steel scraping on glass. The stale odor of these queues led me to think they had been there for days. I felt defeated before I'd even begun.

I picked what seemed to be the shortest of them and ended up fifteen places back, behind three Chinese traders practicing their Russian for *One ticket to Irkutsk, please!* When I was eighth from the head of the line, the cashier plunked a LUNCH BREAK — ONE HOUR sign in her window and left her seat. No one dispersed.

The cashier returned from her break on time. She took fifteen minutes per ticket; with some people buying three and four tickets, my patience grew thin and I began to feel blood pooling in my legs.

Never complain that things are bad; when you do, they're sure to get worse. Where had I heard that?

Husky women in blue overcoats began gathering from the other side of the window, forming a two-headed line. Yes, they were railway workers. Someone ahead of me shouted to them, "Get in line like everyone else! You think you're better than us?"

"Read the sign! This cashier serves only railroad workers!"

"You call this service?"

Some sort of shift had ended. The railway workers' line grew and grew, many of the women shoving in and paying absolutely no heed to the civilian queue, where I was now about fifth from the head. I felt defeated—but the two and a half hours I'd spent in line anchored me to my spot. How could I start all over again?

Those behind and ahead of me seethed.

"Don't shove me!"

"I'm not shoving you!"

"Get off my foot, citizen!"

"When will this all end?"

"They're raising ticket prices soon!"

"If there's going to be a civil war, let's get it over with so things can get back to normal!"

But no one complained when a youth as hulking as a bronze statue, with a flat crewcut (the obligatory insignia of the Russian Mafia), handed his buddy in line ahead of us six passports for six extra tickets for six destinations at six different times. The crowd of once-querulous Russians held their tongues: the authority of the *podstrizhennye*, those with shaved heads, wasn't to be challenged.

At the beginning of hour three, I was still fourth from the front. In the line adjacent to ours, a ruckus broke out.

"Don't give him a ticket! He didn't wait in line! No!" commanded a middle-aged proletarian in glasses as he shoved back a besotted queue violator of about forty-five, reeking of cheap booze, with hands covered in scabby lesions.

"No! No!"

The worker placed his shovel-like paw on the drunk's face and sent him flying out of line with a propulsive thrust. He rebounded off a nearby column, straightened his lapels, and brandished a heavy wooden cane at his assailant from afar.

Some people hissed at the violator; others shouted "Bravo!" to the worker. The tired and oppressed of our line rallied together in praise of his just move ("Bravo! Good man! You showed him—he has no conscience!"). It was so easy to hate the drunk, so convenient to displace all the loathing provoked by this interminable, humiliating queue onto his person.

Minutes passed in hate-suffused ecstasy. But then there were cries from the rear.

"Ooow! Have you no conscience!"

"Aaah! Shame! Who do you think you are!"

The drunk had penetrated our line and was pushing forward.

"Look, Uncle, you'll have to get in line! We've been here over three hours!" said a young man behind me and grabbed the drunk's shoulder.

The drunk whipped his cane through the air and dropped the crook of it around the neck of the young man.

"I'll kill you! Don't you touch me! I'LL KILL YOU!" He jerked his cane spasmodically, and with it, the neck in the crook. The young man struggled to free himself and jumped away, rubbing his neck and wincing.

This man seemed quite agile and strong for a drunk. His threat, barked out crisply and without slurring, made me wonder if he could be intoxicated at all. But he exhaled cheap-booze breath in wafts that reached even my spot in line and his eyes glowered dully, as through a viscous film.

He shook his jacket free of dust and, after cutting across to the line of railway workers, took up a position behind a young blond woman who warned him that he would get his ticket only after five others had gone ahead of him (I wondered why he should be allowed even this, as there were thirty or so in line). He leaned into her; he cocked his head and screwed up his face, as though he were about to cry, and he mewled to her about being a Veteran of Labor and how he'd throw himself under a tram for his motherland, but he had no motherland now, and what had happened to the socialist spirit and where had Soviet brotherhood gone and . . .

The man ahead of him, reacting to the stench of his breath, said, "My God, Uncle! What have you been drinking?"

The drunk's voice turned gravelly.

"Eau de cologne! And damned good eau de cologne!"

He shoved the blond woman into the glass and made a final dash for the cashier's window, but flailing arms repelled him and he rebounded into a spot directly behind me. Just his proximity, with his rancid sweat and eau de cologne stench and scabrous hands, filled me with loathing.

He was pressing at my back.

"Hey," he began mumbling to me. "Hey, let me by, will you? I'm a Veteran of Labor . . . motherland . . . tram . . ."

"No."

"You don't know what it's like to work all your life for the motherland and then have it come apart. I labored for you . . . all my life! Let me pass!"

He was demanding now, not requesting. His voice trembled with suppressed rage.

"No," I said. "Get in back of the line and wait like everyone else."

At this, he jammed the crook of his cane into my ribs. My reaction was instinctive, immediate: I struck with my arm and sent him flying over some suitcases. He landed on his back but with a surprising agility, bounced to his feet.

"Young man, what are you doing!" a woman shouted at me. Another cried, "His cane! Grab his cane!"

He swung his cane back in preparation for a strike. I caught it at its zenith and forced it down, and this drew us face-to-face, his bespittled stubble scratching at my chin.

"You are shit!" he raged. "You are shit! I should kill you for that! Kill you!"

I held the cane down, my arm trembling with his fury, conducted through the staff like lightning through a metal rod. Unavoidably, I was staring into his eyes.

What I saw was my own reflection. There I was, in a Russian backwater town, in a fight with a drunk that could easily result in injury or death for either of us. And it was not my country, although he couldn't have known that, nor was it an excuse for his conduct; but still, I hadn't come to Russia to tussle with derelicts or beat on those deformed by an inhuman system, but rather to meet people and learn about them. I wanted to respect them. If I couldn't do that, then it would be better to remain silent or uninvolved.

I let his cane go. He straightened his jacket.

"All my life I labored to build this country for you," he muttered, "and you disgrace me. *Pozor* [shame]!"

I felt myself no victor. And no one in line had helped me. A mute desperation verging on rage burned in my chest—one woman had shouted at me as though *I* were the instigator, as though *I* were to blame, although perhaps she had not seen him strike me with his cane. Everyone around me was so stolid, so passive, but I had allowed myself to be provoked.

"*Pozor!* After all I, a Veteran of Labor, have done for you! *Pozor!*"

I finally bought my ticket and left the station, feeling alone and vulnerable and somehow debased. Some six thousand miles lay ahead of me—I had to pace myself, to endure, as did the Russians

in line. Yet my conviction, at least in theory, was that passive en-
durance let tyrants reign. It was wrong to tolerate so much.

The system Russians lived under hadn't worked, but they suffered it until it collapsed around them. Now they survived in the
ruins. Only the dead, I thought, or those utterly without hope,
could bear such squalid humiliation on a daily basis, from trivial
insults like waiting for train tickets to larger torments. How could
you start a business here? Develop the will to make something of
yourself? Soviet rule had reduced many to the state of rats, at each
other's throats over scraps. Suddenly I realized—I *felt*, rather—
what this meant. Even a ticket line had provoked me to violence.
Who was to say life in Chita wouldn't have extinguished *my*
spirit, too, or turned me into a raging drunk? How could I not see
my own reflection in their eyes? I couldn't resolve my feelings
about all this, but it was clear I'd have to stay as neutral and tol-
erant as possible just to get through the trip alive.

I ate a late lunch in a diner and returned to the hotel to pack,
still dispirited and somewhat shaken. When the maid at the hotel
learned I had a ticket for the "common car," the lowest class of
train travel, it turned out, she gasped, "Take that ticket back and
turn it in for something in first or second class! You could be
robbed or worse there!"

It was Saturday night. I decided to cheer myself up by going out
on the town, but it seemed the only restaurant open was the one
in my hotel.

WAIT TO BE SEATED, read the sign at the entrance.

I waited. No one came up to seat me. After a few minutes,
I picked an empty table and seated myself.

The restaurant was cold; had the temperature been any lower,
my breath would have been visible. Red and green lights around
the base of the dance floor blinked sluggishly through hanging
skeins of cigarette smoke. The hall echoed with roistering tables
packed tightly with the same crewcut mobsters and their rented
girlfriends who had been there the other night. The fat man had

shaved and was hosting some sort of event at a big table, raising his glass of vodka every few minutes to propose hoarse toasts. His group must have been there some time already; empty vodka bottles crowded hors d'oeuvres plates and overfilled ashtrays on his table. The scent of sweat and vodka breath and burned kebab lingered and mixed with floating islets of cigarette smoke.

The atmosphere put me on edge. An undercurrent of malevolence charged the place, rankled in the toasts, buzzed in the throaty laughter of the revelers. I suppressed my inclination to leave and decided I should accept the scene around me, to try to find something interesting in it. There were, after all, tables at which harmless-looking Chinese sat and socialized and pretty girls ate with their dates; not everyone looked like Russian Godfathers. And almost everyone trotted out to dance and look silly on the parquet floor near the band when their favorite songs played.

I ordered a Chinese beer and decided to relax. If this was to be Russian entertainment on a Saturday night, I'd share it.

"Get up! I didn't seat you here!"

A stout woman standing at my shoulder glared at me from under a threatening beehive hairdo.

"I'm not getting up," I said, mustering all the positive energy I could and smiling. "You were not at your station when I came in. This table is not occupied—does it matter that much to you where I sit?"

"I don't care where you sit, but you owe me a hundred rubles [about ten cents] for the seating fee. Pay up!"

I handed her her rubles and refused to let my mood sag.

The waitress brought me beef cutlets and a cucumber salad, and I ordered another beer.

The dancing set me at ease. Even criminals have a right to make merry, I thought, and it would be better to adjust myself to my surroundings and have a good time. What happened today in the station was a fluke, and anyway, why not drink and forget about it? I took a swill of beer and resolved to do just that.

"Would you like to dance? My name is Natasha."

Natasha stood at my shoulder with her hands behind her back, her eyes beaming from atop high, flat cheekbones. She had on a shiny black dress, such as teenagers wear to their proms, and was a bit plump. I said yes.

On the dance floor, it occurred to me she was probably a prostitute, so when she suggested I was from the Baltics, I agreed that I was, feeling more comfortable with this little lie, which lent me a degree of anonymity that I craved after the station incident. After our dance, she asked me to sit at her table.

Her two friends, statuesque blond Lena with pursed lips, and square, pudgy Nadezhda, who was a Buryat (a Mongol people with their own republic, Buryatia, to the west), had been drinking for some time, and both were pleasantly tipsy and flirtatious, batting eyelashes at me and giggling. All three turned out to be medical students finishing their final year of school.

"Lena and I are surgeons!" Natasha bubbled.

"I'm an anesthesiologist!" said Nadezhda, and gulped a glass of vodka.

"I'm actually an American," I admitted. "I'm traveling across Russia."

Nadezhda cocked her head at me and burped. Lena stared transfixed for a moment, then lay her chin on her hand and smiled. Natasha grew suddenly uncomfortable.

"Oh! I wouldn't have guessed! And you're seeing us like this . . . I don't think we look our best . . . And this place—it's not like a restaurant in America . . . You're used to better—"

"Enough!" said Lena, interrupting Natasha and her apologies. She grabbed my hand and dragged me out to the dance floor. We danced and chatted about her medical career, about how she would soon do her internship in a village health care center. When we got back to the table, Natasha took me by the wrist and led me out to the floor again. More apologies, more talk about what I must feel as an American in lowly Chita, about how this is not what the girls *really* do for fun, about how their life was unworthy and how ashamed she was. She held me very tight, though.

Lena saw this and cut in.

"How rude! Can't you see Nadezhda is suffering? No man has asked her to dance all night, and you spend all your time with Natasha and me. Please ask Nadezhda!"

We returned to the table. Lena prodded me: "Go on, ask!"

Nadezhda was trying to exorcise some grief: she began pawing me and kissing me, and dragging me all around the floor in sloppy drunken waltzes—until Lena cut in and sent her off.

"How rude! Natasha invites you to our table, but you spend all your time dancing with Nadezhda and me! You should ask Natasha to dance!"

Natasha also decided to toss in kisses between apologies, which she drew out into monologues on the vileness of Russia and the paradise she knew America was.

"It must be so hard for you, an American man, in such a place as Russia," she said, tightening her grip around my waist. "You are so far from your family . . . Your homeland is so advanced . . . You have so many things in your markets . . . Not like Chita—"

Lena cut in.

"What have I done now?"

"What have you done? What have you *not* done? You never ask *me* to dance—you wait until I cut in every time! How rude!"

How rude. Lena was by far the most attractive and engaging of the three, and she made no issue of my being foreign, which I liked. She kept her nose high and had a proud look about her that kept her above the sordidness of the restaurant.

We all danced and chatted through the evening. The lights eventually came on.

"Let me take your picture," I said to the girls, pulling my camera out of my bag. They agreed, but only after they dragged all the spent vodka and beer bottles off the table.

I clicked. They asked me to send them a print.

No sooner had I put away my camera than a heavy hand dropped on my shoulder.

"Show me that camera!"

Above me wavered a tall, heavily muscled Buryat with a crew-cut, one of the criminal types who had been sitting with the fat man earlier that evening. His face was all bony brow and fat, snarling lips. He gripped an empty vodka bottle like a truncheon in his other hand.

It was as if cold water had been splashed on my face. I momentarily failed to understand what was going on.

"Give me that camera or I'll s-s-smash it!"

His words were slurred but his resolve clear. I sat in the most awkward of positions for any sort of fight, twisted into a pretzel and staring over my shoulder at his dull mug. I decided if he did not leave I would have to jump up and strike first or risk getting a bottle smashed over my head.

"I said, give me that camera or I'll *kill* you!"

He swung the vodka bottle back over his head. I jumped to my feet, sending my chair tumbling over backward.

At this moment, hands grabbed his arm in midswing and the bottle smashed on the floor behind him. Two Russian bouncers had him by the elbows. They tore him from his spot, his feet kicking, saliva spewing from the side of his mouth.

I stood dumbfounded. I hadn't seen them approach.

They dragged him kicking down the aisle, his feet hooking chairs and toppling them. One of the bouncers knocked the front door open with his foot. In unison they hurled him through it and set out after him.

There were screams and blows, thuds of fists on flesh, then cries, then muffled whimpers and more blows and gasps for breath. Then nothing. The bouncers returned and nodded to the maître d'. She in turn nodded to us.

Natasha grabbed my arm.

"Let's go, Jeff! Oh, what did I tell you about Chita!"

My mind went blank. Lena grabbed Nadezhda, who tottered and burped and whispered in Natasha's ear.

"We invite you home with us for a nightcap," said Natasha

plaintively, as we were passing through the doors. "We are so, *so* ashamed. First, though, Nadezhda must correct herself," she said. "We'll wait for them."

Natasha and I ended up standing by the women's bathroom, a reeking row of squat toilets with no doors, not even on the outside. Those using the squats had to rely on the decency of passersby not to look in and invade their privacy. A girl was crying in the restaurant, retching inebriated sobs that quickened when she stumbled out the door in the grip of a girlfriend, struggling to place one foot in front of the other. She staggered toward us, and as she passed by, emitted a throaty, bilious belch that erupted into an explosion of vomit when she stepped into the restroom. My stomach churned and I felt like retching myself.

Lena emerged with Nadezhda in tow. We walked out onto the street. Cars stood in the cold with engines running, their headlights streaming over their own exhaust fumes and illuminating all sorts of people whose postparty scenes of queasiness and trauma should have remained cloaked in darkness.

"We will walk down to the street at the bottom of the hill to catch the bus," said Natasha. We started off down the hill. A car followed us. A black Volga. It had four men inside.

To my dismay, Lena and Nadezhda picked this moment to burst into song, and Lena, who had been so sober and correct, began affecting a drunken stumble and slurred her song into groggy, disconnected couplets. The car stayed with us, its engine humming.

"We want to celebrate," said Natasha. "We won't think of what just happened in the restaurant."

"But why is Lena acting drunk? She and Nadezhda are making a spectacle of themselves with all these thugs around! Let's find a cab and get out of here!"

"What cabs? There are none! And they're making a scene because they don't care anymore! Look at our life—would you care? *We don't care what happens!*"

The Volga drove away. Lena and Nadezhda saw this and toned down their singing, as if it were an act put on for those in the car.

But soon, other vehicles filled with dark, leering figures pulled up to them, and they danced and stumbled anew. Even Natasha joined in the revelry, and I began to feel that I just didn't understand what was going on around me. When we finally arrived at the bus stop, two cars pulled up by the girls. Both were full of guys. My stomach was turning.

Some sort of dialogue took place between Lena and the drivers. I was amazed and relieved when they pulled away.

Nadezhda broke free of Lena with a cry and jumped aboard the wrong bus. She looked nauseated.

Lena took my arm.

"So much for her! We'll see her in the morning! Having a good time in Chita?"

NINE

Ulan-Ude: Doing Business on Communist Street

The "common car" the maid had warned me about turned out to be quite satisfactory; a samovar next to the conductor's cabin provided hot water; wide upholstered shelves served as bunks, six to an open compartment; a woman offered fresh bedding to anyone with two hundred rubles to spare. I rented my linen and settled into my upper berth for the all-night train ride from Chita to Ulan-Ude.

"Where are you getting off?" quavered a voice from beneath me as we pulled out of Chita station.

I looked down from my perch; sitting in a heap on the lower bunk was a woman in her sixties wearing a frumpy red-and-brown dress and blue jogging pants with threads dangling from the hem. It seemed unsociable to sit alone in my upper berth at such an early hour, so I climbed down and took a seat next to her. She kneaded a greasy blue SPORTO travel bag between her fingers and nodded hello.

A young woman with a rat's nest of brown hair topping a pallid, egg-shaped face came in and placed her bag in the compartment under her seat, which was the lower bunk opposite mine. As I had boarded first, my bag filled the compartment under the old woman and me.

The old woman asked the young one where she was getting off. Balygdy. This upset her. She turned to me, her two steel front teeth glinting.

"I have nowhere to put my bag."

"You can put it under my seat," offered the younger woman cheerlessly, as she took out a bottle of Zhigulyovskoye beer.

"Under your seat? Why do you offer me the space under your seat?"

"Because I have room. Feel free to—"

"Oh, I see! I put my bag under you, but then you get up at five in the morning for Balygdy and while I'm asleep you walk out with it! That's happened to me before." She wrung her hands and shook her head, working herself up as though she'd already lost her bag. "No, thanks. No . . . no."

"I don't need your bag and whatever you've got in it," snapped the other woman. "If you want, I'll wake you up when we reach Balygdy and you can watch me take my bag and not yours." She gulped from her beer bottle and looked out the window.

The old lady fretted.

"What, and wake me up in the middle of my deepest sleep? What about my health? I'm a pensioner and I need my rest." She turned to me. "And now she starts talking about my things. Maybe she thinks I'll tell her what I've got with me. *Nyet!* I will not! And just for her information, I've got nothing at all, except old clothes of no value, and my dinner."

"I don't care about your bag. Do as you like!"

She rummaged in her sack for a book, found it, and opened it, screening her face from the old lady's with its cover.

Rather than listen to this anymore, I offered the old woman the space my camera bag took up under the seat. I'd rather have it next to me anyway, I thought. She accepted gratefully, showering me with all sorts of tender diminutives as though I'd caught a thief red-handed with her bag and saved it from being carried off to Balygdy. Now that the danger had passed, she decided to forgive the would-be thief buried in her book and make small talk with her.

"So you are from Balygdy?"

"No. My mother is. I'm going to visit her."

"Have the Americans bought up Balygdy yet?"

The pallid woman kept her face in her book and huffed at the interruption.

"No, they wouldn't be interested, I suppose," responded the old woman to herself. "They need a place to drive their limousines. Yeltsin and Gorbachev—they've sold Russia down the drain. If they die tomorrow, only foreign businessmen will shed a tear. Look what they've done to our motherland! How's an old pensioner to live?"

She reached into her bag and pulled out a shard of unleavened bread, an orange, and a tin cup, and poured herself water from a bottle in her bag. She then tore off strips of the bread and chomped on them, chasing them with long gratuitous slurps and gurgles from her cup. Her eyes stayed glued gratefully on mine, the gratitude she felt for my good deed not having yet subsided. I looked out the window.

She peeled her orange and began eating it as one would an apple, gnashing her teeth into its orb and sending streams of juice flying about the cabin. One particularly bountiful squirt landed on my book. She peered over her bag and examined the juice on my page, then smiled dully at me. I wiped it off. The result of her next nosedive into her orange was a stream shot as if from a water pistol onto the young woman's tights, which prompted her to get up and leave for the bathroom.

When she was down the hall, the pensioner turned to me and whispered.

"She drinks beer! In my day, young women didn't drink in

public. And certainly not beer! We had a sense of decency then, and manners. Say, would you like to read my paper?"

She handed me the splotched and stained issue of *Sovietskaya Rossiya* ("The only paper that tells the truth for a pensioner!") in which she had wrapped her dinner. It was a week old and covered with calls for citizens to vote against Yeltsin in the referendum that had just passed. Other articles denounced the "Anti-Slavic Adventuristic Involvement" of the West in Yugoslavia and the "Mafia Control of Privatization." I thanked her for it and crawled up into my berth. The white trunks of birch trees and snowy earth tinctured with gold drifted past my window as the sun set. Somewhere between Yugoslavia and *Sovietskaya Rossiya*'s call for Soviet rule I fell asleep.

Dawn came. Outside, empty brown steppe drifted by, bathed in blue light, a steppe so utterly denuded of vegetation, so sterilized of anything living that it resembled moonscape or, at best, a frigid vista of desolation from nearby Mongolia. At length, shacks of dusty wood with cattle scraping frozen earth in their yards began to proliferate, then smokestacks and soot and BLOOM, BELOVED BURYATIA! in huge red letters over a factory lot strewn with rusting machinery.

Ulan-Ude, or Red Uda (the Uda being one of the two rivers that pass through the city, both flowing into Lake Baikal to the west), was once a Cossack fortress town built to secure the Zabaikalye region of eastern Siberia in the seventeenth century, originally bearing the name of Verkhneudinsk. The local Mongol Buryats, for the most part, had lived in the countryside and raised cattle, while Cossacks, political prisoners, and repressed Russian religious minorities, as well as various fortune seekers, made up the town's population. The Soviet era saw it grow from a few thousand to more than 350,000, many of its new inhabitants lured by the higher salaries and work opportunities such undeveloped areas as the Buryat Autonomous Soviet Socialist Republic provided. Clean yellow buildings and starkly modern concrete structures dominate central Ulan-Ude today, but to see the cattle breeders of the past one need only take a tram anywhere outside the center. For that matter, Soviet Square, located on one of the city's highest points, offers a view of east Siberian taiga stretching to the horizon in every direction, and this makes it easy to remember how far away Ulan-Ude is from anywhere else, how much an outpost in the wilderness it remains even now.

I needed to change money, but I arrived at the state bank during its noon closing. As I walked about the low stone and plaster yellow-painted shops and houses in search of another bank, it became clear that the Buryats were a minority in their own capital; perhaps some seven out of ten people on the street were Russian, and signs everywhere except on government buildings were in Russian. There seemed to be little socializing between the two populations—Buryats walked and talked with Buryats, Russians with Russians. The older residential areas off the main streets were all brown wooden multidwelling houses, without the trim and decor of many Siberian homes, standing apart from each other on broad gravel or dirt roads. There were few people out and about and it was hard to find anyone to ask about money changing. I ended up in small commercial shops asking if they would exchange my dollars but got only curt *nyets* and stares.

Eventually, I found myself on Soviet Square under the vigilant glare of the four-story-high head of Lenin in front of the Buryat House of People's Deputies, all steel-and-glass facade in front of which were Volgas with snoozing drivers. The sun shone hot on the yellow buildings around the square and threw Lenin's features into stark relief. In fact, there was a glare to the light that verged on harshness, and it was clear that this unfiltered barrage of ultraviolet rays singed the steppe to the south and east and withered its vegetation, leaving only brown dust and dried grass all the way to Mongolia. In Ulan-Ude, this light sterilized all that it struck, leaving much of the town antiseptically characterless. There were no drunks about, few potholes, and no decaying concrete buildings; edifices there had a shorn, spartan cast, as if they had been sand-blasted free of impurities. In this respect, Ulan-Ude was an un-Soviet republic capital.

Communist Street had a tram line and a number of private kiosks, one of which, Goods for You, caught my eye with its crowd of kids in oversized army surplus jackets and pants with the knees scraped through, begging for Snickers candy bars and Wrigley's Spearmint gum. The young woman inside the kiosk looked up at me in relief when I approached to ask about selling dollars and gave her an excuse to ignore the street urchins.

A passing middle-aged woman in a fur hat and heavy *sapogi* overheard me and glowered at me.

"Listen," she barked, tugging at my arm, "there is no reason to turn to *sobstvenniki* to sell your dollars!" (*Sobstvenniki:* owners of private property; in this case, private shop owners. The word, to older Soviets, implies the immorality associated with capitalism, profit, and greed.)

"I can't stand you, you *sobstvenniki!* You *kioskyory!* When will a strong fist rid us of such elements as you!"

The man in the kiosk motioned me in and slammed the window.

"You see what we have to put up with? We are trying to earn a living, that's all!"

Vika and her husband, Dima, bought fifty dollars from me at a rate better than what I could have gotten in a bank and offered me a seat. She was pretty, with a lilting voice and limpid eyes; he was a bit swarthy with short-cropped hair and a permanently pained look, a sort of endearing look of despair. They had met a few years before as medical students in Baku. After they married, they discovered that, with all the economic changes that had taken place with the collapse of the Soviet Union, it was far more profitable to work in a kiosk than in medicine. Still, they were not proprietors but employees—a large local firm owned and operated the kiosk we were sitting in. Their boss was due by any minute.

"Our boss will come and complain about something, despite our hard work," said Dima. "We spend from seven in the morning to eight in the evening here with only a lunch hour. We make a little more than skilled workers in factories, but at least we're on our own. I worked in a factory and it was unbearable. Everyone got drunk all day. Everyone on the boss's good side, that is. The others had to carry their workload. I just couldn't take it."

Vika added: "What you saw with that woman was typical. We are 'thieves' or *spekulyanty*." (Speculators—those who buy at one price and sell at another—sit at the top of the old socialist hate list, abhorred both for the profit they make and because they sell but do not produce, something even Russians who accept the market reforms find objectionable.)

Goods for You sold more than Snickers bars: its shelves were packed with American chewing gum, foreign cigarettes, Chinese blouses, secondhand slacks, bottles of Pepsi, Polish shoes, lighters, matches, Bic pens, and even a bikini.

Dima agreed with her but admitted to feeling uneasy.

"I can't figure out how it came to be accepted abroad that profit and business are moral and decent concepts. That does bother me. It seems a little immoral."

The door flew open.

"*Zdrasst'ye,* boys and girls! How are we?"

In stepped a tall blond man in a leather jacket that squeaked as he moved. He was the boss, that much was clear. He stood framed by a yellow bikini top and a Mickey Mouse head.

"So how are our little affairs today!" he asked, laying a heavy hand on Dima's shoulder and leering at Vika. She squirmed in her seat and looked away. Dima handed him a cigar box stuffed with rubles.

"This is what we have for today. Seventy thousand or so."

"No, come now! We've done better than that, I'm sure. Where's the rest?" His words were directed to Dima; his eyes stayed fixed on Vika.

He and Dima counted the cash and he left.

"This boss of yours," I asked. "Who is he? An entrepreneur?"

"In Ulan-Ude we have no entrepreneurs and don't even know

what the word is supposed to mean. Look at the Lenin statues around here. Don't they tell you something? The same people—the same Communists—are running everything. This business you see here is all run through crooked deals and old party connections. The only counter to that is the racket—racketeers collect *dan,* protection money, from all of us."

There was a pounding on the glass. We looked up: three bedraggled, bleary-eyed proletarians were demanding vodka. Dima shouted they had none.

I was surprised to see drunks at five in the afternoon appearing from everywhere in groups of six or eight. Dima was not: "At five they're getting off work. They drink like this on the job."

I asked if there was racial tension between Russians and Buryats. "There wasn't much interaction," he said. "Villages were either Russian or Buryat."

After we exchanged adresses, I walked back along Communist Street toward the hotel. At the entrance, a pair of big Buryats held a little Buryat against the wall. "Speak!" they demanded. His eyes jumped from one face to the other in terror. One belted him squarely in the solar plexus, and he doubled over voiceless trying to catch his breath.

"*Spekulyanty!* No-good youths! You fight over who sells us junk at high prices from the sidewalk! You all belong in jail!" shouted a babushka from the bus stop to the three youths. "Damned *spekulyanty!*"

I caught the 9:18 bus south to Datsan the next morning. Dima and Vika had told me I should visit the Buddhist temple there. I knew nothing at all about it.

Buryat women making the pilgrimage to Datsan huddled on the seats of the shabby, creaking red bus, their pear-shaped figures squeezed into seats and spilling into the aisle. Their faces were plump and flat. No one was speaking Russian, except the Russian driver, who wore a checked cowboy shirt and chewed bubble gum as he twirled his fingers through his walrus-tusk mustache. He treated his bus like a bucking bronco and shouted at the women who couldn't get on or off fast enough for him. He delighted in making them squeal as he pulled away with them still hanging on to the door.

Only the faithful remained on the bus by the time we reached Datsan an hour later. Cows gawked from the roadside as we pulled up to the temple gates, which looked as though they might lead into a corral of sorts. I wondered what the fate of the temple was during the Stalin years and the "Struggle with Religion"— maybe it *had* been a corral then, as churches had been turned into stables. The babushkas rushed in ahead of me, adjusting their scarves and chattering in Buryat.

Larch houses with white trim occupied the southern half of the enclosed temple area. The other half was reserved for the temples themselves. There were red-and-orange prayer wheels; in their midst stood white monuments of sorts with gold trim and pagoda-style temples with white walls and red pillars and yellow roofs, all their colors rendered luxuriant by the azure sky above. Inside the central temple, the Dalai Lama was featured both in photograph and portraiture at its head; people entered in silence, paid money to a woman at the door for prayers, sniffed the incense wafting from sticks burning slowly in the center, and set off toward the portraits with heads bowed and hands pressed together in front of them. They prayed at the head of the temple, under the portraits, and left backing out, keeping their faces turned toward the Dalai Lama out of respect. Monks with shaved heads and red robes scurried about and tended the incense. No one paid attention to me, even though I was the only non-Buryat on the temple grounds.

At the edge of the residential area hung a sign: CENTRAL BOARD OF BUDDHISTS OF THE USSR. It was deserted, although all the doors were open.

TEN

A Stone from Lake Baikal

The sun rose over Ulan-Ude station and ringed the fur hats of the Russians and Buryats below on the platform with halos of gold as they said good-byes, some crying, others hugging convulsively and pressing their lips to each other's cheeks over and over again, as if to store up kisses for the long trip ahead and the weeks or months of separation sure to follow.

As usual, I was solitary in my window seat on this train to Irkutsk. Despite all the people I was meeting on my trip across Russia, the journey was a lonely one; I was certain to be leaving soon and certain never to return. The transient nature of these acquaintanceships intensifed them. They magnified the uncertainties of life that hedge the borders of our consciousness even when we are stationary: we don't know when our last meeting with our friends or family will be any more than we are able to predict the moment of our death. We travel through time even when rooted to one spot. I already missed the people I had met and left behind thousands of miles of road back, from Alexander in Magadan to Sasha and Sergei on the Kolyma Route to Stal and Vika in Yakutsk; they had for a short time been vital to me. In fact, I owed my safe passage across Russia to them. The warmth I felt toward them would dissolve into aching sadness after my departure.

The engineer eased our train into motion, and a Russian man with flaxen hair stopped by my seat. His pale eyes sat deep in a face furrowed by exposure to the frosts.

"*Zdrasst'ye.* Looks like I'm in the seat across from you. My name is Grigori."

He cleared a space for himself amidst the mess of vodka bottles and grease-stained food wrappers and cigarette butts littering our compartment.

"I'm from Cheboksary in the Urals. Where are you from?"

"The United States."

A puzzled look dropped over his face and he sat back.

"The United States? Are you serious?" He paused. "Surely the citizen of such a great power would travel by a more luxurious means, perhaps in his own private jet."

"I don't have a jet."

To find an American in Ulan-Ude seemed absurd to him. "It's a foul place, poor. No economy left." Irkutsk, the capital of Siberia, and Baikal, the pearl of Siberia, seemed worthier to him. He thought it was a good idea I was going there and pulled out a white stone.

"This stone is from the shores of Lake Baikal," he said, running his fingers over it. "Baikal is a place I'm very proud of as a Russian. I carry this stone with me and remember my visit there, some years ago, and how eternal the lake is and how short-lived I will be in comparison. The stone, of course, will outlast me, as will Baikal. What I lived through as the boss of a state farm in Cheboksary and now as a buyer for a clothing plant there is nothing compared to what Baikal has seen of our history. This stone helps me remember that."

He reclined in his seat and we watched the *izby* and cows and steppe give way to patches of birch forest and evergreens, still swathed in vapors of dawn tinted gold in places, pink and orange in others. It would soon clear the horizon and burn away these mists entirely, leaving unattenuated sunlight in full dominion over the taiga.

A Buryat teenager with a shoulder bag stopped by our compartment, plopped an assortment of black-and-white glossy photos on the table between us, and walked on. The top one was a photograph of a religious calendar; beneath it lay Sylvester Stallone in a scene from *Rambo,* then soft-porn pics.

I was curious to know what the life of a buyer for a Siberian clothing factory was like.

"Oh, what is there to tell?" he mused. "I make about eight thousand rubles a month [eight dollars]. With bonuses, I can make as much as fifteen thousand. You call that a salary? I've got a wife and three children. The wife works at a construction firm. She makes half of what I do. We get by, though. Before all the changes, I was working in agriculture. Times have changed."

I asked him about his year as a farm boss.

"I ran a *sovkhoz* [state farm], but I had to leave there. All the farm workers were stealing. They had to—their seventy-ruble-a-month salary wasn't enough to live on. But it's impossible to bear if you're honest. I mean, ten percent of the seed we were allotted actually got into the ground. It begins disappearing when it's shipped to us. Then more is stolen when it arrives, and even more when it is stored in our holds. Farmers just take it for their own use or sell it. Then, even after it's planted, they steal it out of the ground at night. As I said, we ended up farming ten percent of our allotment."

"And then, I assume, the cold climate makes growing things difficult," I added.

"No! That's wrong! Western Siberia is very fertile. I planted a small crop of wheat and peas by my office window and kept track of it, just to see how it would grow. By the season's end, I had a wall of wheat and a patch of peas so thick you could barely walk through it! People ruin our agriculture, not the weather."

The Buryat teenager returned and pointed to the photos on the table: did I want to buy them? No, thanks. He pointed to his lips. He was deaf, it turned out; I assumed he meant talking was useless. I shook my head, and he grabbed his pictures and left.

"When I caught some farmers stealing, they tried to kill me," Grigori said. "I said 'enough' and went over to the factory. Who needs it? The *sovkhozniki* would often vandalize machinery. They'd leave tools on the ground so that harvesters would run over them. Or they'd steal parts. No one was being paid, harvests were lost . . . That's the way it is even today with our collectivized agriculture. We always are short of grain, but we could produce more grain than all the countries of the world combined."

"What about privatizing agriculture and letting people own their own land?" I asked.

"Maybe that works in the West, but here? Who would end up with control over our lands? Not the people who worked them. Criminal elements bent on exploitation would buy it all up through connections."

By this time, we were drawing up on a vast sea covered with gray ice floes that were slit in places by passages of water rippling with the wind and stretching northward into a horizon where ice, water, and sky melted into a turquoise mist. Baikal. We both fell silent. Our train skirted the southern rim of this, the largest and deepest of the world's lakes, and the most ancient. Around its sandy shores villages sat exposed, their *izby* pitifully small, the puny birches and larches around them offering little protection against the wind.

Grigori said, "I have no answers." He sat back and stared at Baikal.

Russians have a penchant for believing the worst. They think foreigners are too naive to see the machinations and clever evil-doings by which politics and national life operate in Russia. They believe that in the West people are honest, or at least less devious.

Our talk dwindled as the morning wore on. I got up, still wearing my overcoat against the chill on the train, grabbed my camera
bag, and walked down to the rest room at the end of the car. It
was occupied, so I stood and waited. We were approaching the
village of Baikalsk.

"Ticket!"

I was startled. A husky woman in a blue uniform stood behind
me.

"I said ticket!"

I told her I had given my ticket to the conductor, as usual, at the
start of the trip.

"Sure you did! And you just happen to be standing here with
your coat on and bag in hand as we approach Baikalsk!"

I didn't understand. What was so absurd about my using the
rest room? I kept my bag with me for obvious security reasons.
And I wasn't going to get off at Baikalsk.

"Where is your ticket then?" she repeated. Before I could answer, she said, "You are trying to steal a ride from Ulan-Ude!
That's illegal! We can fine and arrest you!"

"What? I bought a ticket, as I've told you."

"Show it to me."

"I've given it to the conductor."

"What is her name?"

"How should I know? She's sitting at the end of this car—let's
go ask her."

"You say you don't know her name! Next, when she has no
ticket for you, you'll say it was a different conductor!"

She stretched her words derisively, taking a sadistic delight in
her display of bureaucratic prerogative to intrude on people's privacy and make them jump through hoops. I got sick of this and
set off down the hall to the conductor, who was sitting in her
cabin. When she produced my ticket, the woman in the blue uniform dropped my "case" without a word and walked on.

The conductor explained that trains got a lot of *bezbiletniki*
(ticketless ones). "People try to ride as rabbits [slang for 'without

a ticket'] and they never actually sit down—they loiter with their bags by the car door."

I had nearly been arrested in Tynda due to a technicality concerning my visa. I had suffered through that humiliating line at the Chita train station, to say nothing of the abominable melee over rooms at the hotel desk. Bureaucrats, infamous even in czarist times for their malicious incompetence and tyranny, were fast becoming the most loathesome aspect of Russia for me; every Russian despised them. I recalled Grigori's story of how the peasants sabotaged the state-run farm where he worked; the system was at fault here, but no one seemed to have any idea of how to change it, and worst of all, few had the energy to do anything more than endure it.

North toward Irkutsk, fog drew an oppressive curtain of gloom over forests of pine and larch. The train set off between low hills, past villages of mud and slush and rotted plank sidewalks. Around three that afternoon, we roared onto a bridge over the great Angara River, frothing and surging west with a non-Siberian impetuosity.

I caught glimpses of a great city of old stone houses, factories and smokestacks and plumes of smoke drifting into fog, and columns of Zhiguli taxis and speeding black Volgas and brown Kamazy. The activity convinced me that, for the first time on my trip, I was *arriving* somewhere, that I was progressing westward and leaving somber, uninhabited eastern Siberia behind. My mood lightened.

Like Yakutsk, Chita, and Ulan-Ude, Irkutsk was originally a Cossack outpost founded in the seventeenth century to bring the local tribes, in this case Buryats, under czarist domination during Russia's drive to conquer Siberia. But that was where the similarity ended. Its stately stone trade houses and elaborate wooden residences intricately embroidered with Russian *rezba* (lacy wood carving) testified to a past of grandeur, during which Irkutsk reigned as the capital of Siberia and came close to being the central city of an independent state in the early eighteenth century under its ruler, Prince Gagarin. Its proximity to China and Mongolia allowed it to grow as a trade center, and the Irkutsk Oblast was itself rich in sables and gold.

But, as with all Siberian cities, the legions that populated it were, to a great extent, exiles, and the city hosted almost all the key players from the 1917 revolution, from Stalin to Kirov to Molotov. Other exiles, especially Poles, of whom there were some eighteen thousand after the Russian suppression of the Polish revolt of 1863, helped Irkutsk develop into Siberia's most sophisticated city. For the first time since I stepped on the plane to Magadan, I breathed freely.

The next morning I headed down to the bank of the Angara. The weather was mild in late April—in the thirties and sunny. Irkutsk had a well-developed riverside: a paved embankment offered running space for joggers, picnic tables stood by the water, small craft, anchored firmly in the swift current, searched for fish. There were remarkably few people, though. I walked out the bridge onto the little island opposite the Hotel Angara and saw a teenage girl trying unsuccessfully to train her dog to speak and a man bathing naked in the freezing river water. Otherwise, it looked as though the city was on vacation.

I spent the rest of the afternoon wandering amidst the grand wooden residences around the center. The feeling that I had "arrived" kept revisiting me. Irkutsk, unlike the other Siberian towns I'd seen, had acquired a historical patina, a soft polish that evoked the persistent and cultured effort of exiles from European Russia and Poland to recreate the comforts of civilization in this east Siberian taiga.

Lunch hour found me at the Café Bylina off Kirov Square. Cafés in Russia bear little resemblance to counterparts in Paris or Rome or Budapest: coffee is a rarity, no one is sitting and chatting, and the cold keeps people huddled indoors. They might just as well be called snack bars or even bars, as half the customers stand around guzzling vodka straight out of tall glasses.

The main dish was *pelmeni*. *Pelmeni* served with vodka in a tall glass. Or *pelmeni* served with "Drink." "Drink" looked like cherry Kool-Aid. The barmaid was swift; she flung *pelmeni* deftly into bowls and shot them down the bar to customers, and ladled "Drink" effortlessly into plastic cups or measured *sto gram* (a hundred grams) of vodka using her fingers against the glasses. She had on a tall chef's hat and never cracked a smile.

The bus I rode to Lake Baikal followed a road that paralleled the Angara, ascending and descending the gentle, eroded folds that gave a subtle texture to the Irkutsk Oblast's taiga. Huge blocks of ice, some as big as houses, rushed down the river toward the lake in a churning, precipitate frenzy.

An even ceiling of clouds cut off from view the tops of mountains across the river. Sheets of descending snow wandered across the leaden face of the water as if in search of dry earth to powder. Several kilometers out into the lake, an icebreaker chopped a path through the lake's cracked, frozen crust. There was a dock below, beside which was moored a small ferry. I wandered down the bank toward it.

After descending all the way to the lake, I reached into the water between floes and touched it—it was icy and crystalline. Baikal is one of the few bodies of water in the world untainted by plankton or algae of any kind. You could see clear to the bottom in water hundreds of feet deep. People in Irkutsk had told me that there were seals and walruses in the lake that swam from the Arctic Ocean through a tunnel. Others said that there was no such tunnel. But what was certain was that about a third of the species of fish in Baikal were found nowhere else: the lake was an ancient microcosm, a sea unto itself, a preserve of creatures long since extinct elsewhere, if they had ever existed beyond its bounds.

A forlorn wind haunted the birches, murmuring through the pines, breathing life into the groves of larches, and whispering the secrets of a mythical past over the ice floes. Buryat legends about Baikal were numerous; its environs had always been sparsely populated and the abode of spirits and gods.

The ferry swiftly backed out through the slush, turned south, and motored off into the snow squalls hovering offshore.

I walked on; my aim was to get to Listvyanka, a village a few kilometers north on the shore, to catch the last bus at six. The road was lonely, the snow flurries thickening.

No one was around. Everything was closed, as it was a Sunday. Boats creaked and cracked ice in their moors, agitated by the wind. I pulled out my camera and began taking pictures of them, enjoying the way my wide-angle lens caught the curves of the bows.

"No! No! No!"

A man emerged from one of the boats and shouted in English at me. PATROL was written in black letters on the bow of his craft. I saw I must have photographed a police boat of some sort.

A loudspeaker emitted an ear-splitting introductory screech.

"It is forbidden to photograph us! Forbidden!" said the voice in angry Russian. I waved in compliance and put away the camera and started back to the road, but then in English I heard, "Excuse me! Excuse me!" over the loudspeaker, as if they wanted me to stop. I played dumb and walked on.

"Man with camera! Return!"

I made it to the bus stop.

The bus to Irkutsk pulled up at that instant; it was six o'clock. I jumped aboard and it drove off into the flurries whipping about the lakeside, leaving the policeman balancing on the gangplank.

ELEVEN

Tomsk:
Searching for Salvation

What had there been about Tomsk in the news lately? The TOMSK sign at the Tayga station triggered a pang of fear, a sensation of danger. But *why?*

At Tayga I switched to a northbound train. North from there meant the end of solid earth until the Arctic Circle. Bogs and more bogs, bogs of peat, bogs of mire, bogs of midges. But it was still winter in Siberia, and anything damp or wet was rendered hard as steel by the frosts.

After three hours of frozen bogs, dismal larch villages, roads rutted with black muck, and dirty snow, we drew into Tomsk. Snow, light and fluttering like down from a burst pillow, flurried and whirled around the low gray and yellow buildings of the center. A family of Tadzhik refugees was migrating across the parking lot, the grandfather, white-bearded in a long blue robe, accosting those who came his way, begging alms, the son in a black skull cap dragging his sack over ridges of frozen slush. Behind them followed a flock of children with runny noses and a mother who herded them along with a little switch, like sheep.

Directly across from the station stood the Hotel Tomsk. I went in and asked for a room there. The clerk took my passport, flicked through its pages, and shook her head.

"I have no right to register you. You have a visa for Moscow, not Tomsk. You must receive permission from OViR. I'm sorry."

Tomsk was one of Siberia's oldest towns, founded in 1604 on the river Tom as a Russian military outpost to defend western Siberia from the nomadic Tatars and other hordes. As the surrounding lands were settled, it became a prosperous trade center as a result of its rich veins of iron ore and coal and its peat bogs; eventually the city hosted Siberia's first university and technical institute. During the Soviet era, geologists discovered oil and natural gas in the vast northern oblast and began their exploitation. Tomsk's secluded location far from prying foreign eyes made it ideal for military and atomic industry, and secret numbered cities were built up around it. The whole area was closed to foreigners until the year before I came. Recently, Tomsk had been in the news, but I couldn't remember why.

OViR, as a part of the secret police bureaucracy, was located in the gray faceless building marked DIRECTORATE OF INTERNAL AFFAIRS at number 18 Kirov Street. There were three entrances and I was bandied about from one to the other until I located a guard who allowed me to ask a question. OViR, he said, was on the second floor and all the way back. I found nothing on the second floor and all the way back except bulky men in gray suits with wide foreheads. One said OViR was downstairs and around the corner and led me to the staircase. I descended. In the courtyard the guard pointed me to the right. There were several unmarked doors, but people were entering only one. I followed them.

Some twenty-five men and women in parkas and muddy boots thronged around the door to room 313. An hour passed. No movement. I had had enough; the door opened and, as someone was exiting 313, I slipped inside.

I was confronted with three tables piled chest-high with red Soviet passports. A blond woman scribbling behind one of the piles muttered at me, not bothering to lift her head.

"What do you want?"

"I'd like to register. I'm a foreigner."

She looked up.

"Tatyana Vasilyevna! Come here at once!"

A corpulent woman in a blue uniform threw the door open from the side room and charged across the carpet.

I explained myself and handed her my passport. She snatched it and stomped off into the other room, slamming the door.

The door flew open again and the officer reappeared, retracing her crisp steps across the carpet.

"Tomorrow between ten and twelve you will register!" she clipped, slapping my passport into my palm. She turned smartly on her heel and marched back into her office.

The door slammed again.

Back at the hotel I explained what had happened. The receptionist agreed that I could stay the night as long as I registered in the morning. I was annoyed, though, and had no mind to waste my next day traipsing around the OViR building again.

"Then OViR will come here to visit you," she cautioned. "They are the authorities. We must obey them. We *must*."

So I would.

> *Dear Citizens of Tomsk and Guests of Our City!*
> *We invite everyone to sermons about Jesus*
> *Christ from 30 April until 5 June at DK-GPZ 5*
> *daily at 6:00 p.m.*
>
> *Sermons will be read by pastors from the U.S.A.*

I found this announcement in the *Tomsky Vestnik*, a local newspaper. The ominous "DK-GPZ 5," which sounded like some sort of top-secret military designation, turned out to stand for a House of Culture at a factory on the other side of town. Out of curiosity, I took a cab there. I mistrusted evangelists, and I wondered how they fit into Russia, how Russians in this secretive city surrounded by peat bogs would react to them and their sermons of openness and trust and good faith.

Crowds of youths, some as young as twelve or thirteen, were horsing around and tussling with one another at the door. An older teenager guarding the entrance let me into the lobby, buzzing with children and adults with shopping bags swarming around a table and filling out little blue forms.

"Fill out this form completely and you will be registered," said the smiling young woman behind the desk, shaking a mane of flaxen hair over one shoulder with a twist of her head. She stared at me, as if we already knew each other, her eyes glimmering sea-green, then looked bashfully down at her forms.

"I can help you fill it out. Only when you bring your card and have it signed by us for each sermon will you receive your complimentary valuable gifts."

A woman barged through the registrants to my side.

"*Devushka,* why do you need my address and phone number? For what purpose?" she asked with a hoarse voice. She was of the Stalin generation. Putting her name on a list was serious business.

The girl smiled.

"It's only for the gifts. If you don't want them, you don't need to bother."

The woman threw her card on the table and pushed her way out, saying she would sign her name to nothing.

I found myself staring at the young woman. It was not only her looks that held my attention; she was poised in the face of boorishness; her manner was gentle despite the crowd of rude registrants. Crowds had bruised and fatigued me lately. Russians as a rule showed even less patience than I did in lines—it was the norm to butt elbows and jostle for anything from chewing gum to shanks of beef. Yet Galina, as she introduced herself, smiled at everyone and took no offense at their pushiness and insinuating questions. She seemed above it all.

Registration wound down and people trickled out of the lobby into the auditorium. Galina got up and introduced me to Rick, a bearded man from Washington State with a broad smile and easy laugh. Rick stopped laughing and paused in midbreath when I told in him that my trip through Russia was related to writing a book. He straightened his tie, peered over at my note pad to check the spelling of his name, and then adopted a very professional tone with me, as though I might be an adversarial reporter of some kind searching for hints of sex and scandal and air-conditioned doghouses. He said he and several other Americans of the Seventh-Day Adventist faith were here giving sermons and had been in Tomsk for three weeks. He asked what I knew about the radiation level. Had I heard anything recently? I hadn't.

The sermon began, at first resembling an American variety show more than a homily on salvation, with a sing-along to "It's a Great Morning, Your First Day in Heaven," led by a tanned, bearded man in his thirties who introduced himself as Rod. No one sang along because all the lyrics were in English. A simultaneous translation flashed above him on a screen, but to no avail. The Tomskans sat dourly and fingered their registration cards. But the Americans up on stage had pluck, and without losing an ounce of cheer or dimming their smiles for a moment, they moved into act two.

Rick followed Rod, looking credible in his tweed jacket and tie; he gave a lecture on the dangers of smoking. He also attempted a sing-along, with the same result as Rod. Gospel good cheer and public displays of joy of whatever kind were out of place in Russia, but then these were Americans on stage and how were they to know? Some Tomskans shifted in their chairs, others wondered aloud about the complimentary gifts and when they would be given out. I felt a penetrating disconnection: the Russians were there for gifts, the Americans for faith, I for neither.

Senior Pastor Arnold, a tall man with white hair and wearing a starched white tennis shirt, appeared to deliver the sermon itself, the theme of which was that humanity awaits salvation much as a troop of Arctic explorers adrift on an ice floe prays for a rescue team. Not bad, as salvation similes go, but does all of humanity look like the Cleaver family? On the screen flashed slides of white Americans circa 1954, bouffants and greasy kid stuff and all.

Arnold closed with the predictable admonition: accept salvation and live eternally, or reject it and die. The Tomskans were silent. He shuffled his papers into order on the pulpit and invited everyone to his next sermon, the topic of which was to be "The City of Babylon and Sin"—plugged with a slide of a languorous, buxom gypsy woman in gold bracelets beckoning to the audience with an outstretched vessel of wine. After an hour of June Cleavers in knee-length skirts and blouses buttoned to the neck, the image was overpoweringly arousing and a murmur of titillation rippled though the audience; that would be one sermon they would be sure to attend.

This was hardly the way to close a sermon in slushy, peat-bogged Tomsk, where people craved escape and yearned for the exotic; the Tomskans would probably rather follow the godless Babylonians on their carnal odyssey to damnation than join a saved humanity doomed to bobby socks and sensible stockings. After more than seventy years of regulation, rules, and forced ideology, the last thing Russians wanted to do was exchange one dogma of self-abnegation for another.

In the lobby, Galina introduced me to Rod and Pastor Arnold and pulled me along with the crowd into a bus waiting in the parking lot. Rod and his wife, Ella, invited me to dinner in their hotel.

"Where's the restaurant?" I asked, as we jumped off in front of the hotel.

"Just come on in!" said Rod. We would eat upstairs, he said.

Three big trunks with padlocks stood against the walls on the shiny parquet floor of their room.

"We don't eat the food here," said Rod, jiggling the lock loose on his trunk. "We've brought everything freeze-dried from the States. Before we came, we weren't even sure there *was* food here. We heard people were starving. And with the accident and all, we wouldn't eat it anyway."

"What accident?"

"A nuclear power station blew up around here last month, some fifteen kilometers outside of town. We've heard all sorts of differing reports on how serious it is. We're nervous about it."

That was what I had heard about Tomsk! Russian television had broadcast an abbreviated, no-need-to-panic news flash on it a month ago, which was less than comforting, since a similar bulletin followed the Chernobyl catastrophe. Thank God, I said, it was outside of town.

"Outside of town means right about there," said Rod narrowing his eyes as he pointed through the window to a group of gray buildings down the river. "That's the secret city, Tomsk Seven, where it happened."

There was dispute, they said, about how much damage had been done to the environment. The Russians were saying very little radiation escaped, but after Chernobyl, he didn't trust them. All this was of great importance to them: they had come for six long weeks and had brought their teenage son.

"What shall it be? You're our guest—you decide!" said Ella, throwing open the trunk lid. Freeze-dried backpackers' meals in rows of silver foil lay next to green packets of lemonade, powdered milk, and plastic picnic knives and forks. All were vegetarian dishes, she said. I picked spaghetti, peas, and carrots. These were popped into a tin on a ministove and boiled, and made a decent, filling meal we washed down with lemonade.

Although I found their sermon and song-and-dance routine banal, Rod and Ella were charming. It was good to be in the company of my own kind for a short while, eating spaghetti and speaking English and laughing and swapping Russia stories. They told me about all the problems their organization had had here: mayhem in customs on arrival, thousands of dollars going missing with a shifty cashier in Moscow, and confusion about schedules once they got to Tomsk. I matched these with a similar litany of grievances I'd suffered through in setting up the Peace Corps in Uzbekistan, and the frustration I'd felt as a traveler in Russia poured out of me. When Arnold came in, our talk jumped all over the world as he and Rod began telling missionary tales from Jerusalem to Borneo and elsewhere. Phone calls in Russian interrupted us now and then ("When are the valuable gifts to be dispensed?"), but we talked until late in the night. I knew nothing about Seventh-Day Adventism and wasn't really interested, but, to my surprise, they never brought it up. And, even more to my surprise, none of them showed the sappy Good Samaritanism or supercilious piety I had expected; they were just out in Russia doing a job and worrying about the radiation like everyone else.

At midnight, it was time to go. Rod said to me, glancing at a trunk, "Oh, I almost forgot. Do you need any gifts?"

"'Valuable gifts,' you mean?"

"Yeah. They can come in handy. Take a handful!"

He threw open the trunk and waved his arm over the sweet-smelling bounty of perfumes, hotel soaps, crayons, seed packets, and dried foodstuffs. I grabbed a handful of perfume samples, figuring they might be useful in getting better service from the *dezhurnye* in the hotels.

The next morning, Galina came by the hotel and met me in the lobby. Tagging along was her plump churchmate, Tanya. I hadn't remembered inviting her—this annoyed me for a moment as I recalled how she had eavesdropped on us when I asked Galina to show me Tomsk. Galina didn't seem to mind, though, and Tanya was pleasant enough.

"You will have to be out by noon unless you register with OViR," the receptionist reminded me in a flat tone as we passed her desk. "Noon. You must follow the rules."

Galina and Tanya looked away. OViR reminded them of who I

was. I had to be kept track of; I was a subject for inquiry by the secret police; I was suspect, here without a sponsor.

It was snowy and blustery outside. We trudged along Kirov Street saying very little. They didn't have to come with me, I said; I could manage on my own. Galina's eyes were dull; Tanya tittered nervously and looked away. When we reached the back door, they said they'd wait for me, and hurried out of sight of the guards.

At room 313 there was no line this time. I walked right in. The same passports stood in the same stacks on the desks; the same bland-faced woman shuffled yellow forms behind them.

"I'm here to register."

She looked up and raised her eyebrows.

"Tatyana Vasilyevna!"

She kept her eyes on me. A sickening feeling stole over me: I had become another worthless peon, guilty before trial, begging for mercy from the unscalable throne of Soviet bureaucracy.

The woman who'd told me "tomorrow!" the day before stomped through the doorway and didn't seem to remember me.

"What do you want?"

"I'm an American. I need to register."

"Passport!" she commanded, as though she were shouting "Hands up!" to a dangerous criminal. She snatched it away and disappeared into the side office, just as she had done the previous day.

Ten minutes later she came flying through the door.

"Sit!" she commanded in English, pointing to a chair in the back. I sat.

"Ver in passporrrt veeza Tomsk?" She waved it accusatorily in front of my face, as though it were a bloodied knife bearing my fingerprints. "*Ver* in passporrt—"

"You can speak Russian."

"You have no visa for Tomsk," she stated perfunctorily, slapping my passport onto the little table. "You cannot be here!"

"I'm sorry, I *am* here. The U.S. and Russia have an Open Lands

Agreement that stipulates freedom of travel for Americans in Russia and Russ—"

"I am telling you you haven't got Tomsk in your visa! I'm not asking about agreements!"

I kept calm. I even smiled.

"I'm sorry, I'm explaining to you that there is no need for Tomsk to be written into my visa. It is not there because it doesn't have to be there. The Open Lands Agreement gives us the right to travel freely in Russia."

She paused. She picked up my passport and drew it to her face, then sighed.

"You *have* freedom to travel but only with OViR's permission." This was a softening.

She sat down next to me. Her eyes looked tired, defeated.

"*What* are you doing here?" she intoned, almost as if in pain.

"I'm here as a tourist, and only for a few days. I thought I'd see some of Tomsk's famous wood-carved houses."

She stood up and walked into the side room with her head lowered.

Several minutes later she called me in. Passports were massed in piles all over her desk and the desk of her colleague, a young man with a crewcut in a gray suit. He looked up expressionlessly from his papers and shook my hand.

"You claim to be a tourist. Have you any documents to support this?" she asked.

"What sort of documents would I have?"

"A group registration card of some sort. As is the case all over the world, tourists here follow certain official procedures in organizing their vacations."

"Actually, I'm not sure tourists generally follow official procedures to go on vacation. At least in America we think of tourism as being spontaneous. Even fun."

"This is not America."

I knew that was coming. "Listen," I said. "No, Tomsk is not in my visa. I realize my visit here has caused you discomfort, but I'm planning on leaving in a few days. What are we going to do?"

"Do you have your ticket out?"

"No. I was going to buy it today."

She straightened in her chair.

"We have no right to stamp permission to be here in your visa. Because it is multiple-entry. We must stamp a separate piece of paper."

She rummaged in her stacks for a piece of scrap paper, and slammed her stamp down on it.

Galina and Tanya and I took off on a walking tour of Tomsk. *Rezba* in chocolate-colored wood decorated many of the houses around town. Tomsk was old. But the bitter cold and wind and snow flurries hurried us along. May was still a cold month in Siberia. We ended up in a pizza café downtown.

Tanya picked at her pizza with a fork.

"Life here is gray and pointless. We've joined the church to get away from it. There is nothing to do here. Nothing."

Galina added, "We call this 'the gray life.' We wonder, sometimes, even about our own church. The old people in it are so strict and joyless. And the Americans who come bring us things like seeds and soap, as though we're beggars. It's degrading to see our people line up for 'valuable gifts.' They should have more pride."

Tanya got upset.

"They give us 'humanitarian aid' in the form of soap. But have you seen the bars? They're so tiny!"

I told them that they were hotel soaps; that's why they were so small. They stared at me. What was hotel soap?

Galina, despite her defeated mood, looked beautiful and soft, backlit as she was by the dim window. An unconditional despair, a kind of primal despondency, marked her features, from her *sapogi* drawn over dainty feet to her fine hair forced down under a thick, depersonalizing scarf. She looked as though she had been sad all her life, living in a lightless gloom that she knew would never end and over which there was no point in shedding tears. There was nothing ahead to strive for, nothing in the present to cry over not having.

"We are still followed and hemmed in," Galina said. "Even now. My teacher in high school used to call my house at night to make sure I was home and not out running around. When I got a low grade in Marxism, she would call me in and demand an explanation. *Don't I have a right to do poorly?* I asked. No, no. I had to sit and explain. And explain. And now it's obvious that it was all nonsense. So what does she say to that? 'Tie me to the stake, shoot me! I'll be a Leninist till I die!' Why would I study to be like her? Should I strive to be so stale and harsh? What kind of examples are there for us?

"I was baptized by Seventh-Day Adventists—Russians—in the Irtysh River near Semipalatinsk. I feel good about that." She sounded as though she were trying to convince herself.

Galina was twenty and studying at a pedagogical institute. Tanya deflected questions about her occupation and said it was "classified." Was that a joke? Neither of them laughed.

"Hasn't anything gotten better over the last few years? Since socialism collapsed?"

Tanya sighed.

"We have no interest in politics. We take no part in them. Why should we vote? Everything is decided by Moscow anyway. There can never be democracy here. You will not be able to understand this, being an American. You see, life for us is hard here because we are young and have so much time left. There are even drug addicts on the streets here, not like in America."

We had drug problems in America, too, I said. And worse than in Tomsk, to be sure. Both shook their heads at me; *nothing* could be worse than Tomsk. Then Tanya went off in a rambling discourse: there was high unemployment in Russia ("Not like in America!") and crime everywhere ("Not like in America!"), and young people were bored ("Not like in America!"). It was two against one; when I tried to explain how Americans had to deal with these same problems, they drowned me out in a chorus of protest. *Everything* was rotten in Russia, not like in America.

Galina had the reserved, soft, tragic charm peculiar to Russian women, but in spite of it, once we got away from the grim topics, she laughed and giggled now and then with Tanya about things she secretively referred to as "girl talk." When Tanya was out of earshot at the pizza counter I asked Galina to go to a movie with me that evening. Her face grew long and she picked at her food; no one in Tomsk goes to the movies. What else did they do? I asked. Nothing. She stayed home in the evenings. Guys drank too much and smoked, and she didn't like that. My request for a date got lost in commentaries on Russian life. Then Tanya returned and we left the café for another walk in the snow flurries.

I asked them about the accident at the nuclear plant. What had they heard? Galina knew the details.

"In April there was an explosion at a radioactive chemical plant in Tomsk Seven, one of our secret nuclear cities. Radioactive gas leaked into the atmosphere. The authorities said the wind blew it away from town, that there was no danger, but who knows?"

Tanya asserted that "Tomsk is like Chernobyl now, but they're hiding the truth from us. We will never know what really happened. It's probably so radioactive that staying here longer than a few hours is harmful. The radiation level should be at ten micro-roentgens an hour. Here, I heard it's four hundred and twenty-seven. Over twenty is dangerous."

A lump formed in my throat.

"Aren't you worried? You sound so matter-of-fact about it all. Aren't you scared?"

I was. All sorts of thoughts of radiation poisoning and back-ground radiation and safe exposure time raced through my head. I thought I felt neutrons bouncing off me as we spoke.

"In America, this wouldn't happen. But it's normal for us. We're used to it."

"People here have been dying of radiation for a long time,"

Galina said. "A friend of mine developed leukemia last year. The doctor told her it was from radiation, but he refused to put this in writing. You see, it is forbidden to write about radiation here. Officially, there are no accidents."

"We're used to it," Tanya repeated.

We passed a stone arch commemorating victims of the Bolshevik terror. Both yawned at it ("Nothing will ever change. Our government will always repress us"). But a little farther down stood a building with an illuminated digital screen reading nine, then ten, then nine. They told me this was a public Geiger counter set up to calm Tomskans after the accident. Tanya smirked and pointed out that since it was indoors, its reading meant nothing. More government trickery. Another yawn.

We ended up at the train station where I wanted to buy my ticket for Novosibirsk. The Tadzhik refugees had moved in and occupied half of the waiting room. They were arguing violently over something, flailing arms and gesticulating, stomping slippered feet, their brood of children running around in circles and crying, an ailing grandmother wailing from a straw mat by the window, raising her arms to the heavens as if she were calling on God to take her soul.

Galina came alone the next morning to see me off. She had on a dark gray overcoat and a red scarf that enriched the glow of her blond hair and tinted it with scarlet. We walked arm in arm to the station, suddenly aware of the closeness that had developed between us. On the platform she smiled, but a dullness returned to her eyes when the loudspeaker blared my departure. What could I say? As I was about to jump aboard, the words *come with me to Novosibirsk* tumbled off my tongue. She agreed right away, as though she had been expecting me to ask her all along. Her eyes livened. Tomorrow, she said, meet her at the station. We kissed and I pulled myself up the ladder into the train.

TWELVE

Omsk:
Saying Good-bye to Siberia

Galina came to Novosibirsk, and we spent two days together. I was smitten with her, and my infatuation edged out the *toska* that had shadowed me across Siberia.

Evening was fading into pale blue and gilding fleeces of clouds in the west. Galina and I stood on the Novosibirsk station platform, my departure having materialized from nebulous talk of leaving and the casual perusal of train schedules into a yellow ticket in hand and a hissing diesel ready to go. I promised to arrange for her to visit me in Moscow later in the year, and she agreed to come, with hot tears streaming down her cheeks all the while. To Galina, the thought that she would ever leave Siberia seemed a fantasy, a notion too cruel in its improbability. Tomsk was her world; surviving the crush of gray days there extracted so much energy from her she had none left over to dream of going elsewhere, to struggle or to defy. Before we had a chance to say much more, the conductor shouted to me. I threw my bag on the train, kissed her, and climbed aboard. We pulled out of the station and she stared numbly at me as the train drew around a bend. Galina turned away, head down, just as the curve stole her from my sight.

Deep forests of somber birches slid by. Omsk was ahead, the last city of Siberia before the Urals. My cabinmate was sullen and deep in a book; our compartment was overheated and musty. I crawled up into my bunk and read there until I fell asleep, with Galina and her tears still glinting before me.

"Omsk! Get up! We're in Omsk!"

A conductor shook my leg and disappeared through the door. I was startled. The cabin was a furnace and I found myself in a sweat. I grabbed my bag and slipped out of the berth and through the door.

The air hung in swaths of vapor tinctured with orange from the sunrise. Trees seemed to breathe a warm breath, as if they had not seen frost overnight. My overcoat and heavy socks suddenly smothered me, made me even hotter than on the train. Omsk felt like Arkansas, not Siberia.

Later that morning, after taking a room at the Hotel Omsk on the Irtysh River embankment, I set out to find food. The air was even steamier by then and the sun beat down through the moisture, inducing a springtime languor I had not even dreamed of finding until the Volga. A breeze picked up now and again and toyed with the thick leaves on the trees; it had been spring here for weeks. The warmth made me delirious with relief. I luxuriated in every step I took

Omsk was a small city built primarily around a couple of thoroughfares clogged with taxis and clanking trolley buses with clumsy electric contact rods that often slipped off overhead wires. There was a good bit of road work being done—men poured tar into potholes, flattened it with steamrollers, and banged away ferociously at the pavement with jackhammers. Across from one of these sites was a park. I took the sausage and bread and cheese I had bought and sat down in the sun with the local paper and opened it to the personals section.

*Girls! A middle-aged well-off American Jewish male is
seeking a wife for immediate move to U.S.! She doesn't
have to be Jewish, but she should be between twenty
and thirty years old, beautiful and shapely, and good-
natured. Send your photo and self-addressed, stamped
envelope today for questionnaire. You could be the one
for me!*

In my shirtsleeves I browsed through the paper on the park
bench, melting into the spring and sun and heat. The oaks in the
park were budding, sparrows tussled in the grass, crows squab-
bled and pecked at orange rinds in the fountain. The Irtysh me-
andered by the edge of the park, muddy and reed-filled and
skirted by a pleasant concrete embankment where parents
strolled with their children and dogs chased sticks. Siberia had
disappeared.

My eye caught red. Little red leather pumps on tiny feet. They
stopped. I looked up from the personals.

"Is it hot here in the sun?" asked the old lady, bent forward as
though searching for something to rest her weight on. She was
wearing red lipstick that matched her shoes, and her hair was
dyed an even brighter red. Her eyebrows danced. She hobbled
over and regarded me expectantly, as though we knew each other,
as though she could expect only good things from me. Her coral-
print dress was splattered with every color in a tropical reef, and
over that she had drawn a purple sweater.

"I'll sit here for a moment if you will allow me."

Her hazel eyes sparkled, her thin red lips parted, revealing in-
tact white teeth. Her tanned skin was free of age spots, and her
smooth cheeks and temples were almost without a wrinkle.

"My name is Anna Fyodorovna. What's yours?"

I said my name once and she stared at me, then asked me to repeat it. She angled her ear toward me for better acoustics.

"Oh, my hearing is going now. I just can't seem to get your
name," she said, squirming with embarrassment on the bench.

"My name is Jeff. I'm American."

"Oh my, is this true? And here I was thinking you were saying something like 'Georgi' and I just wasn't understanding it. I thought my hearing had gone completely. You are the first American I've met!"

Anna Fyodorovna asked me what I was doing in Omsk.

"Traveling around our Russia?" she answered. "Ah, well, I can't say this sounds like much fun these days. But why not, Seryozha? You are young and you should see the world. I myself have seen much of Russia, too, as a doctor in the army during the war. They transferred me from Omsk to the front, and then afterward to Moscow. So there I lived, a pretty young girl with a prestigious job in the capital. It was a different time then. People were kinder, more upstanding, more honest. Moscow was one of the world's finest capitals, like your New York, or Paris in France. It was clean and all the buildings were old. Tell me, are there Russians in America?"

"Quite a few, especially in New York."

"That's good. Good for America—she accepts all the needy. I can't say I'll ever get to America, but I do visit my brothers in Moscow every couple of years."

She paused and looked out to the river.

"My days were different. I remember when the Father of Nations, Iosif Vissarionovich [Stalin], passed away. We all grieved, we all cried. Not like when these leaders of ours before Mikhail Sergeyevich [Gorbachev] died. We *grieved* for Stalin. I was a beauty then and I put on my best dress to go to his funeral down in the center of Moscow. People were screaming! People were pulling at their hair! Our Stalin! How could he be dead? *Could* he be dead? Some people said he wasn't, that it was a trick. Well, the crowd got so upset. People started pushing, then running, then some fell down and were trampled. A crushing wave caught me. I was lifted from my feet by these screaming people, and I felt my shoes coming off. I was just carried along over trampled people. We rounded a corner and I was ejected onto a square, without my shoes and with my dress all torn. I sat there for the rest of the day, afraid to move into the crowd. I never got to his body. I think it was two kilometers away. I don't know how many hundreds died in the stampede, but maybe for them it was better. Some just couldn't live without the Leader."

Anna Fyodorovna's face had lit up and flushed with the reminiscence. I asked her when she had moved back to Omsk.

"Omsk was always my homeland. I never had a mind to leave it, really, but the war made all of us think of our duty and not ourselves. Stalin died and as is usual in our foolish country, the new leaders decided to undo everything that he had put together. They transferred me within a few weeks straight back here. I couldn't have stayed in Moscow if I had wanted to. But my two brothers married there and got Moscow *propiski* [residence permits], so they stayed on. They are all I have in the world. I'm a little old lady all alone here."

"You were never married, I take it?"

She smiled, as if resigned to this fate so unusual in Russia—very few people, especially women, lived single lives past the age of twenty-five.

"Never married, and no children! Ha!" she exclaimed, as if daring anyone to find fault with her. "Seryozha, it's getting too warm for me in the sun. May I invite you home for *pelmeni?*

I accepted her invitation. Why was she calling me Seryozha, though? We got up and walked toward the store where she needed to buy food for dinner.

"This store here on the embankment always has what I need. The Finns built it—as you can see from the outside. There's no way our simpletons could have built such a structure."

I couldn't tell the difference, really. It was called Okean, Ocean, a title only a tad more imaginative than the standard Soviet Fish Store seen all over the former Soviet Union, and rather inaccurate because the nearest ocean was thousands of miles away. But inside, it had well-stocked freezers (unlike Soviet stores, where fish are simply laid unrefrigerated on the counter), and hundreds of black-and-gold jars of honey lined its shelves.

"I've got to find my little fish . . . salted fish . . . I love them, Seryozha. I love them more than anything else in the world."

Her fondness also embraced the Finns who provided it ("Finland, I think, is a beautiful country. They care about pensioners there. I wish I could have seen it"). The freezer that had been earmarked for her fish was empty, and this nearly panicked her; she walked to and fro, moving her hands in little circles as though she might conjure up her fish by some form of prestidigitation, all the while peeking into the same freezer over and over as though it might spontaneously materialize there at any moment.

"My fish . . . My little *rybka* . . . This is the first time . . . The cashier here said they would never run out."

In fact, she had confused freezers and was looking in the wrong one, said the store girl in her tall white paper hat. Anna went over to the freezer and peered inside, then drew out several tiny packets of what looked like silvery minimackerels. At the cashier's, she pulled out a bantam red purse and fingered through the bills ("my pension"), which amounted to little more than a couple of thousand rubles. The fish cost three hundred.

We walked to the river. The breeze blew strong and cool, hydrofoils glided up and down the reedy Irtysh, the water mirrored vernal azure hues in the sky. Spring arrives in western Siberia before it does in eastern Siberia, and because of the bleakness of the winter it is doubly green, doubly imbued with the musks of new cycles, nests, buds, and sprouting grass.

"Omsk is a rich town," said Anna, as she dangled her bag of fish and walked down to the embankment. "It gets its name from the river. The Om, that is, which flows into the Irtysh up ahead. Stalin made it richer when he exiled the Volga Germans into Siberia. Thousands ended up here. He knew not to trust Volga Germans during the war. They turned out to be much harder workers, more industrious than we are. You will see them in the markets. Many still speak German."

"Are you a native Siberian?"

"My father was a Pole. You can see this in my features. I'm

pure Slavic. Pure." Russians say the Tatar-Mongol occupation from the thirteenth through the fifteenth centuries spoiled the Russian gene pool; Poles have had little mixing with non-Slavic peoples by comparison. "My mother was Ukrainian. No, we were not from Siberia. We ended up here, and that is all. But I'll never forget my Polish background. I was in Sochi on the Black Sea, at a resort where your millionaires smoke their big cigars, and heard a group of people speaking Polish. I ran up to them and asked if any were Kuszczynkis—which is my last name—and a couple were! We talked for a while. But I was scared to ask for their address, so I just let them go. I shouldn't have done that."

Anna Fyodorovna's building was divided into several sections on two sides of a street, and I had some difficulty locating the address. I was half an hour late. When I got to her door, she was emerging with a look of anguish on her face.

"Oh, Seryozha, I thought you weren't coming! I was going out!"

"I'm so sorry. I couldn't find the address."

"What could have been the trouble? Never mind, Seryozha, come on in. I'm so sorry, I couldn't make *pelmeni* for you." She lurched from one piece of furniture to another, as though aboard a storm-tossed boat. "You can see I'm swaying like a drunkard. I'm having an attack of high blood pressure."

I asked if I could bring her anything or get medicine from the pharmacy for her—she said no. She stumbled around in the kitchen and emerged with soup, most of which, owing to her tremors, ended up on the plate under the bowl.

"Have some soup—I can't offer you more." She placed it on the table and lay down. That made her feel much better.

"If I may ask, why do you call me Seryozha?"

"Well, I've got to call you something, right? I could never remember that name of yours!"

I got the impression that at some point in her life, someone who meant a great deal to her was named Seryozha. That impression grew stronger as she repeated the name over and over again, of-

ten very tenderly and with a wistfulness in her eyes. I even asked
if this might be so, but she answered evasively.

The lace curtains on her balcony windows fluttered with a
breeze from the Irtysh, which filled her apartment with river air.
Boats chugged by below, sending their echoes into the old stone,
Stalin-era building Anna Fyodorovna lived in. Her furniture was
of rich, dark wood; the pictures on her walls hung graying or yel-
lowing from decades past. Her apartment was frozen in time
somewhere in the 1950s.

I ate my soup, a borscht of some sort, and she brought out a
plate of potatoes for me. Everything was fresh and delicious, and
I told her so, but she only apologized for the lack of *pelmeni*. I noticed a portrait on her wall of a family that might have been from
Tolstoy's time.

"That was Father. He had a temper. And my mother. She never
worked a day in her life. She only raised us. Those are my two
brothers. And that was me at twelve."

Her austere look was surprising; she looked utterly cheerless.
So did everyone else.

"How did you say you ended up here in Omsk?"

"Oh . . . We ended up here . . . not of our own will. Those were
different times. Father was a pan, a Polish nobleman. He moved
to the Ukraine before the revolution. You know, during the revolution, the Red Army was rounding up all the pans and killing
them. So he fled here, where he met my mother. He worked hard
and became a school director. And he somehow managed not to
get sent off to the gulags during the thirties. Look at me! Not one
wrinkle! That's my Polish blood."

I finished the soup and potatoes. Anna Fyodorovna sat up on
her couch.

"You travel around Russia now, you say. Russia has always
been robbed, raped, and pillaged. World War I, then the civil war,
then Stalin and all his purges. He put all our smart people in jail
or killed them. For thirty years he held us like this." She made a
fist, an iron fist. "He could only keep power through terror—that's

what he was good at. When the war came, our soldiers were filthy, hungry, and poor, but we still won. I saw all this—I was a lieutenant colonel doctor at the front. Now look at who we have: Gorbachev and his queen, Raisa. The West bought him out. And Boris Nikolayevich [Yeltsin]? He is no leader for Russia. We need authority. Russia cannot do without it."

"Like under Stalin?"

"Of course! He bound us together; he kept us in fear; he gave us authority."

She brought tea out from the kitchen, but her hands shook so violently it almost ended up on the floor.

"Omsk is the best part of Siberia. We feed forty oblasts, at least we used to. Our crops are always plentiful, our state farms rich."

I finished my tea, hurried along by Anna Fyodorovna, who said she had to go out into the street for fresh air. We walked to a shady area of the embankment and sat down.

"Seryozha, you are not married. My advice to you is get out of Russia. Don't marry a Russian woman—marry a Ukrainian or a Pole. Russian girls are spoiled, not so moral."

She felt her blood pressure rising, she said, and said she would go to meet her lady friends on a nearby bench, but invited me to dinner the next night, asking me to call first ("I may have to call the first aid—I may be in the hospital").

"Thank you, Seryozha, I'll go to my women now. I'll say goodbye to you here."

She waved a feeble hand and walked gingerly toward some old ladies on a bench, swaying as though her boat was soon to capsize.

The next day I called Anna Fyodorovna as she had requested, but she felt too ill to have me over. She wished me a happy life and safe traveling.

Getting out of Omsk and leaving Siberia behind was my next priority. Later that week I visited the railroad ticket office behind Detsky Mir, the toy store, off Karl Marx Street, two days in advance of my intended departure to be sure to get a seat on the train to Chelyabinsk. The huge lobby was eerily vacant. In Russia, no tickets are ever purchased without bludgeoning crowds. Something was wrong; it couldn't be so easy. It just couldn't be.

When I told the cashier my last name, she blinked and asked for my passport.

"We are authorized to sell tickets to Russian citizens only. There is a special office for foreigners. You'll have to buy your ticket there." A bureaucratic goblin danced behind her and made a face at me. "I'm sorry."

To her credit, she *did* look sorry. But I was annoyed and suspicious.

"And how will my ticket differ from a Russian's?"

"It will be inside a shiny cover. And it will cost hard currency. Dollars. At least I think."

This was the first time I had run across the old Soviet two-tier price system on the railroads. It could turn a ticket worth a dollar's worth of rubles into something costing fifteen or twenty bucks.

I pointed over to the "special office"—it was dark and had a curtain drawn over its window. "It's not open—I want to buy my ticket now. I want to know on what legal basis you are refusing to sell me a ticket."

"There has been an official decree."

"I'd like to see it."

"Ahh. I will call my supervisor."

She slipped off her stool and back into the network of little glass passageways and gesticulated to a bulky keeper-of-the-order in a flaming red jacket, who shook her head and flung a sharp *"Nyet!"* in the cashier's face. The cashier came back to the window.

"Please, my supervisor will be happy to speak to you about this matter. At the next window."

Happy was not the word. I moved one window down. It had no head-level voice holes as did the other, but only an inch-high slot at waist level for me to speak into. Her voice, however, would be carried by a full-strength intercom. This was bad.

"What is wrong?!" blared the woman through the speaker.

I bent down to the waist-high slit and began my explanation.

"What?!" she blared. "I can't hear you!"

"I'm asking for the decree that forbids—"

"Buy your ticket from the special office! It will be open tomorrow!"

"I am asking for—"

"You'll get no decree from us!" she barked in an ear-splitting garble through the screeching intercom. "I'm telling you, you will buy your ticket as you are told! If you board with a regular ticket you will be thrown off the train and the cashier will be fined! Be at the special office at nine sharp tomorrow morning to buy your ticket!"

She slammed shut the glass over my voice slot and walked away.

I returned at nine the next morning, delaying my plans to walk around the old part of Omsk. A charmless woman in a pale blue polyester skirt and jacket with an old Intourist pin sticking out of the lapel sat jabbering to a fat lady, plopped on what looked like a bar stool, wearing similar garb and with thick black hair on her legs that had been mashed into flesh-colored leggings.

"Excuse me," I said, interrupting their conversation, and earning two dirty looks for doing so. "I'd like a ticket for—"

"Come back at eleven! No tickets until eleven!" shouted the cashier, turning back to her jabber.

"I would like a ticket now."

"You would like a ticket NOW?" questioned the hairy-legged woman from her bar stool. "You will not get a ticket NOW. You will return in two hours for your ticket!"

I was incensed.

"Why all this rudeness? Please, just sell me a ticket on the train to Chelyabinsk! It leaves in seven hours. I have plans today; I can't spend all my time running in and out of this office!"

"We have told you when you will buy your ticket. It is not up to us to schedule your day."

I threatened to complain to her supervisor about her attitude.

Naturally, when I asked for her name, she wouldn't give it to me ("'Comrade cashier' to you!"). It would cost no more than the ticket for a Russian, she told me, and I would pay in rubles. I would get it in two hours and not before.

Two hours later, I showed up again. Both women were still sitting in the same positions gabbing. I asked for my ticket. It cost three times what the Russians would pay. I pointed this out.

"Look at your ticket—the cost is the same."

The column marked Cost *was* the same (around seven hundred rubles), but another column marked Commission showed eleven hundred rubles. The total of eighteen hundred was obviously not the same. I pointed this out. The fat lady stepped up to the glass.

"What you are getting so upset about is the commission, not the cost of the ticket. We charge a commission—how do you think our salaries are paid?"

"This is utterly ridiculous," I said. "I can read and I know what a commission is. You said my ticket would cost the same as a Russian's. If I have to pay more, I'd like to know what I get extra!"

"You get a shiny white cover for your ticket," she said.

At this point I nearly lost my temper. I told them that such price scaling based on nationality was blatant discrimination, that it irritated all guests of Russia who had to pay more for the same poor service. I said this sort of thinking belonged back in the Soviet era and made Russia look bad. I knew it was useless to go on in that way, but I felt stepped on, and besides, my sightseeing day had been ruined with all this bureaucracy.

They looked at each other and said that they had never seen a foreigner complain about the service at their window. Never. I grabbed my ticket and left.

I still had until the evening to see some of Omsk. The market was something I hadn't seen. Anna Fyodorovna had mentioned that it was full of hardworking Volga Germans; it might be interesting to go down there and meet a few.

Dust and papers and dirty wrappers blew around in circles at the iron-gate entrance to the market, which was largely outdoors. It was as charmless and drab as every other market in Siberia. Rows of middle-aged Russian women were selling knickknacks, swarthy Azerbaijanis and Georgians hawked vegetables. There were no Germans, but I did see a Chinese section where leather jackets and boots were being sold. The vendors were little Chinese women wearing the same clothes they were peddling. One grabbed me and began shouting "coat leather" in Russian and pointing down to a baggy jacket of paper-thin crusty hide, about as shoddily sown as one could imagine. I feigned interest, though, hoping to start up a conversation.

"Jacket—leather—quality—good. Jacket—on—you?"

I tried it on. A passing Russian woman told me it fit like a sack, was too tight in the shoulders, and looked cheap.

"Jacket—leather—quality—good!" the vendor repeated.

"I'm interested in where this is from—is it from your hometown?"

She gave me a puzzled stare.

"No Russian—Chinese leather!"

"I know. But where are you all from in China?"

She got nervous and rattled something off to the Chinese men behind her. They both stared at me. One thought occurred to me: I had heard that the Chinese welcomed having their pictures taken, so I took out my camera.

"*Nyet! Nyet!*" shouted the little woman in a near panic, flailing her arms at me. A man jumped up from behind her and threateningly jabbed his finger at my Nikon, and in his multitonal language made it clear that I was not to take a picture, or else. I placed my hand over my chest and shook my head in apology, and walked away.

Omsk's central avenue was more like a racetrack, with its speeding drivers jostling for position on a laneless strip of asphalt. The breeze from the Irtysh gave the city a seaside feel, and I soaked up the heat from the sun, still strong even at six in the evening.

I picked up my bag at the hotel and stopped off at the kiosk in the lobby to buy a soft drink. At the counter ahead of me were two Georgians in sateen jogging suits buying vodka, though they were already drunk.

These were the last faces I saw in Siberia before taking the evening train to the Urals.

THIRTEEN

Chelyabinsk:
Bogs of Fire and Bioenergy

Aboard the train, I awoke around five in the morning, some two hours ahead of our scheduled arrival in Chelyabinsk. I pulled myself up to the window to see the Urals, the southern portion of which we should have entered by now, but dawn had cast a coppery light over land that, rather than having rippled into low mountains, spread out into a new degree of flatness. Birch groves, some quite scrubby and ailing, stood in swatches, scattered about on table-flat steppe, the short grass on which had been bleached and dried limp by a sun that shone much brighter than in Siberia, even at dawn. A village slipped by, a collection of prefab modern shacks as might be found in some of the poorer areas of the southern United States; it was utterly lacking the greens and blues and white trim of the *izby* of Siberia. Still, the early morning light infused the mist floating over it with iridescent spectra that the smoke from the chimneys teased and dissipated, and breathed the warmth of day into the cold grays and browns of the dwellings.

Later on, the sun rose and turned the night vapors into steam. The birches disappeared, and great flat stretches of marshland resembling rice fields came into sight, the grass sparse and reed-like, the water stagnant.

Chelyabinsk was yet another city on my itinerary that had been known for its nuclear and defense industries and had been, until recently, completely closed to foreigners (as was almost the entire Ural Mountain range). It had been a fortress town established in 1736 to secure the southern Urals from nomadic Kazakhs, and the great road south and east to Siberia and Asia crossed through it. Before the Soviet era, its massive prison building was the largest structure in town, and convicts being marched east were rested there. Otherwise, Chelyabinsk remained insignificant until Stalin's industrialization drive began in the late 1920s and transformed it into one of the country's leading industrial zones, with eventual disastrous consequences for the ecology. The city's megafactories poisoned the environment for thousands of square miles with their emissions, and, worst of all, at least one nuclear accident rumored to have happened in 1957 at a secret installation outside the city reportedly had contaminated a huge area with radioactive waste. I heard varying stories from Russians in Siberia about this, the consensus being that the Chelyabinsk oblast was the former Soviet Union's most polluted. Some said radiation within the city itself was high; others warned of a lake nearby used as a nuclear dumping site that would kill a man if he were to stand on its shore for an hour.

The day aged quickly in Chelyabinsk, succumbing to a haze of pollutants that thickened over the tops of buildings and shaded the skyline with hues of rust and ferrous brown. The people looked rusted. Stray dogs on the street had furs of rust. Buildings everywhere bore a gritty patina of rust. And very shortly I tasted something metallic, and a dull ache set in behind my eyes that turned into a throb if I breathed hard.

I jumped on a tram to go downtown after checking into the hotel across from the station, but it took another route and rattled off into oak- and poplar-lined suburbs carrying a contingent of proletarians, no two of whom had a full set of teeth between them. Some were in their twenties, others a bit older, but none looked to be more than forty-five. Factory waste had frazzled their hair into scraggly patches and corroded their skin into rawhide. Blood vessels red-netted their noses and bony cheeks. All wore mutations of shoes, shoes with distended bellies and swollen heels. I listened to their talk as we lurched and swayed with the rails; one man had drunk his month's salary a week ago and had to borrow from his brother; another was going to drink vodka on his shift due to start in half an hour.

Workers teemed at every stop and forced their way aboard in silence. The tram soon filled and then overfilled. These workers and their talk of shifts drew me to the conclusion that I was headed somewhere big in Chelyabinsk, and I thought of asking where. But then the tram drew past a sex shop, creaked around a loop, and everyone hustled and scuffled off into the gravel and disappeared through a gate across the road. A hazy vista of a huge gray lake and a cityscape of concrete beyond it caught my eye and drew me in the opposite direction.

A jumble of dark larch huts closed around me as I plodded softly through the black powder earth toward the lake's embankment. Black miniboulders of coal two or three feet high sat here and there, and my steps puffed up coal dust. Workers passed me in twos and threes, and some older women in head scarves chatted by a gate. The dirt path led me down around the huts to a swamp and a reed patch.

"Are you looking for the Glubinskis?" shouted a little boy in a gray engineer's cap.

"Me? No, I wanted to get across this swamp to that rise over there to see the city from the lakeside. How can I do that?"

He walked over and peered at me. He pushed his cap back.

"Are you from Moscow?"

"No. I'm from farther away than that."

"You can't cross the swamp from here. I can show you a way. My name is Dennis. I'm six years old and next year I'll go to school."

Dennis looked older than six and carried himself with a confident, unassuming grown-up air that reminded me of children in Arab countries. I asked him what he was doing hanging around the swamp, and he told me he lived in it.

"That house with the tar roof is mine," he said, pointing to a shack next to the reeds. "Mom and Dad are at Che-Te-Ze."

"What's that?"

"Che-Te-Ze? The factory! Right there."

Behind the swamp towered colossal smokestacks and walls with toupees of barbed wire. The Chelyabinsk Tractor Factory, known locally by its initials, Che-Te-Ze in Russian, was famous throughout the old socialist world.

"Smokestacks smoke," he said. "They pollute the air here and damage our environment!"

"Are you really only six? You have quite a vocabulary for a six-year-old."

"Well, I read a lot."

"You do? About pollution?"

I tried to remember when I learned to read and what I read. All I could remember was a book about a red fox and another about a frolicking pig. Treatises on the environment were not in the first-grade curriculum, as I remembered.

"I read about pollution and chemicals and factory waste matter. Right now the pollution hasn't affected my respiratory system. But soon it will. We get very sick here from the gases. Let me show you around."

He started with the swamp, motioning me to come nearer to it.

"You don't smoke, do you?"

"No. Don't tell me you do!"

"Of course not. But I want to warn you not to throw matches in our bog or it will blow up," he said, matter-of-factly. "Look at the swamp water."

It glinted in opalescent shades of green and blue, like a bluebottle fly's back.

"That's all chemicals from the factory. Diesel oil! It sucked a boy under last year and he drowned. And once a man got drunk and tried to drive through it. He got sucked in with his car, too."

That excited Dennis and he grabbed my hand and led me around the larch *izby,* crammed together on islets of dry ground. Bumblebees hummed in the daisies shooting up amidst the weeds, and both of us swatted mosquitoes as we walked. My feet tangled every few steps in discarded wire running through the grass. Dennis dropped my hand and bounced across springy shards of a ruined house the swamp had already begun to claim. Crows cawed and the ashen air simmered with heat. The pollutants Che-Te-Ze's smokestacks were belching forth settled in a greasy film on my skin, and my head throbbed.

Dennis led me across the swamp to a dirt road. Two trucks rumbled past, dragging trails of black dust that spread into Vs like comet tails. We ended up at lakeside; the blowfly water glimmered iridescent ("It's all chemicals!"), stretching still and lifeless to a vague horizon of apartment blocks and smokestacks quivering mirage-like in the afternoon heat. Dennis grabbed a chunk of coal and tossed it into the water. It went *ker-plunk* and sent a ring of ripples over the glassy stillness of the lake. Not a bird stirred, not a fish bubbled from below, not a frog croaked on the bank.

"My parents won't let me go farther than this. Good-bye!" he said, as he took off running in zigzags back over the wired earth.

Che-Te-Ze seemed like the factory to see in Chelyabinsk but entrance to it was still strictly controlled; I would need a sponsor to get a pass. One of the local newspapers might be able to set this up, I figured, so I picked one, *Vecherni Chelyabinsk,* and visited its office on Sverdlovski Prospekt.

Alexander Dragunov, the chief editor, arose from behind his

desk to shake my hand; his face was large and rugged, as if carved from granite. He had spaces between his teeth and his hair was sandy blond. All in all, he looked like an unfinished statue.

"So, you are in Chelyabinsk to write about this factory? It makes sense. Foreign firms are interested in Chelyabinsk these days. There's more industry, more metallurgy here than anywhere else in the Soviet Union, but, as you know, it was an entirely closed city due to all the secret atomic and chemical installations around it. Now, everyone is curious to know what's here."

"Secret installations?"

"They are still closed, as far as I know. They are military and known only by numbers: Chelyabinsk Forty, Chelyabinsk Seventy . . . The scientists and others who work there are isolated behind barbed wire, but they're well paid and the stores they had open to them had absolutely everything in the old days—only Moscow could compare! Chelyabinsk Seventy, some forty kilometers north of here, was where the nuclear accident happened in fifty-seven. We still don't know the details. Anyway, the tractor factory, now privatized and renamed as Uraltrak, will be interesting for you to see."

Alexander called the editor of the factory paper to arrange a tour and talk for the "American guest." He then offered me a car and driver to take me out to the factory.

Svetlana, the editor, was a stout little fireball of a woman in her forties, with gray piercing through her black short-cropped hair. She was tanned and this set off her lips, which were painted in arresting red. She introduced me to another journalist from her staff, Vitaly, a sallow, bony man with oversized watery eyes.

"We do not find it surprising that you have chosen our factory as the subject for your book. It has a grand history that everyone in the West should know."

Svetlana, through practice or a gift for oratory, spoke as though she were delivering a soliloquy on stage, measuring her tones, bringing her voice to a crescendo in places, easing it into restful pauses in others.

"In 1929, Stalin launched the industrialization drive that gave birth to our factory. Che-Te-Ze was to be a model plant, to show what socialism could do. He sent our experts to your Mr. Ford in Detroit to ask for help. The factory was to be the largest in the world and capable of producing the best and most tractors. Mr. Ford feared our competition and turned us down. It's no secret that he didn't want to be seen helping the Bolsheviks either. Caterpillar refused to help us. Our people left with nothing, but Stalin said, 'Build! And build fast!' so they did. We eventually did get some help from the West, but for the most part, it was our creation.

"For four years our workers labored to create this factory, draining swamps and erecting an entire minicity around it. It has its own theater, cinema, hospital, railroad, and house of culture. For years they lived in barracks outside the factory. Three families to a room. Eventually, they moved into communal apartments. Everyone worked with spirit because Stalin said we must industrialize fast and at all costs, and we did. Maybe you know that our factory was originally named the Stalin Tractor Factory.

"During the thirties, Che-Te-Ze produced its first tractors and all over town affiliate factories sprang up. Chelyabinsk became entirely industrialized. A technical school was established in town to train workers for Che-Te-Ze. Then when World War Two began—"

"I don't mean to interrupt, but you haven't mentioned anything else about the thirties. What about the purges, if I may ask?"

"Ahh. Our first director was found to be an 'enemy of the people' and was executed. And so was our second director. Everywhere, in every workshop, at every tool stand, managers and workers were found to be 'enemies' and shot, or sent off into gulags in Siberia. The luckiest were fired from their jobs, the luckiest! Only the war stopped this. I don't know how many good workers we lost to the Terror."

She paused. Vitaly sat uncomfortably on the edge of his seat. He looked like a jumble of bones in a suit.

Svetlana continued: "The war came on and changed Chelyabinsk. Entire factories were evacuated from western Russia out to Che-Te-Ze and set up on its grounds. For example, the Kharkov Diesel Factory moved here. Che-Te-Ze became known as Tankograd. It went military. Thousands of workers were brought in from Central Asia to increase the staff. You can imagine what living in unheated dorms did to these people used to the heat of Asia. It killed many. Everyone worked day and night. All employees were reclassified as military, and our plant became a military installation. We saved Russia with the tanks we built here—every Russian knows that.

"By 1986, we were up to producing thirty thousand tractors a year for our country, socialist Europe, Africa, Asia, and Latin America. You should know that all the other tractor factories in the world at that time produced only ten thousand a year!

"When socialism collapsed, we stopped producing tanks. Up to then we were still in part a military installation, but it was a state secret. God help you should you mention to anyone that we were building tanks here—you'd be sent straight to jail—but everyone knew it.

"We had fifty-five thousand workers, but we're down to twenty-five to thirty thousand. Now there's not enough work, few orders. We're trying to conclude contracts with companies in Canada and West Germany, but it's rough."

Vitaly showed me around the factory grounds, or at least a small part of them. A very small part. The grounds indeed looked like any small city. Gardeners tended roses in flower beds, people hawked jackets and milk and fruit by the entrance. When shifts changed, as they did during my tour, armies of laborers trudged to the gate and were met by an army trudging in. Shiny yellow tractors stood assembled in rows on railcars as far as I could see in every direction. There was too much to take in.

Svetlana invited me to dinner at a friend's apartment. On the way she stopped to buy liquor and asked me what I drank. Over her protests, I asked for something nonalcoholic.

Before my trip I had had no particular aversion to alcohol; now, the rows of kiosks selling little besides vodka depressed me. The sweet stench of vodka mixed with human saliva even has a special name in Russian, *peregar,* and is one of the more common smells of Russian life.

I explained my desire for a soft drink by telling Svetlana that Americans drink less and are not used to vodka. She smiled.

"Ah, I watch your movies and I know your national drink is whiskey. Perhaps *that* is what you are used to. I'm sorry we have no whiskey here."

Svetlana took Lena's apartment by storm, introducing me as she chided her for not having completely set the table, for not having finished the main dish, for this, that, and the other thing.

"We are late and you're still not ready! My God—what will our guest think!"

Lena batted her eyes at me. She was soft and feline, with opaline chestnut eyes and long brown hair wrapped in a loop and pinned in a fluffy ball behind her head. She wore her plumpness comfortably, exuding sensuality.

When we sat down in the living room, Svetlana told Lena her table was too small, her hors d'oeuvres meager, and her main dish bland. Lena took it in stride, spreading fish dishes, kasha, meat, cucumbers, beets, cabbage, dark bread, and compote around the cognac bottle in the center of the table. She moved as fast as she could, but Svetlana nagged at her still: "My guest is tired ... He's expecting a good meal ... I gave you enough notice ..." and so on.

Lena's husband, Viktor, walked in and unleashed a big brown dog that bounded around us in glee and threatened food dishes with his rotary tail. Viktor asked if he could pour me a cognac.

"Americans don't drink!" barked Svetlana from across the table. I thanked him and asked for some compote.

"I think I understand why you don't drink," he said, piling my plate with cucumbers and beets and sausage. "Bioenergetics, right? It's taken hold in the U.S. I myself don't drink. The more I read of bioenergetics, the more I come to understand my own aura, my own dietary and bodily needs."

"Perhaps our gallant men would choose to ignore their needs for a moment and join us women in a drink!" suggested Lena, who had poured herself and Svetlana shots of cognac. "It cannot be that only us girls will be drinking this evening."

"I think bioenergetics has been clear enough on the subject of alcohol, Lena," said Viktor. "I prefer to follow its doctrines and abstain, like Jeff."

Svetlana couldn't let this pass.

"I'm sure, Viktor, that you know the fundamental bioenergetic postulates do not *prohibit* drinking but caution that it be done with the proper energy flows. You are only fouling your aura with such dogmatism! I will drink. To our guest!"

I was flattered though I had absolutely no idea of what they were talking about.

She and Lena tossed their heads back and downed their shots.

Viktor's aura was quite impervious to criticism and his buoyant good humor shielded him from the barbs the two women aimed at him.

"Svetlana," he said, spearing a beet with his fork, "how can you accuse me of dogmatism in bioenergetics when you know full well that I renounced Ivanovism due to his rigidity and dogmatic approach? Jeff, you might be able to provide some insight here. How do Americans practicing bioenergetics view alcohol?"

"I haven't heard of bioenergetics, to be truthful."

Viktor placed his fork on the table and adjusted his glasses. His face went blank. Lena poured herself and Svetlana another shot of cognac, elbowing her to raise her glass for another toast.

"You haven't heard of bioenergetics?" he said, pleading with his eyes for mercy. "But in America everyone—"

A woman with curly gray-brown hair and a pug nose appeared

at the dining room door and pirouetted, twirling her flowery skirt as she did so, tossing one arm above her head in jubilant aplomb.

"Tatyana! We're so happy to see you! Let's drink to Tatyana!" Lena shouted and raised her glass.

Viktor offered me more beets and kasha and told me he had, in strict observance of bioprinciples, worn no hat all winter, despite thirty-below weather, and had increased his biosphere immeasurably by keeping open the pathway down which cosmic energy travels from the sky to the earth; headgear blocked this energy and starved one's biosphere. He next intended to forgo wearing shoes, he said, to prevent the natural side effect of "excessive augmentation" of his biosphere, resulting from the "most natural and evident counterconsequence" of cosmic energy flowing in freely through his head and "finding itself obstructed in its passage to the earth. This can allow it to build to uncomfortable levels," he assured me. Svetlana hummed agreement as she sawed at her meat cutlet. Tatyana urged him on.

"Viktor, you are on the path to excessive augmentation if you don't give up your shoes! You know what that can lead to!"

"I know, I know, I just can't seem to overcome my fear of going shoeless."

Lena and Svetlana clinked glasses again. It then was decided that our bioenergy could do with replenishment—a walk along Chelyabinsk One would do the trick.

The lake was deep blue and still as a mirror, bound by a grassy shore with trees spreading their canopies here and there along the path. Che-Te-Ze loomed like a sleeping beast on the far shore, its gray-and-red smokestacks turned coppery by the golden light of the evening sun.

Great swarms of mosquitoes danced in the clear air and descended around us. These were not the skinny whiners of southern climes, but fat, fast bombers. They flew into our mouths and up our noses. We all started swatting at them, but they distracted no one from the topics at hand.

Svetlana warned everyone that a solar eclipse was due Friday.

No important work should be undertaken that day. I said I wasn't changing my plans for an eclipse.

Viktor spit out a soggy mosquito, as one might a sunflower seed husk, and cocked his head at me.

"Don't you have your own private astrologer?"

"I don't. I'd have to say that astrology is less popular in the U.S. than here in Russia."

"But your official papers publish horoscopes! This cannot be!"

I explained that newspapers in the United States were not "official" (state-owned), but businesses, and that horoscopes interested some people and not others. That certain newspapers published them was not an indicator of their legitimacy.

"You see, Jeff, astrology was once something we were forbidden to learn about. Eclipses came and left and we suffered all the ills that befall a person when he ignores them. What little information we had came through the civilized Baltics. We've been so screwed by our government and the powers that be that we rely on other sources of information when we need to know something. We rely on each other—you might say on rumors—and on Radio Liberty. Whatever our old socialist government hid from us or attacked or banned we agree with now. Sakharov was banned. He's an idol these days among us. Solzhenitsyn and his books about the gulags were banned. We've all read him now. Astrology was forbidden . . . You can see the point I'm making."

I could see the point. The repression ended up doing more than eliminating dissent, it had chained reason to suspicion.

To change the subject, I asked if people ever swam in the lake. At this Viktor stripped to his underwear and said the radioactivity in Chelyabinsk increased their resistance to disease and lengthened life spans. He flapped his arms, raced to the water, and dove in with a flat plop.

Tatyana jutted forth her jaw and spread her arms wide as though she were about to entreat the gods.

"The lake! The lake!" she exclaimed, looking to the heavens. "It was the source of our second life! We should tell you, Jeff, how the lake led to our rebirth!"

Viktor shouted from the water, "Tell him, Tatyana!" wrapping his arms around his torso, all ashiver, like a giant white fish, and turned to splash about. Svetlana stripped off her shoes and went in up to her ankles, tittering. Lena stood alone and swatted mosquitoes.

"A year and a half ago," said Tatyana, in a tone of subtle gravity, "I was strolling across the ice here—it was January and around twenty below—when I saw a group of people out in the middle of the lake standing around a hole in the ice listening to a man deliver a sermon. No one was shivering—does that tell you anything? They had discovered a source of inner warmth. I listened for a moment and raced up and got Viktor and Lena and called Svetlana. We all came out on the ice and stood listening to this man and—"

"And they were not wearing hats!" shouted Viktor as he emerged from the water Popsicle-blue.

"That's right! They were disciples of bioenergetics . . ."

The next morning I returned to Che-Te-Ze. Svetlana had announced a tour of the foundry with one of the workshop bosses.

Mr. Bobrov loved Che-Te-Ze; that much was clear from his detailed expositions on the history of his foundry and what it produced and in what quantities. He was proud of all the details, but I couldn't assimilate them rapidly enough, having no background in smelting and metal pouring. This surprised him, he said, as I came from a "land of smelters and big factories . . . where foundry work is of the highest quality." I told him I was from Washington, D.C.—not exactly a smelting town.

"Well, anyway, you know, we are supposed to be turning into capitalists and model ourselves after you. Perestroika. But why? Why do we have to mimic the West, like parrots? We are Asian, not Western. Take this factory. All my life, the collective was the most important thing for me. I labored for it. I knew why I had to work. But now? They turned it private and call us a 'joint stock company.' Who knows what that is? Company for me is friends and family and so on."

He dragged me up and down the dark corridors of his workshop where everything but smelting and pouring was taking place; metal hooks swung by our heads, tramcars with coal in them rumbled over shaky rails, steam and dust shot out of terrifying machines that hissed and screamed.

"The foundry is next," he kept saying. He discoursed at length about smelting, types of steel, molding and casting and water temperatures and ovens and British technology versus German versus Russian. Whenever I stopped and asked to talk to a worker or take a picture, he told me that we had no time, that we had to make it to the foundry soon or we'd miss the shift. Desperate to see something, I stopped him in his tracks and, with all the tact I could muster, reminded him of what we had agreed to do.

"OK, OK." He looked defeated and nervous. "We'll have to get permission from the boss who manages that particular workshop. But you see, it's not a good place to be. Criminals serve out their sentence there. It's hot and dark and dangerous. The workers sometimes get drunk and . . ."

The foundry was dark, save for columns of dust lit by lurid beams of sunlight piercing the gloom of the workshop from windows above us. Vats of molten metal bubbled and sparked, shadowy men in hard hats poured lava into casks and carried them away. I asked Mr. Bobrov to explain what exactly was being done. "This is not my sector," he said defeatedly. I took out my camera and got off a few shots, but Bobrov grabbed my arm and told me it was time for lunch, that we could come back afterward.

When we finally arrived at the door of the smelting section, the workers were stripping off their protective clothing. They were done for the day.

"Well, we've missed it! No time for photos now!" said Bobrov, barely concealing his delight. "Let's look at some fixture-casting and cooling apparatuses!"

I asked one of the workers if that was really the end of the day—it was only three o'clock. The next shift began at four, he said. At four, I made sure I was there again, and I used several rolls of film shooting the molten metals and flames. The precision of the pourers and the physical risk they ran was awe-inspiring—with the heat and red light I felt as though I were deep within the bowels of the earth. Tense, unsmiling men hurried hither and yon bearing vats of molten steel that would destroy a limb in an instant if knocked over. Bobrov stayed as far away from it as possible, kneading the rubber mat at the door with his feet and pushing his glasses high up on his nose.

When I finished, he grabbed my arm and led me out.

"Even though I know everything there is to know about the foundry, I'm scared of it every time." Maybe that was why he had fussed and faltered all morning when I asked to be taken there.

The next evening Svetlana took me to dinner at Viktor and Lena's again. It had rained all day and the streets ran like rivers. Svetlana and Lena began to drink vodka, but without much toasting.

Even Viktor seemed glum. He sat down next to me and peered into my plate.

"You do not mix your peas with your meat," he said.

Lena rolled her eyes and plunked her spoon down on the table.

"Oh, for God's sake, will you drop it!"

"Will you not interrupt!" retorted Viktor. "Our guest is trying to eat!"

I put my fork into my meat. Viktor froze at this, and stared at my fork. He looked up to me and smiled. I asked him whether something seemed particularly intriguing to him about my eating habits.

"Ahh! I'm glad you asked!"

He had been waiting for this, it seemed. Lena popped back a shot of vodka and banged her glass down on the table.

"You see, I believe your eating habits confirm what I have seen of American dietary practices on television; strict separation of food types. Meat eaten alone, followed by vegetables, then beverage. Meat—vegetables—beverage. Meat—vegetables—"

Svetlana sucked on her teeth.

"Americans have very defined dietary habits," she said. "Some based on the principles of bioenergetics, some—" here she sucked an incisor—"some not. So do other peoples. Take black people. If you take bananas from a black man, he'll die. It's a fact: a black cannot live without his bananas."

I wanted to say, "That is bull." Instead, I took a deep breath and said that race had nothing to do with taste in food. Svetlana maintained that a Russian would "die without his black bread."

Viktor, who disagreed vehemently with the banana statement, also disagreed with this, saying that many Russians prefer white bread, "as do Americans." Tempers flared; Lena thumped her shot glass on the table and called for order.

I looked at my meat and peas. Viktor picked at his beets. Svetlana reminded us that the solar eclipse had happened today. We finished eating in uneasy silence and watched television, a sour mood having overtaken us all.

FOURTEEN

Magnitka:
Vodka for a Faded Beauty

The snow caught up with me the day I was leaving Chelyabinsk for Magnitogorsk, making its way through the smoke hanging above the town in rusty skeins and dropping on the bus windows like a shower of wet rotten leaves, thick and clinging and tainted with factory waste. Chelyabinsk's outer districts were beginning to stir under a film of soot and turgid slush. These were the muddy dragging hems of Russian Ural life, an urban purgatory reminiscent of Dickensian tenements and nineteenth-century packinghouse squalor; dark brown aluminum-roofed sheds, scrap machine-tool innards, and rusted domestic oddments scattered over vacant lots; columns of proletarians trudging their way to creaking trams they would take out to the industrial conurbations jutting up along the city skyline.

Soon we passed these and pulled out into the lakes and bogs beyond, then into groves of birches with their rust-coated leaves and trunks and snatches of tangled undergrowth, and finally, onto rolling steppe that resembled low mountains abraded by millennia of winds, but steppe nonetheless. It occurred to me that I might only be imagining it undulated more than any other steppe because I was hoping to see the Urals.

An Uzbek family sat in the first row, the father squat under a rectangular, black-and-white Central Asian skullcap, the mother sour-faced in a scarf and picking her nails, the son in a Russian fur hat propped jauntily on his protuberant ears. Ahead of them, on the sheet of glass separating the driver's compartment from the front seats, hung a poster of a naked blond shielding a candle flame with her palm.

As the snow thinned, the wind picked up and lashed at the bus, whipping it forward over expanses of steppe, dun-colored and scratchy with brown stubble and wisps of weed. The sky spread from the horizon like a sheet of corrugated iron and unleashed salvos of rain pellets and hail that thwacked the bus roof like marbles dropping on a glass tabletop. We stopped occasionally near villages rising in dark relief against the sky and ejected passengers, leaving them to trudge home alone over hundreds of yards of open field. Indeed, I thought, Russia often seemed made up of such woebegone, remote expanses. Could an an entire country be hinterland?

About two hours after Chelyabinsk, we hit Plast, a muddy village of boarded-up houses with shivering cows chewing their cuds at the side of the road. The driver called a forty-minute break and drove off to get gas.

I wandered around. The kiosk outside the station sold only Mars candy bars, beer, and soda water. Behind it was a Soviet-era poster of a square-jawed young worker with his arms outstretched calling upon citizens "Not to wait, but to act!"

We waited. An hour passed. Then another thirty minutes. Passengers began grumbling to one another that something was wrong. A bus marked MAGNITOGORSK finally pulled up, but it was not ours. The driver shouted at us to get in. But, what about our luggage?

Like a swarm of locusts, we indignant passengers descended on the manager's little window.

"What has happened to our bus?"

"Where is my bag?"

"Where is our luggage?! We demand our luggage!"

"This is inhuman service! What kind of people are you that you rob old pensioners of their belongings!"

Former Soviet life is all bridled frustration and bitterness. The dead-faced bus riders uncorked their rage, and all at once, those who had sat in silence for two hours began shouting, shoving, grousing, shaking fists, and berating the station manager.

"Citizens!" she shouted through the holes in her glass. "You must remain calm! For your own safety we have changed buses for you. Your bus had a breakdown at the gas station."

"What about our luggage? Our luggage!" we shouted in unison. My journal was in my overnight bag—I was not leaving Plast without it.

"Your bags will be sent ahead on the next bus! Step away from the window and disperse!"

This was no minor dilemma. Bags, however cheap and however objectively valueless their contents, mean more than anything else to travelers. We grumbled and fretted and became of one mind: we wanted our bags, we would not leave without them. But as is often the case with crowds, responsibility for action lay between us ("Someone's got to do something! Such disorder!"), and we all stood around and waited.

The thought of losing my trip journal prompted me to act first. I asked the manager where our bags were, and if it would be possible to retrieve them and place them aboard the new bus ourselves. Several passengers overheard me and seconded this suggestion; those of the Stalin generation stood and stared and waited fretfully to see how it would play out. The manager made a phone call and turned to us.

"You may pick up your bags at the repair station," she shouted. "It's across the road through the gates."

In another locust-like rush, we abandoned the station and streamed across the road through the gates into the garage, following no one in particular but finding the bus all the same. We picked up our bags, dragged them over to our new coach, and threw them into the luggage hold.

For the next five hours, we wound along the steppe road serpentining away toward a receding horizon, the leaden sky and bleak land wearying and offering no solace, no hope of arrival anywhere, snuffing out consciousness throughout the bus like a general anesthetic. Heads bobbed back over seat rims, eyelids grew heavy and dropped once, twice, then finally stayed down. Sleep did not flatter these Ural mountain dwellers: stubs of teeth and bare gums were now exposed. Faces went flaccid, wizened and drawn-out, with hollowed eye sockets and skin like soggy sandpaper wrinkled with fatigue, worn raw. The land outside had shaped them and carved every wrinkle into their visages. It was almost barren; it produced only enough for survival, but could always threaten famine. It was too expansive to master, make one's own. It was an element to win scant rations from, but never to nurture into luxuriance or plenty.

At Petropavlovsk we hit gravel road. Shortly afterward, the innumerable gray and black smokestacks of Magnitogorsk rose from a depression ahead, and between them snaked the Ural River, a silvery ribbon reflecting a band of clear sky clinging to the western horizon.

Magnitogorsk was not a town but a forge, a purgatory of furnaces and smelting works where black steppe earth was being purified into orange light and glowing embers. Many of the smokestacks belched flame; others spewed sparks and incandescent flotsam that danced in furious circles before expiring and drifting earthward. The bus ended its run at the train station in the center of town, out of sight of the smokestacks.

I rode and rode on this tram and that, looking for a hotel, and finally came upon a dormitory behind a technical institute.

A little woman appeared followed by a man in a blue sateen jogging suit.

"I'm sorry, our regular rooms are full. All we have is our single deluxe suite. Are you prepared to pay for it?"

"What does it cost?"

"Almost two thousand rubles," she said, wincing at such a high price (about two dollars).

The little woman ran up to have it cleaned, leaving me with the man in the jogging suit. He smiled, puffed a thick stream of smoke through a gap in his teeth, and asked me where I was from. He was surprised a foreigner would come to Magnitogorsk.

"Why is that? These huge metallurgical plants have foreign customers by now, don't they?"

"That's what we'd like, but the reality is that our plants are doing so badly, no one is interested in us. Half of the workers here are on leave without pay. Others have been fired. You see, we want to sell our iron to the West for hard currency. Why should we send it up to Chelyabinsk for rubles? That's our idea, but it's hard to find customers abroad. We end up bartering our goods to Western companies in return for consumer items, which is bad for salaries, of course. We've been on the verge of collapse since our plants were privatized a year ago. That's why I say I see no reason for you to come here. Magnitka—that's how we locals call our city—is in ruins."

We talked for quite some time. This man worked for the Lenin Metallurgical Kombinat across the river, the largest plant of its kind in the entire former Soviet Union. He had just returned from Gorno-Altai, where he had relatives, and told me that no one there lives past the age of forty-five; they all die of cancer brought on by the fallout from years of aboveground nuclear testing done in nearby eastern Kazakhstan.

I asked about the ecological situation in Magnitogorsk, which was almost as infamous as that of Gorno-Altai.

"As I said, I see no reason for you to come here. Our ecology here was destroyed sixty years ago with the construction of the kombi-nat. And we have a *zapretka* [forbidden city, secret military instal-lation] over at Beloretsk. Who knows what they are doing there? We have no Geiger counters to test. Could be radiation. And a lot of it. Right here. By the way, don't put on a clean shirt while you're here! It'll be dirty ten minutes after you walk outside."

The area around Magnitogorsk originally belonged to nomadic Bashkiri tribes of cattle farmers. The Bashkirs accepted Russian suzerainty in 1557, but it was not until 1743 that Cossacks estab-lished a fortress here, the *stanitsa* (Cossack settlement) of Mag-nitnaya. The early settlers noticed a peculiarity in their compass readings that led them to discover some of the largest magnetic iron ore deposits in the world just under the surface of the earth. In 1747, two Russian industrialists named Myasinkov and Tver-dishchev began mining the ore and shipping it north to be pro-cessed in furnaces in the town of Beloretsk. But the enterprise was unprofitable: Magnitnaya was far from everything civilized in Russia and two hundred miles from the nearest railroad.

Stalin wasted no time once he had secured his grip on power and pushed for mass industrialization, launching an all-out cam-paign for the exploitation of the iron ore in the Magnitnaya moun-tain region. His planners called on the American McKee Com-pany for assistance, and the Soviet government set aside $2.5 million in gold to pay the contract, on the basis of which McKee was to oversee the construction of the proposed Lenin Metallur-gical Kombinat.

By the end of June 1929, a railroad into the site of the new town had been completed, as well as temporary quarters for workers and a small electric station. By December 1, 1929, more than three thousand people—planners, workers, and engineers—had arrived and were working away, building the massive plant on the left side of the Ural River. Just above it, they erected Sotsgorod, a city complex housing the workers and hundreds of foreigners involved in the project. In 1930, the party, following Stalin's ever more demanding policy of rapid industrialization, decided the plant should produce not 750,000 tons of iron a year, but 4,000,000, ignoring the effect this would have on the environment and the health of the city's residents. In February 1932, the kombinat was belching forth hundreds of thousands of tons of pollutants, but sending iron to industrial plants all over the USSR.

The iron for every third shell the Russians fired at the Germans in World War II was mined here and processed at the kombinat, and the city grew and grew, spilling onto the right bank of the river, until its population was estimated at 600,000. Magnitka, despite its foul air and ruinous environmental impact, was, at that time, the Soviet government's symbol of the modernization of the country and the bright future to which socialism would lead. A new, modern, industrial future, with Stalin at the helm. The death of old agrarian Russia. Today it spells ecological disaster and has environmentalists the world over wringing their hands at the still lethal doses of pollutants emitted by the factories there. The monstrous kombinat is a dinosaur that will not die.

Everything was closed in Magnitka that Sunday evening except for a few kiosks selling chocolate and alcohol and one restaurant on Marx Street called the Beriozka. The Beriozka looked closed, but the cold wind and snow flurries drove me inside it. The entrance hall was cavernous and dark. I stared into the shadows to let my eyes adjust to the gloom, and caught distended, wavering echoes of music coming from above. Like a blind man, I felt my way around the wall to the staircase and ascended.

Upstairs was a huge deserted restaurant hall with tables set, musical instruments resting on the bandstand, and red velvet window curtains drawn shut, twitching convulsively to a draft. But no people, no musicians. I asked if there was anyone there. No answer. I turned to leave.

As I stepped into the stairwell I heard a woman's voice from behind me. I turned around. Just then, two men emerged from the stairwell; I was surrounded.

"What are you doing here?" asked the woman. Her tone was sharp and stabbing. She was dressed in a waitress's outfit—a black skirt with black pumps and a red blouse. The two men wandered past me toward the tables.

"Is this restaurant open?"

"Of course it is. Why didn't you sit down instead of loitering in the aisle?"

"I wasn't loitering. I would just like to eat."

"Eat?" She extended one foot and balanced her weight on its heel, tipping her head to one side and examining me. "And will you be drinking vodka?"

We walked into the hall. She took out her pad and pen and motioned me to a seat at a table behind the two men.

"No. What dishes do you have?"

She sat down at my side and put her face directly in front of mine.

"Vodka, cognac, champagne."

Her eyes were fixed on my lips. I pulled away from her.

"You have only alcohol?" I asked. "Haven't you got any food?"

"Oh." She sat back. "We do. Chicken. And cucumbers. And soup. The men are having soup. So should you. What will you be drinking?"

"I'd like a soft drink. And I don't want soup."

Dominating the skyline of Magnitka, the Lenin Metallurgical Kombinat beckoned with the drama of smokestacks puffing red dust, coughing up gray matter, spewing steam, spouting geysers of flame or belching soot and cumuli of smoke, standing uncountable in the haze of their own wastes. This vision of industrial purgatory extended across the entire territory of the kombinat along the Ural, and I watched it as one might the Yellowstone geysers or even waves crashing on a seashore, entranced by the ever-varying yet eternally constant ebb and flow of waste gases and fiery emissions across the districts of the complex.

The kombinat's pollutants coalesced into a yellow-brown miasma and drifted south over the steppe and low mountains, by-passing the city. But this, it seemed, could not always be the case: every building, house, structure, car, and sidewalk wore a coating of the same brown-gray industrial grit. The people of Magnitka themselves were wizened with it—it creased the furrows around their eyes, the part in their hair, the spaces between their teeth. They looked spent and enervated, like coal miners emerging from shafts after an arduous shift. At least some of this haggardness could be attributed to diet: when Magnitogorskans shopped for food, they had but slews of ailing, gnarled vegetables or gristly meat to choose from. Only depleted soil steeped in pollutants could yield such stunted produce.

I walked down toward the water. Dividing Europe from Asia, the Ural meanders infirm and choked with algae, feverish with steaming water ejected into its flow by the kombinat. Just under the smokestacks, fishermen waded through the shallows tumid and bubbling with factory excrement, sullenly casting their lines in the scum. Signs hung from trees near the bank there urgently warning people not to bathe by the thermoelectric station; it was tough to imagine that anyone would want to. No boats floated on the river; apparently it was not navigable. The Ural looked dead.

Svetlana at Che-Te-Ze had given me the phone number of a woman she said I should call in Magnitogorsk if I wanted to visit the kombinat. I tried and tried at intervals throughout my first day to get through to her, but the line was always busy. So I took the tram to the address. It made no sense; Yelena's office seemed to be in a apartment high-rise. I found the building and then the address, a flat on the ninth floor—it had to be a residence, not an office. I rang the bell and heard feet scuffle to the door, and felt myself being scrutinized through the peephole. Silence.

"Who's there?"

"It's Jeff Tayler." Silence. "I'm looking for Yelena Markova."

"No one by that name lives here!"

Feet scuffled away from the door. I rang the bell again and asked once more. This time, the door opened.

"I thought you asked for Yelena *Markovna,* not Markova. Come in."

Yelena's mother was bony and spent-looking, dressed in a ragged robe and shod in slippers with holes worn through at the big toe. A dishrag tied over her head covered her sparse brittle hair. She moved aside cheerlessly to let me pass.

I stepped inside. The apartment was sunk in flotsam and knick-knacks and tattered tidbits of pack-ratted oddments. Not a single square yard lay clear of clutter; not a single square foot of upholstery was unpatched. The old woman kept her eyes averted from me and it seemed as though my presence intruded on this wretched disorder, which she would prefer to bear in solitude.

Head down, she moved past me and took a seat in the living room, so I followed and did the same. A discreet leaden glow suffused the chamber—it was sunset, but clouds obscured the light and transformed it into a sterile ashen luminescence that chilled rather than warmed, and beamed dimly as though a diffuse reminder of the twilight we all face in our declining years. I had thought I might get a good look at the kombinat from the window there, but it faced the bare steppe and served only to draw the desolate emptiness beyond the town into this old woman's home.

She held her arms crossed tight over her chest, as though she were cold. I apologized for having bothered her, but she waved her hand at me dismissively and looked away. A gust of wind blew open the tiny *fortochka,* or ventilation window, above the main window. She closed it and sat down again.

"Look at our climate. It's been turned upside down by all these Magnitogorsk factories and power stations," she said. "It should be spring now—it's almost June—but what do we have? Cold, and a cold that's killing our crops. Summer is like winter and winter like summer. In April, it was sixty degrees outside. We were suffocating. We couldn't turn off our heat in here. Last year frosts hit us in summer and ruined our peaches and apples and carrots— we grow all this outside town on our private plots—and we went hungry. And now, here it is, almost June, and they've cut off the heat and stopped giving us hot water!"

She kept her eyes riveted to the ground and emitted a sigh that induced a crackling in her chest and brought on a gasping consumptive fit of coughing, during which she drew a handkerchief from her robe and expectorated into it quietly, with a muffled gag. She never raised her eyes.

"I'm sick," she went on. "I worked at the kombinat for twenty-five years, and it's wrecked me, ruined my health. This air here, it kills us—it's all gas and smoke from the plant. Babies are born sick and the young people die like flies. If cancer spares you, lung disease won't. I'm not going to complain—just send me to heaven. The sooner, the better. You are American. You must know that our Sotsgorod used to be called the *Amerikanka* because Americans built it and lived there. During the thirties, that is. I've been here since 1931, since I was a little girl. My parents came to build *this place*."

She chuckled bitterly at the last words; "this place" to her was fatal and worthless; all iron and steel and pain and broken dreams. Her chest rasped and she turned away her head as she drew her handkerchief out of her pocket again and covered her mouth, as if in suspense. She held it there for a few seconds, and the rasp recurred, followed by a seizure of hollow, mucus-laden coughs that alarmed me so much I stood up to help her, but she looked away and waved me off, ashamed of her infirmity.

Yelena was late, and her mother suggested we telephone her. When we called her she told me to come to her office the following morning—she would be busy until late that evening.

I was in no mood for tram travel after that. The wind was gusting and drove dust over the chopped-up steppe around the apartment blocks as a gale blows hoary sprays of water over the sea during a hurricane. At the tram station I caught a taxi. The driver had another passenger. After I got in, they resumed their conversation.

"You've read *The Godfather*, right?" the driver asked the man in a black hat in the seat behind me.

"That's old stuff. No, I'm talking about what our Russian boys are doing to America now! Our Mafia has really taken over the U.S.—I've been reading about it."

The cabbie smiled.

"Yeah, I've heard as much," he said.

"This Mafia of ours is terrorizing the population in the U.S., and would you believe it, it's even got the blacks out of the ghettos! None of the sappy politicians they have there managed that, but our boys have. You see, Americans are spoiled—from cradle to grave, they're handed everything from Mercedes to mansions. It only took a few of our streetwise boys a short time to take over there."

This news pleased the cabbie.

"You don't say?"

I'd heard similar nonsense from other Russians. Among the uneducated, such pride in the new Russian "racket" or Mafia nurtured wounded national esteem; if they couldn't rival the West militarily, they'd outdo it in guile and criminality.

The man in the backseat pulled his hat down around his ears and continued.

"You see, our boys use their brains over there. No American ever dreamt of diluting gasoline with water or falsifying receipts, but this is child's play to us. Our boys have 'em jumping through hoops! You could say the Soviet system sharpened their senses and created a new breed of man. That's what the 'Soviet man' is—the cleverest of crooks!"

He and the cabbie guffawed and we slammed into a pothole.

My "deluxe suite" in the technical school dormitory consisted of a wide room with two beds, a television, and a broad window overlooking the backyards of brown wooden houses, some with manicured gardens that showed a great deal of fastidiousness in their upkeep. The walls of my room were shoddily papered; from peeling slits, tiny brown roaches emerged and tested the air with tentative antennae. I had my own bathroom, though the toilet had no seat and the bathtub faucet only occasionally produced hot water.

There was a knock on my door. I answered it, but no one was there. Then another knock; again I answered it and found no one. When the third knock came I was ready and flung open the door in annoyance. In marched a slender brunet with a cigarette in her hand.

"May I come in?" She batted her lashes as she sat down on my bed.

"And may I come in, too?" asked a buxom blond in a denim jacket, also puffing on a cigarette, who slipped in after her and shut the door.

I stood there for a moment feeling rather invaded, assuming them to be prostitutes. They rolled their cigarettes in the tips of their fingers and drew in their cheeks with long puffs. The slender brunet saw a look of mild alarm in my eye and stood up.

"I'm sorry. We have come to invite you to a party next door. We don't accept noes here. You will be eating and drinking with us. It's no use trying to stay in here to write—we'll be making too much noise for that."

I locked up and followed them out into the hall. Next door, tiny, mouse-like Sveta, the student-maid for the dorm, was dishing potatoes onto plates set around a table studded with vodka bottles. She said hello and welcomed me. Two thick-browed youths, both named Sergei (one was from Volgograd, the other from near Chelyabinsk) clinked glasses and swilled a couple of fingers' worth of vodka. The air smelled of fried food and cigarette smoke; the girls' breath was redolent of vodka.

Lyuda, the blond, sat down across from me and told me that the Sergei to her left was her husband. He seemed very drunk and stared at his glass. Sergei from Volgograd asked me to drink with him, but I declined, not being a vodka drinker.

"Oh, I remember. Americans drink only beer. Come on, Sergei, let's get up and get some from downstairs."

The Sergeis stood up and left. Sveta came in with a plate of potatoes and onions for me. Her face was beaming.

"You don't mind, do you? I told them where you were from and they were upset you were alone. Don't drink if you don't feel like it. Have some potatoes!"

I didn't mind at all; in fact, Sveta and her friends' warmth revived the low spirits that had settled over me in this gritty town. The other two girls emerged from the kitchen with cucumber and tomato salads. Both, I noticed, swore freely and chomped on bubble gum, but I liked their prolish aplomb. They toasted each other and downed shots, their necks loosening and their syllables bumping into one another. Lyuda's face reddened and she stood up, throwing open her arms.

"I want to dance! I want to sing!"

She grabbed a hairbrush, turned up the volume to the Vetlitskaya song on the boombox, and twirled around. With a fervent, almost desperate panache, she tossed forward her arms and sang along:

> *Don't call me any more!*
> *Don't ask me for anthing more!*
> *I'll return to you all your gifts,*
> *I just want to know who you've dumped me for!*

Olya snapped at her to sit down, and she did, obediently. It was as though someone had doused her with cold water. Her panache evaporated and she downed another shot of vodka.

"I *hate* this loathsome town," she said, her face flushing with vodka warmth. "I'm only twenty-two. Because of the water here I've already got five gold teeth. I'm here only because of my husband and his job. What will be left of me when I leave?"

She doubled over as if rent by a pain in the gut. Olya shrugged, poured herself another shot, and asked me why I would vacation here. When I explained that my trip was not a vacation, but a sort of expedition to learn more about Russia, Lyuda cried out to herself and kept her head to her chest.

I examined her when Olya got up to help Sveta in the kitchen. Lyuda had the features of a true beauty—high, clear cheekbones, limpid blue eyes, and a tiny pursed mouth with full lips. But these lineaments had been abraded: the skin on her cheeks was stretched and flaking; her eyes did not shine; her lips were cracked at the corners and covered a discolored front tooth. In a few years, she would be as coarse as the rest of the proletarians traipsing around outside.

A thick-skulled fellow with wiry black hair pulled a drunk blond man in a leather jacket into the room. Olya and Lyuda looked up and asked what they wanted. Drinking partners, they said. The wiry-haired fellow asked for a comb; Lyuda handed him Sveta's hairbrush, and he started dragging it through his mop. Sveta popped out of the kitchen with more food. They said they would return with a bottle and left.

"You gave him my brush?" said Sveta reproachfully to Olya. "How could you!"

Within an hour, the drinking fest had grown to include the two Sergeis, Sveta, Lyuda, Olya, and the newcomers and their bottle. Everyone was shouting, drinking, toasting, running down Russia and expressing admiration for the West. Everyone but me—I started to explain the passion for Russia that had sustained me on this journey, but my words sounded ridiculous in grimy Magnito-gorsk, so I shut up.

The wiry-haired fellow clinked his glass with his spoon to gain the floor.

"I am a worker, a truck driver. I don't know much about the West, but I do think that a Russian *muzhik* [literally, peasant, but also simple, hearty fellow] and an American *muzhik* would get along and share vodka, because they are both *muzhiki* and that is what matters. You live your way and we live ours. But we're all *muzhiki*."

He drank to his words.

Lyuda glumly excused herself and her husband, who had been snoring with his head against the wall, and led him out. The evening dwindled until the vodka dispirited those who drank it and an expressionlessness stole over their faces. Only Sveta, who didn't drink, chirped and flitted about the room cleaning and straightening up. She looked at the groggy mugs around the room and shrugged at me.

The next morning I visited Yelena in her office at Magnitostroy Trest (Magnitostroy stands for Magnitogorsk Construction). She would be a striking woman in any country; her eyes glistened an almost turquoise shade of blue, her silvery hair was shimmering and cropped boyishly short. She and Svetlana in Chelyabinsk resembled each other as professional women often do in Russia; both possessed a candid, articulate charm intensified by wholesome good looks built along clean, sharp lines, petite, well-shaped noses, high cheeks, and firm jaws.

"It has been hard for you to get in touch with me, I know. I was out planting potatoes yesterday in our plot."

I mentioned something about Russians maintaining ties to the earth even when they moved to cities.

"Ties? I scrape in the earth and mess with potatoes because I have to. I want food to eat that I know I can trust, so I grow it myself. Just because I fix my own car doesn't mean I enjoy being a mechanic. I have no choice. This is our Soviet reality.

"Anyway, what can I tell you about Magnitogorsk? Our city is like no other in Russia," she said, rummaging through papers, searching for a story outline. "Magnitogorsk was conceived back in 1925. 'Iron! Mine that iron! And fast!' was the slogan. Build fast, industrialize, make Russia a modern country—Stalin pushed that line hard. The Comintern recruited the foreign experts we needed to build our city. You know, not many foreigners outside the Soviet Union wanted to be seen helping the Communists, so the government used the Comintern to recruit. It was so successful that it was hard to find a Russian expert here in the thirties."

I said I had noticed that all the factories were located across the river, and that the prevailing wind seemed to blow the smoke out of town. I wondered if this was an accurate observation.

"Absolutely not. We have a joke, 'When the wind blows to the right, those on the left bank laugh. When it blows to the left, those on the right bank laugh.' No one thought of the ecology here, or health. We've even begun to run out of water. What do they do but drill more wells! It's idiocy. They don't realize that all our water comes from one water table. It's now so depleted that they've begun cutting off water to the apartment blocks, like ours."

Yelena arranged for press secretary Yevgeni Naumovich to show me the plant. He agreed to set aside an hour for me.

"You see, I usually deal with big-time magazines—*Time, National Geographic,* and the like—they set up meetings with me months in advance and that's the way I like to work. But what the heck, I'll show you what I can in my free hour."

We drove into the kombinat through a security checkpoint off the Komsomolskaya Square central entrance, over which stands a huge Lenin statue against a backdrop of dozens of smokestacks belching rust-colored dust or puffy plumes of steam.

"Quite a view, isn't it? We've got some thirty factories here in Magnitka, three of which are metallurgical combines on the left bank, but this Lenin Kombinat is king. It pumped out 800,000 tons of dust a year through its smokestacks until last year, when production was cut and emissions reduced to 650,000 tons. And believe me, these cuts worry everyone most—we're all afraid for the future of the kombinat."

"Does anyone plan to do anything about the pollution? Is there a way of reducing the emissions besides closing down the plant?"

"Oh, yes. The Germans have offered to build such emission controls systems into our smokestacks, but at a cost of one hundred million dollars. Who has that sort of money? We are a private enterprise as of the first of September 1992, and have been struggling. State funding has ended. We now do nothing with the government except pay it taxes. We have to find our own buyers, arrange our own contracts."

At Yevgeni's suggestion, I spent the rest of the day wandering around old Sotsgorod above the factory. Little there distinguished it from the rest of Magnitogorsk, except that its buildings were older and sootier and there were quite a few private residences on its tree-lined streets. From all the high points in Sotsgorod the view was the same: the Lenin Kombinat and its smokestacks. Toward evening I hopped in a taxi and asked to be taken back to the dormitory.

"You're not from around here," said the driver, accelerating as he barreled through the busy lanes of trucks and cabs and errant pedestrians, "so I'd like to ask you what you think of our *air?*" He gritted his teeth at the last word.

"People croak like flies here." He clenched his teeth. "Nowhere else will you see so many thirty-year-olds in a cemetery. *Thirty-year-olds*. Lung disease kills them, and cancer—yes, cancer. All that floating radiation from the accidents in Chelyabinsk landed on us. Shit, I'm telling you, it's genocide here, genocide! But no one's on trial for it!"

We were now bearing down on the dormitory, flying along next to the tram line and very nearly destroying our axles in the huge potholes that covered every street in Magnitka. I mentioned that there were roads in similarly bad condition in Tashkent.

"I doubt that," he said. "Our roads are eaten up by the toxins in the air. They're the worst in this whole cursed country of ours. You tell me: if the air eats up our *roads,* what the hell does it do to our *innards?* We have to feed our children iodized salt to clean the poisons out of their systems. It does no good anyway. They all die young. It's genocide, genocide!"

We screeched to a halt and I paid him. He tore off, swerved broadly in a U-turn, thumped through a pothole and lost a hubcap, and sped back toward Sotsgorod—"Socialist City."

FIFTEEN

Crossing Bashkortostan to the Volga

In Russia, manholes are always suspect: either their lids are not fully in place and, if you step on one, you risk breaking your leg off at the knee as the wobbly metal cover gives way with a clang under your weight, or there are no lids at all, and you find yourself plunging into the sewage tunnels below.

I had my bag slung over my shoulder and was walking up to the Magnitka train station, my eyes dully fixed on the manhole in front of it as my thoughts wandered over the all-night trip I was about to make to Ufa on what had to be one of the slowest trains in Russia. It covered the two hundred miles in fourteen hours, or roughly a little more than fourteen miles an hour. How could a train move so slowly?

I was within three feet of the manhole when the lid trembled and clanked, like the top on a pot of water reaching a boil. Startled out of my train daze, I jumped to the side, but the lid did too, clanging like a church bell on the asphalt. An arm slithered out,

followed by the rest of an old man in blue overalls smeared with
raw sewage. He staggered to his feet and adjusted his glasses, sur-
veying the square for a second with his hand as a visor while his
eyes grew accustomed to the light, then walked away, leaving the
cover off the hole. He stank and left fecal footsteps on the concrete
square.

On the train, I shared a compartment with two old women speaking the Bashkiri Turkic dialect. Both had flat faces and sallow
skin and bodies shaped liked big pears. I took the top bunk and
daydreamed, staring out the window.

Low dun-colored mountains hunkered in the dusk to the north-
east of Magnitka. Beyond the tracks, power lines crisscrossed over
gravel roads traversed by bulldozers and cranes and dump trucks,
all of which were working in the iron mines along the way. Here
and there, bleak larch houses reminiscent of Siberian *izby* without
window trimmings appeared, surrounded by even bleaker larch
fences.

A Kamaz kept pace with the train, bumping over potholes on
the mud road beside the track, its driver bouncing on his springy
seat and looking up at us. All these empty steppes and stunted
mountains and my Bashkiri compartment mates reminded me
strongly of Buryatia, of the tableland leading to Mongolia I had
passed through in eastern Siberia. Briefly, a sense of remoteness,
a pang of the numbing disconsolation I had felt there returned to
me, then memories of Galina—where was she now? I missed her,
but she seemed infinitely distant, as if she belonged to another
world or age. The mournful descent of night prompted me to close
my eyes in search of sleep and peace and the quick passage to a
new dawn.

Bashkortostan is one of the autonomous, non-Russian republics of the Russian Federation. The Asiatic Bashkirs appeared
in the Urals a thousand years ago, long before Ivan the Terrible
expanded the Russian state to include the neighboring Tatar and
Bashkiri lands in 1552. They were fine horsemen and warriors

who participated with valor in Russian campaigns against European enemies, but grew restive under the bureaucracy and excesses of Russian rule. They staged revolt after revolt and retained a strong sense of national identity that persisted right up to the revolution of 1917. The Soviet government granted them the status of autonomous republic (which meant nothing, really), but the years of Stalinist industrialization wrought profound changes in the national life of the republic, and the oil fields in Bashkortostan became some of the most productive in the Soviet Union. They are the foundation of its economy today.

Like neighboring Tatarstan, Bashkortostan's native population is Muslim, and according to Russians I had met during my trip, religious sentiment there was increasing and causing tension between the Bashkirs and Russians. The question of Islam is of vital concern to the Russian Federation: Muslim Tatarstan and Bashkortostan border the Russian heartland and contain massive oil and natural gas fields on which it depends for fuel and hard-currency revenue.

Day broke, drizzly and dull, as we were pulling into Ufa the next morning. The three cabbies in front of the station, burly and fat-knuckled in mud-covered *sapogi* under the awning of a vodka kiosk, quoted me a price of six thousand for the ride to the hotel. It was too much and I told them so.

"Look around this place," gloated one, chomping on a cigar butt. "See any other taxis? At six in the morning we're all you've got."

As I turned to walk back inside, a pudgy man with white hair waved nervously at me. He was standing out in the lot, shifting his bulk from foot to foot and sniffling, rain running in rivulets down the side of his face.

"You need to go the hotel, I take it. Two thousand rubles. I'm honest and I don't work for the Mafia, unlike those cabbies there. What do you say?"

"Let's go."

He led me to his mud-spattered Zhiguli parked with one front wheel on the curb and the other in a crater of brown water so wide that I would have needed a canoe to cross it to reach the door. He begged my pardon and asked me to wait until he pulled out.

"Ufa! No sewer system!" he muttered, and threw his Zhiguli into reverse. His second front wheel splashed into the mud and he lurched into first, dragging the whole vehicle through the huge puddle and pulling free of it and into the middle of a lane of on-coming traffic. An approaching taxi swerved and honked furiously.

"Get in! Quick!" he shouted. "I don't want any trouble! The Mafia—I don't work with them. I'm a freelancer and if they catch me picking up passengers they'll beat me." He cursed and reached out his window to jiggle the windshield wiper, which lay flat and impotent on the glass.

We pulled out of the station lot onto a narrow road lined with dense trees. Ufa seemed to have been cut right out of a forest, and the road was infernal, strewn with axle-smashing potholes, some of which were several feet in diameter. Viktor, my cabbie, swerved erratically to avoid them and very nearly drove us head-on into an oncoming bus.

"Curse this wiper! Curse it!" he shouted as he fiddled with the limp rubber rod on the other side of his windshield. "That's Russia for you—fix it today, and it falls off tomorrow!"

He allowed the car to wander dangerously as he plucked at the wiper, reaching out his side window to do so. We shot through a puddle on the left side of the road and doused a woman with a grocery cart, lurched onto the sidewalk to avoid an approaching Kamaz, and trundled back into traffic, narrowly missing a taxi passing in our lane. Viktor pulled his arm inside.

"It must be something with the electrical system. My turn sig-nals—if they don't work the police could fine me." He began flick-ing his turn signal knobs in a flailing way that fatalistically por-tended their failure. They were out, too.

Viktor jiggled his turn signal knobs and muttered as Ufa shot by. Actually, from the window of my lurching taxi, it looked mani-cured and finished as a city everywhere except for the roads, which were rivers of muck, expansive puddles, or outright obstacle courses of freely strewn axles, potholes, or other tire-popping debris. I held onto my overnight bag, which lay on my lap, and figured it could serve as a cushion of sorts in a collision, the possibility of which was growing ever more likely as we entered the congested city center, all mud and soaked pedestrians and cars swerving around potholes.

"My turn signals! . . . The militia! . . . Got to get a look at the signals!"

He rolled down his window and stuck his head out, looking toward the rear and dragging the wheel to the left. The militia car coming toward us flashed its lights in alarm.

"Viktor!" I shouted, and clutched my bag.

He pulled the car out of the lane at the last second, just missing the militia car's fender. When he realized whom he had very nearly crashed into, he turned suddenly down an unpaved side street. From behind, we heard the militia ordering us to pull over. Viktor ignored them and we flew on through gigantic mud holes that threatened to suck us under entirely, dousing everyone plodding through the muck on either side of us with torrents of water.

"We'll cut through the circus. We'll lose them in the Moscow circus," he said. "You ever been to the circus?"

We pulled into a flat paved lot with multicolored cranes standing around, the only touch of color in the rainy landscape. Nothing else suggested a circus. The militia were nowhere to be seen.

After circling for a few minutes, we sped out onto October Avenue, and Viktor fretted about "what Russia will never want for, bad roads and idiots." It was a faceless, gray thoroughfare of speeding trucks and dirty Soviet taxis. But the hotel was near and I was relieved about that. As soon as this thought crossed my mind, it appeared ahead of us on the other side of the road, which was bisected by an impassable tram line. We passed it, there being no way to turn around. When some way down we did reach a crossing, Viktor stuck his hand out and waved frantically to those behind, signaling his left-hand turn across the tracks.

A car skidded to a halt behind us, and its driver leaned on the horn. Apparently Viktor's hand had not been visible in the rain. A swearing match followed, during which Viktor lost track of the traffic around him and the tram line. When he finished his curses he huffed indignantly and started into his turn.

Alarm bells rang from an approaching tram—in a split second, Viktor saw we were about to cross a track down which a tram was speeding at us and decided to risk it anyway, hitting the accelerator and sending us across the rails in a lurch. We flew past the tram's front end into traffic in the oncoming lane, and three or four cars swerved and honked as they screeched to a halt. Briefly there was confusion about who would move first. Viktor decided he would; he did a half-circle and pulled up onto the curb in front of the hotel.

"Like I was telling you—in Russia, you'll never run out of bad roads and idiots. Remember that—bad roads and idiots!"

I turned on the television in my room at seven that evening, local news time in autonomous Bashkortostan. A plump woman with flowers pinned to her shoulder, kohl under her languid Turkic eyes, and wavy black hair woven into a sensual braid, announced the reading of the news (in Russian) and described the day's events in the republic: Bashkortostan border guards were awarded medals for serving with distinction, American businessmen arrived to discuss joint ventures, a Bashkiri director had revived a moribund state sanitarium outside of Ufa, and two Bashkiri sculptors were honored with a report on their work. The newswoman read from sheets of paper, which she shuffled noisily between items, just as Soviet anchormen did years ago. Every other sentence contained the formulaic unit of "the Autonomous Republic of Bashkortostan," just as old Soviet broadcasts repeated at length "the Central Committee of the Communist Party of the Soviet Union."

This was depressing. Nothing about the news indicated any investigative initiative on the part of the journalists; it sounded like the old Soviet propaganda, with a few words changed around. This was unlike Russian television, which reported on crime and unrest and turmoil, even if it was biased in favor of Yeltsin.

The anchorwoman adjusted the flowers on her shoulder, called to attention "all the Muslims of Bashkortostan!," and asked them to attend *namaz* (prayer service) for the Islamic Feast of the Sacrifice to be held soon at the Palace of Culture. Dead air followed and I turned off the set.

Old wooden houses with magnificent intricate carvings above their doors crowded each other along muddy streets in central Ufa. Modern avenues nearby looked prosperous with new coats of paint, clean glass in the shop windows, and no litter on the sidewalks. What was most surprising was that these shops were state enterprises yet still well maintained. Few on the streets were Bashkiri; most looked like Russians and were speaking Russian, and almost all signs were in Russian, though some were in both languages.

"Why should I work; why should my son work? Our 'autonomous' government just announced a seventy-five percent income tax. Is that civilized?"

My taxi driver's eyes drooped with fatigue. He was an old Russian.

"I told my son, 'If you don't want to steal, don't work for the government; be a taxi driver.' He ignores me and says he's going to be a *spekulyant*. At least be moral if you can't get rich, I say. He won't hear of it. In my day, we worked for our country, and it was shameful to say you wanted to get rich."

"Was your day Stalin's time?" I asked.

"Yes. Stalin . . . we were building our country then. We worked because we had spirit, we sacrificed for our homeland. When I came to Ufa, it was a small town, but during the thirties they built oil refineries and airplane factories and machine-tool factories. This is a prosperous place now, one Russia can be proud of."

"Russia? What about the Bashkirs? Isn't this Bashkortostan?"

"There are more Russians and Tatars here than Bashkirs! They're outnumbered three to one. We get along, though we don't intermarry often. They're Muslims and won't marry Russians."

Later on, the *dezhurnaya* on my floor asked me how my sight-seeing day had been.

"You know," she said rather shyly, "we've all been wondering why you stay here. On our floor, that is, instead of the eighth floor."

Her conspiratorial tone suggested forbidden fruits and secret treasures. She stood up and touched my arm.

"They didn't tell you? About the . . . eighth floor?"

The eighth was the top floor. She averted her eyes when she led me to the elevator and hit the button, as though she were doing something naughty. We rose with a hum.

The doors opened to a luxurious world of plush green-and-blue wall-to-wall carpeting, clean white walls, and polished oak furniture. She introduced me to the reigning *dezhurnaya,* a smiling pretty blond woman in a fresh blue suit who looked like an SAS flight attendant.

This was the hard-currency *dezhurnaya;* they showed me a hard-currency room with pink walls and a fan in the bathroom and a glistening white hard-currency bathtub and a separate, shiny, hard-currency toilet ("Look at it—it shines like glass!"). The room had two single beds ("Foreigners don't like to share rooms, so when they're here one bed is always empty") and a minibar, too. It cost seventy dollars a night (my clean but drab ruble room downstairs went for five dollars).

In the lobby I was shown the hard-currency bar and a gift shop with hard-currency candy and a high-cheeked young woman who sat at attention as we entered, rearranging M&M's and Mars bars in the display case. All items were on sale for hard currency at three times their ruble equivalent on the street.

"Hard currency" (*valyuta* in Russian) is more than a designation indicating freely convertible banknotes, and its adjective, *valyutny,* confers a special dignity and value on any noun it precedes. What may be purchased in Russia with *valyuta* is by definition infinitely preferable to what can be had for mere *dengi,* or "money." Items sold for *valyuta* had *valyutny* prices in excess of their ruble value. Russians with foresight kept savings in dollars, which protected them from inflation and served as an investment of sorts, since the exchange rate for the dollars always rose. Rubles, or *dengi,* were just workhorse bits of paper that served for what Russians referred to as "their" produce or products, and any items described as "theirs" or "of the fatherland" were implicitly inferior.

At times, it was hard to convince Russians in the outback that I wasn't crazy to have left the *valyutny* world to live in their country. My passion for Russian history and literature seemed irrelevant compared to the country's poverty and endless political discord. Russia, they said, was a place to resign oneself to, or better yet, to leave. It was distressing to me to hear so many educated, capable individuals set their sights on immigration when so much could be made of their huge, resource-rich homeland if they were to stay and work for positive change. *Valyuta* was a symptom of national malaise, of disgrace, a voucher of credibility in a system of fiscal insolvency; as its prestige increased, Russians' faith in their own system diminished.

In the morning, I was on a train shooting out of Bashkortostan and across boundless green expanses of steppe sprinkled with violets and daisies and a riot of other flowers. Azure skies with billowing white cumuli hung above us and birches began to appear. The steppe wavered and turned undulant, with *izby* along muddy lanes. We passed Dimitrovgrad and sped into the Russian heartland around the Volga. My cheerlessness left me and I opened the window to smell the nectar-scented breeze and watch the swallows and jeweled warblers flitting in the underbrush of the birch groves. Blood coursed through my veins and my spirit lifted, as though this day could only prove to be a wonderful one, filled with hope and the possibility of something different.

We emerged onto treeless hilly terrain and then, suddenly, roared onto a bridge crossing the Volga, which spread wide as the sea and reflected the lapis lazuli luster of the sky in every direction. On the distant horizon, its water held a quality of light so like that of the sky that the distinction between the two faded away. In an instant, the feeling that I had "arrived" settled over me and put me at ease. The Russian heartland . . . the Volga River . . . the *true* boundary of Europe—I had made it.

— SIXTEEN —

The Volga

WELCOME TO THE HOMELAND OF VLADIMIR ILYICH LENIN . . .
WELCOME TO THE HOMELAND OF VLADIMIR ILYICH LENIN . . .

The train flew past the high grassy banks of the Volga and drew into Ulyanovsk station with a prolonged squeal and a hiss and a round of explosive clanks. Only a few people with sacks of potatoes and rickety carts disembarked with me. The station was gloriously empty and clean, bathed in soft sunlight and freshened by breezes from the river, echoing with the recorded announcement reminding everyone of the only reason Ulyanovsk was on the map: it was the town of Lenin's birth; and it still bears his true family name, Ulyanov.

The latest National Geographic map called it Simbirsk, indicating that the town had been returned its historical name, but when I tried to buy a ticket to Simbirsk in Ufa the cashier had no idea where Simbirsk was.

"Sim-what? Where in Siberia?"

Outside the station, three bold placards stood in the sunlight. One read ULYANOVSK — THE HOMELAND OF V. I. LENIN! The second said that ULYANOVSK IS AN IMPORTANT CENTER FOR THE PROPAGANDA OF LENINISM! The third, under which a pair of Tadzhik refugee families were encamped and arguing noisily, declared that 1.5 MILLION TOURISTS VISIT ULYANOVSK EVERY YEAR! The tourists had stopped coming long ago and the streets were nearly empty — except for the Tadzhiks quarreling under the placards.

Mama Tadzhik, a fat woman with long black braids and wearing an orange robe, flailed her arms as she berated her child in Farsi and finally whacked him on the head with a plastic sandal. *That* is what Leninism is really all about: sandal-whacking poverty and public-square shame and shoddy satchels under bright red posters with exclamation points. It had all come to this; no longer did police hide the displaced away in jails as they once did. The displaced in Russia have come out to take their rightful place in the sun, fouling up the contrived scenes punctuated with bright banners. I stood waiting for the tram and watching them, the thought nagging me that these were very poor people who had been duped and exiled and murdered for seventy years by people who knew just what they were doing but called it all something grand for their own empowerment. The Tadzhik woman finished her tirade and glared at me as if to say, "What are *you* looking at?" It bothered me that I was a tourist to someone else's shame. The tram pulled up and I jumped aboard.

The fortress town of Simbirsk was established in 1648 to protect the Russian heartland from the Tatars on the east bank of the Volga, and, until their pacification, was a principal military and customs outpost on the border. Stepan Razin, the leader of a massive peasant uprising during the mid-seventeenth century, used Simbirsk as his center.

An intoxicating warmth stole over me as I wandered around Ulyanovsk on my first day, a sense of well-being I hadn't expected to feel until Poland. It was a feeling of achievement, of arrival; it was as if I had made it across hostile Siberian barrens that were neither East nor West, but certainly not West, and reached *home*. In some visceral way, I suddenly realized how European Russians are; I came to see the West (western Russia, that is) as Russians did: it was civilization, it was home, it was where flowers scented warm breezes with nectars, and where nightingales trilled from the crests of drooping acacias. Russians belonged west of the Volga; the eastern territories they had conquered since Ivan the Terrible remained places of exile and estrangement for them, just as I had discovered they were, spiritually, for me.

Ulyanovsk sits several hundred feet above the Volga on green hills; steppe winds and the river below refreshed it and drove off pollution. Its streets were tarred and manicured, smooth sidewalks ran along them, there was no mud, nothing was torn up or under construction or half-finished or defiled in the usual Soviet way. Traffic flowed light and orderly, and cars slowed for pedestrians. Trams were numerous and strikingly uncrowded.

But Ulyanovsk was remarkable in another way. Its conservative local government was devoted to preserving "peace and tranquillity" in the oblast and, for this reason, had allowed very little reforming and perestroika to ripple the calm surface of life there. Specifically, this meant that food prices were kept so low (through state subsidies to producers) that ration tickets were issued to residents to prevent hoarding by people from nearby expensive regions. If privatization was under way, it was low key, if not downright invisible. Even kiosks were fewer in Ulyanovsk than in the rest of Russia.

What struck me most, though, were the pure Slavic features of the people. Their blond hair flowed over tanned, clear skin, and high cheekbones. Their eyes shone blue and green. The women of Ulyanovsk were stunning, and many were a good deal taller than average, which created the impression that the streets were fashion runways, given the sleek modern lines of their attire and the subtlety of their makeup. Ulyanovsk felt like Europe; it at least disposed me to relax and enjoy life more than anywhere else I had been in Russia.

But if I was able to enjoy Ulyanovsk, many of my Russian friends were not: "Visiting Lenin's hometown is tantamount to paying tribute to Hitler," was how Valya in Kiev responded when I called and said I was going there. Others said, "It's a pointless idea, visiting Ulyanovsk. We don't believe in Lenin now." I came, however, not to pay tribute to Lenin, but to get some understanding of the place that shaped him.

Two years after the Soviet Union collapsed, menacing dark bronze Lenins with outstretched arms still dominated almost every square town across Russia. They pointed toward a future that once made the miserable, meatless, bread-line present endurable. They stood gallant in windblown overcoats, defiantly looking ahead to the dominance of iron-fisted uniformity at home and the triumph of communism abroad.

These Lenins were unremarkable; no one marveled at them or paused to examine them. But in Ulyanovsk they were remarkable for their absence. Hardly a single one stood in prominence anywhere. His slogans, still engraved on walls or painted above factories elsewhere in Russia, had apparently never been numerous in his hometown. In no other city in the former USSR was I so rarely reminded of Lenin and the Bolshevik past; in no other city was it so possible to drift along breezy city streets and simply enjoy the bounty of the Volga and fresh steppe winds. Why was this so? How was this possible? If they hadn't renamed the place, why had they so scrupulously removed all other traces of his regime? It made no sense.

The Lenin Memorial Complex is a historical preserve in the center of old Ulyanovsk. The houses trimmed in ornate wooden latticework were not more impressive than others standing throughout Siberia and the Urals, but the total impression they created was of a turn-of-the-century neighborhood anyone would like to raise kids and grow old in. The house where young Vladimir spent the most time, at 68 Lenin Street, is now a museum.

I was the only visitor to the museum that morning at the end of May. A tiny old woman rose when she saw me enter and showed me into the first room.

"This was the Ulyanov family's living room," she chanted in a Volga drawl as I stepped up to the rope. Ferns drooped in wooden plant holders, a black pianoforte reflected sunlight streaming in through the window, and polished oak chairs and white walls under a lofty ceiling all gave the place a Swedish ambience, spartan enough to intimate taste and a culture of restraint.

I walked on, with the little woman in tow.

"This is Volodya's father's study," she said, calling Vladimir Ilyich by the diminutive of his name, as a mother would. "He was inspector of schools for the province of Simbirsk. He worked at this desk and died of a stroke on this very couch." She drew her arm ceremoniously across the room. The oaken desk was heavy, his personal stamps lay on top of it, and a large yellowed map of his province hung on the wall.

The little woman followed me like a shadow, walking just out of my sight, into the next room, a hallway of sorts, with old portraits of the Ulyanov family. I noticed the striking resemblance between the family features (broad cheeks, clear skin, slightly slanted eyes) of Lenin, his brothers Dmitry and Alexander, his sisters Olga, Anna, and Maria, and the facial lineaments that had so enraptured me on the streets of the city. Lenin himself looked almost cupid-like—soft and innocent—in his high school portrait.

It has been suggested that he was part Kalmyk (the Kalmyks are a Mongol people settled in southern Russia); I mentioned this to my guide, pointing out the vaguely Asiatic cast to his cheeks and eyes.

"No. No. This is not true," she said firmly but still in her Volga lilt. "Our Volodya was a pure Russian. Nor did he have Jewish blood in his ancestry. This is slander against Volodya thought up to ruin him and his achievements. He was the most Russian of Russians." (Lenin's enemies made much of his inability to roll the Russian *r*, a mild speech impediment associated with a Yiddish accent in Russian.)

On we walked into the Ulyanovs' dining room, with its chessboard and huge map of Europe and northern Asia (Russia), and up to Lenin's own room on the second floor. His favorite works of Russian literature, Gogol's *Taras Bulba* and Turgenev's *A Hunter's Sketches,* lay open on his desk, next to a little white cot. He studied in this room until he went off to law school in Kazan.

I was about to walk out when the little woman called me over and introduced me to Tatyana Mikhailovna, the museum's acting director. Tatyana was about thirty and with her professorial gray skirt, tweed jacket, and glasses would have looked quite academic were it not for the warm smile and wonderful soft lisp that added something even more captivating to her singsong Volga intonation.

"I am only a watchlady," said the old woman, "but Tatyana can tell you more about our Volodya. She has studied all about him."

In Tatyana's study, I said that Lenin's family lived quite well, judging by the museum.

"Oh, I wouldn't say that," she protested with a smile. "This was a modest home in those days and reflected Lenin's mother's Swedish ancestry. She decorated the house in a spartan style not quite Russian, in my view. It is rather bland."

"How has the museum done since the Soviet Union collapsed?"

"It has been tough. The government wanted to close us or give the house to someone to live in. They would have done this, but the citizens of Ulyanovsk wrote a petition to our mayor and asked that the museum be allowed to function as before. Why erase history? Why hide it? History is history. It's important to us all. They listened to us and let us go on functioning, but with a minimum of funds. We've been on the brink for some time. But to get back to the important point: I personally felt that I would be ashamed to tell my children we closed the museum—it would be as though I wanted to hide the history of our country. We have hidden so much, lost so much. Let this house remain as a reminder of our past."

I asked her what had happened to the beautiful churches for which the town had once been renowned.

"This is our grief. We had twenty-nine churches here and two monasteries. During the campaign against religion in the thirties, all were razed. *All.* No foreign invaders destroyed them, no war leveled them. We did this to ourselves."

And why so few Lenin statues? I wondered. Had they been torn down?

"Oh, no. We never overdid our Lenin past. This preserved neighborhood is enough. Anything more would be tasteless, would it not?"

This was remarkable. I nodded in agreement. *Of course* it would be tasteless, but what had taste ever had to do with the millions of tons of bronze poured into leviathans that were intended to do nothing more than drill home the crushing might of the state and man's puniness next to it? Maybe people in Ulyanovsk did not know how defiled the rest of their country was with examples of "tastelessness."

Out on the street again I marveled at the idyllic, nineteenth-century charm of the place, until I reached a promontory from where I imagined the churches and cathedrals of yore would have been visible. I stopped and felt a rush of pain—of course, not one was to be seen. Centuries of heritage and culture had been wiped out in a few months of ideological idiocy. Perhaps the damage done to Russia by the Soviet decades *was* irreparable, maybe I was looking not at a country being reborn but a land of people who had permanently dispossessed themselves. Perhaps, it occurred to me, it made sense to leave and look for happier climes.

A silly thought, I concluded: reason had nothing to do with my becoming enamored of Russia, and it would play no part in my leaving, if I ever chose to do so. The empty, churchless hills I faced were part of the very tragedy that lured me to the country.

Lenin's house and neighborhood were, oddly, the most "European" places I had seen in Russia. The maps on his walls were of Russia and Europe; the decor of his residence was stately European. This all harks back to the central Russian dilemma: where do Russians belong, in Europe or in Asia? So often, communism has been attacked as something anti-Western, but Marxism was European in origin, not Russian.

But even the Russia of the czars, while looking to Europe for style and technology, followed its own Slavic-Russian cultural and architectural traditions. The beauty of Lenin's old neighborhood stands as a testament to the vitality of a culture Lenin destroyed.

— SEVENTEEN —

Building Peace in Saratov

Dawn was dogging me, breaking earlier and earlier with the approach of the summer solstice, flooding my room with light only a few hours after I fell asleep; in Russia's latitudes, this meant, by early June, first light before four in the morning.

I caught the dawn express for Saratov, a town south of Ulyanovsk down the Volga. The train had been en route all night from Kazan; the air inside the common car was clammy, and the heat made the musty train smell like a compost heap of rotten produce. The windows wouldn't open.

The steppe outside spread tenebrous under dark clouds. This was poor land, spent soil. North of Syzran we entered wooded fields, then forest. Soon fresh breezes blew away the torpor of the steppes, and the sky relented into transcendent billowing clouds against a sapphire backdrop. People straightened in their seats and perked up. Six hours later, we trundled through poplar-lined, sun-baked neighborhoods with boys on bicycles and girls with white hair bows, reminiscent more of an Alabama suburb than a Russian town on the Volga, and drew into Saratov station.

I'd set up a meeting with the director of the Peace Corps mission here, Karen Woodbury. Karen had been in Saratov almost since the program's inception some ten months before, and we had met once in Moscow. She offered me a place to stay with one of her volunteers. She was at the train station with her driver, Volodya, in a white flowing skirt and sandals, distinctly Californian in a setting almost Californian with its sun and breezes.

Volodya started up the Peace Corps Ford station wagon, but twice on our way out of the lot militiamen wagged their batons at us, and Volodya had to scramble for his papers and vehicle documents. This preoccupation with security in Saratov did not surprise me. Until recently, it had been one of the Soviet Union's most closed cities, surrounded by military-industrial complexes and bristling with ICBM silos. Why had the Peace Corps chosen such a site for its program? Even with the collapse of the Soviet Union and pending disarmament, the stratified *nomenklatura* and hard-line Communist apparatchiks would have remained in control of the local administration and could hardly be expected to welcome a bunch of Americans loose in their territory.

Assad, a naturalized American from Pakistan, answered the door of his apartment in flip-flops and an Izod shirt. He had a smooth, easygoing charm which at first seemed more suited to a country club barbecue, but which I later realized would carry him through a tough Peace Corps assignment pivoting on personality and a delicate approach to a miserably frustrating task. He was a Peace Corps business consultant. His apartment gleamed with white walls, a fresh parquet floor, and windows that extended on three of its four sides and gave the place a breezy balminess.

While Assad made me pizza, I asked him what it was like to be a volunteer with the Peace Corps here. I knew the basics: there were some fifty volunteers spread out over several Volga towns, they'd arrived in December of 1992, and all of them were to work as consultants to private businesses just starting up.

"It's tough. A big part of our problem here is that the Peace Corps expects us to operate on a level with these U.S. AID officials. They drilled into us that we were to serve as conduits for U.S. government aid to Russia. At least that's the way my job was explained to me. But the Peace Corps treats us like volunteers who should be out building bridges in Africa. We aren't given proper financial or logistical support. We're supposed to advise Russians on how to start their own firms. But most of the volunteers don't have any business background. There are a lot of unqualified people.

"It's all been more than a little frustrating. In Moscow, maybe they agreed to accept us, but we're not in Moscow; we're out here in the sticks. The Russians here are skeptical of us and some have openly told me that any American worth his salt would be working in the States and not volunteering in Russia. They say we have to prove ourselves before they will give us any concrete support like phones, office space, translators. This equipment is all in our agreement, but what we get instead of it is: 'You'll have to prove yourselves' and nothing more. They don't believe we're valid."

The most disagreeable element of all this was that Russians in Saratov, according to Assad, took no interest in the "help" they were offered, perhaps even resenting it since it had been foisted on them by Moscow. "Americans thought up this program and told the Russians what they were going to be doing after we got here," he said. "They tolerate us with suspicion. They don't want us."

This all sounded very imperialistic and cynical: the U.S. government proposed the Peace Corps to Russia, the Russians didn't want to refuse, the Peace Corps then identified fields in which it would work, chose the volunteers, and sent them in, leaving them to dangle when the Russians found no use for them.

Assad explained this to me without a note of bitterness, however. He would stick it out because he saw that learning Russian and living with Russians would prove a valuable experience for him personally, even if his work at the business center turned out to be a failure. When all else failed, he retreated to his kitchen, well stocked from spice shops all over Saratov, and cooked Pakistani food.

THE NAME AND CAUSE OF V. I. LENIN ARE IMMORTAL— THEY LIVE ON IN THE HEARTS AND MINDS OF THE PEOPLES OF OUR COUNTRY AND THE LABORERS OF THE ENTIRE WORLD!

Perhaps it was too much to expect that the lobby of the Peace Corps office in Russia would bear anything but a bust of Lenin and a proclamation such as the above. It belonged to Mostostroi, the government agency responsible for bridge building, which occupied part of the building where the Peace Corps was located. It also served to remind visitors to the Peace Corps that the past was not dead, nor was it forgotten.

As I waited for Assad at the office, I struck up conversations with the Russian staff, who were the secretaries, drivers, accounting assistants, doctors, and language tutors. They did not mince words about these "Americans with no culture, no appreciation for even their own history and literature." They were tired of these volunteers who "act like children, whining all the time about how bad it is here. Who asked them to come?!" The worst of it was that not one of the volunteers could communicate decently in Russian, they said.

Assad arrived and we left for the marketing lecture he was to deliver to the advertising department of a Russian company. It was a hot day. White poplar seed puffs drifted through sunbeams in the lecture hall. The air was steamy. The talk was due to begin in five minutes, but the hall was still empty. Assad tightened his tie and fiddled with the Pepsi and vodka bottles and shoes he had brought as props. It seemed no one was going to show up.

At two minutes to ten, Assad glanced at his watch. A murmur

like the swarming of bumblebees rose and grew stronger. Thirty
Russians with notebooks burst into the auditorium and took seats
in the back rows, licking the tips of their pencils and raising their
eyebrows expectantly. Assad asked them to move closer; they
closed their notebooks with crisp patters, got up, and, to a man,
filed punctiliously into the first two rows.

The translator tucked in his white Izod shirt and introduced
Assad to the audience, but then Assad asked to introduce himself
and did so in halting Russian, explaining that he was twenty-
seven, had a master's degree in marketing from the University of
Chicago, and had worked for Hewlett-Packard for three years in
the States.

A silence followed and seed puffs drifted about the room. He
stepped back to his large posters outlining marketing principles
and adjusted his tie.

"I'm not here to tell you how to market products in Russia," he
said. "I don't know Russia. I don't understand Russia. I'm here to
explain what marketing is."

The Russians kept their eyes on him, pencils at the ready. Assad
moved over to his prop table.

"What do Pepsi, shoes, and vodka all have in common?"

A man stood up and asked the translator for permission to
answer.

"You may answer."

"Thank you. They are all consumer products!"

He sat down. Another silence followed.

Right. Assad followed with a brief description of marketing
principles, the gist of which was that Russian producers should
consider who their customers would be before creating a product
and that customers don't buy products, they buy solutions to
problems. The translator mangled a couple of key points: after
Assad hopped around on one foot, imitating a woman clumsily
trying on a pair of shoes at a kiosk, he asked if there were not better places to sell shoes; the translator stumbled and rendered this
as, "Is not the kiosk the best place to sell shoes?" The audience,

somewhat nonplussed, agreed with him, perhaps out of respect
for his authority as an American expert. There were murmurs
that Assad was talking down to them, that they knew all this. No
pencils scribbled away; gazes drifted to the poplar seeds hanging
in the air.

Assad finished and opened the floor up to questions.

"What exactly is the aim of the Peace Corps in being here?" one
man thundered in a bass voice.

"To help business and markets, to improve quality control, and
to streamline the financial operations of companies."

The man stood up again.

"But what can you tell us about *Russia* and its market? What
do you know that we don't already understand? Specifically, tell
us how we are to market our products in an economy of deficit,
criminality, and bribery."

The audience leaned forward in unison. *That* was a question
that stabbed at the heart of the matter. The Mafia, inflation,
shortages . . .

"As I told you," said Assad, loosening his tie in the heat, "I'm
not here to tell you how to market products in Russia. I'm here to
tell you what marketing is. It's up to you to do the marketing. People are buying; there *is* a market. You should learn to approach it
and work with it."

Another silence pervaded the hall. I got the impression that the
Russians were used to being lectured, that the Socratic approach
was puzzling to them, that they mistook it for lack of substance.
The woman next to me muttered under her breath, "The American cannot understand us! What is he doing here?"

A man with two separate mops of hair protruding from each
side of his bald top, in such a way that he resembled the archetypal
mad professor, jumped to his feet and threw his hand up, like an
eager schoolboy anxious to be called on. Assad nodded to him.

"First, how does this science of yours, which you call marketing, help you live?" he asked, gesticulating with thrusts of his fore-

finger for emphasis. "And second, do you have a wife and children? Thank you!"

He dropped to his seat as rapidly as he had risen. A chuckle rippled through the audience.

The translator mangled the question and Assad thought the man was asking about his degree's applicability in the field of marketing. I raised my hand and told him what had been said, which I would not have done were I not curious to see how Assad responded to a distinctly Russian overture for personal information during a business encounter.

"Marketing helps me to live because I see products all around me and I have an idea of how they came into being. And no, I'm not married."

The professor stood up again.

"Are we free to go?" he asked flatly.

"Yes."

The audience thanked him and filed out. Assad collected his props and we left the hall.

EIGHTEEN

The Fate of Lenin's Brothers, the Kalmyks: Elista and Exile

We want a voluntary union of peoples ... that would
not allow one people to use violence against another.
V. I. LENIN

My bus to Elista, the capital of the Republic of Kalmykia, bounced down the main paved road leading out of town, passing lattice-trimmed wooden houses with bright blue and green window frames, running alongside lanes of earth perpendicular to our road, lanes entirely sunk in frothy puddles and riddled with gorges of raw mud that bore no sign they had ever been negotiated by a vehicle more substantial than the occasional donkey cart. Several such carts trundled over the mushy ruts with heaves and sways of their loads of firewood or hay. Even the walkway along the main road was unpaved, and people balanced their way across wooden beams tossed over the broadest of puddles or probed for hard spots in the muck around the edges. The sky was dumping rain; the pedestrians quickened their gait.

Our bus rocked along as it forded the frequent scattered pot-holes on the main road, sending water splashing onto the walk-ways and driving those on foot to flatten themselves against the fences as we passed to give us the broadest berth possible. A little Kazakh boy beat at the surface of the water in one puddle large enough to be a toddlers' pool; from another, a dog drank until the splash from our passage through a nearby pothole frightened him into a skitter. Flowers bloomed in thickets overgrowing fences around some of the houses, and their pungent aroma drifted through the ventilation slit on our roof and saturated the close air of the bus, commingling with the smell of sweat and forming a va-por that induced a mild light-headedness.

We came out of Astrakhan onto empty rolling land of green and brown pastels, smeared with shallow murky lakes and marshes formed as a result of the delta's frequent deluges. A steppe eagle, russet-hued and with a wingspread wider than a man's out-stretched arms, pumped the air above, keeping pace with the bus, and then veered off over the swamp. Wandering cows slowed us down; twice we stopped for several minutes to let them cross the road or meander off onto the shoulder.

Half an hour later, we emerged onto dun-colored steppe under a canopy of fulminating clouds. Lightning flashed and licked at the flat land and metallic signs over dirt tracks leading away from the road. KOLKHOZ POBEDA, SOVKHOZ NORMOVOY. Farther on, gray concrete-and-tin shacks huddled in clusters at Yashkul, then followed the even bleaker, more dilapidated Ulan-Erge, above which hung a peeling red-and-white sign reading GLORY TO LABOR! Ulan-Erge looked ready to sink into the mud.

We trundled along for some seven hours across this Kalmykia Deserta until the oasis of Elista appeared, heralded suddenly by rows of trees by the side of the road. There's no transitional terri-tory between steppe and city there—Elista is a settlement of en-tirely post–World War II concrete housing blocks and straight Soviet avenues transplanted from a Soviet draftsman's board into Kalmykia's arid barrens and left to decay, with trees thrown in around its periphery. Elista had for years been a closed city, although that it and Kalmykia still existed at all was testimony to Khrushchev's thaw and his denunciation of Stalin. Stalin had banished the entire Kalmyk people into Siberia and the far north during World War II for "treason." Khrushchev rehabilitated them and permitted them to return to their homeland. But the Kalmyks and their tiny autonomous steppe republic remained a living reminder of one of the most absurd injustices ever inflicted on a people by its government. I wanted to find Kalmyks who could tell me of their ordeal.

I went to the Museum of Natural History.

"Wipe your shoes!" blurted a old Kalmyk woman with fat sagging jowls when I walked in. She looked me up and down and waddled into a back room and shut the door with a bang.

I walked to the first exhibit, the "Weather Room." There were footsteps and a slight wheeze behind me.

"This is not a free museum," said the Kalmyk babushka. "Pay for your ticket!" I followed her back to her desk. She drew a multileafed sheaf of printed paper from her desk and began to snip and chop until she had cut me three fifteen-ruble chits.

"This is not a free museum. No . . ." she wheezed, as if I had objected or not heard her the first time. "No, sir. You have to buy your ticket before you visit it. It's not free."

She was implacable.

"You wipe your feet, then you come to me and ask for a ticket. Only then do you visit our exhibits. It's not free."

I had steeled myself to this sort of surliness; it no longer bothered me. I thanked her politely and hurried back to the weather room. Weather rarely gets displayed in museums, but that it did here made sense on the steppes, where the sky ruled the earth and where, also, it presented vistas of greater beauty and majesty than flat dusty lands. The little display cases showed four views of

Kalmykian steppe, one for each season. The winter view showed flat land dusted with snow. The summer view showed flat land dusted with dust. Spring in Kalmykia was flat and dusty, too, but with a glaze of green. Autumn could be distinguished by the absence of both green and snow, and looked least interesting of all. The captions pointed out that the ground temperature during the summer reaches an infernal 160 degrees and said that dust storms are common.

The nature exhibit consisted of a map showing the location of Kalmykia's oil, gas, and brick clay deposits, and bristled with pedantic slogans from Soviet days urging Kalmyks to take care of their land ("Relate carefully to nature!" demanded the Communist Party Central Committee) and the flora and fauna on it ("Relate carefully to every living thing!" urged the Elista city soviet).

Another room was devoted to Kalmyk history with more banalities: quotes from the Kalmyk national epic, *Djangar,* stressing the need for patriotism and urging Kalmyks to give their blood, to the last drop, for their motherland.

The final room contained the shocker—Stalin's portrait on the front page of *Pravda* (July 3, 1941) over the text of his address to the Soviet people on the Nazi invasion. His steely, mustachioed visage dominated the room, and the exhibit smacked of the "Cult of Personality" in a place where, by any human measure, Stalin should be reviled. To make matters worse, the entire World War II room was devoted to the battle of Stalingrad. Where was the deportation of the Kalmyk people? How could this museum, seven years after the beginning of perestroika and two years after the collapse of the Soviet Union, not contain a single artifact, a single exhibit, a single document concerning the defining national tragedy of the Kalmyks?

I fumed about this and walked straight into the next room to the guides' desk where two attractive young Kalmyk women where standing.

I asked one of them, "Why is there not a single mention here of the deportation of your people? What about perestroika? Glasnost?"

She shifted her stance and tilted her head thoughtfully to one side.

"Ah, the deportation. Yes, the deportation," as though searching her memory for an incident she had read something about in passing. She sniffed daintily and her glance darted about the room. "May I ask who you are and why you are interested?"

I explained myself to her. She found it difficult to believe that a "Westerner," as she put it, would be concerned with the fate of the Kalmyks. Her suspicion was palpable.

"The deportation . . . is something we all know about. It is . . . our history. We haven't yet gotten around to . . . displaying it."

I told her I had come to Elista and the museum expressly to learn about the deportation. She excused herself and left the room. Within minutes she returned and asked me to follow her.

"Enker will talk to you. She is our ticket lady."

The same woman who had groused at me for not wiping my feet sat at attention behind her desk. Her demeanor had changed: she radiated something akin to bemused sympathy. I sat down opposite her.

"You want to know about the sufferings of the Kalmyks?" She laughed as though I had made a funny face. "We're all old now. I don't think about my fate. I just want to live in peace until my day comes, my last day!" She laughed again and threw her head back.

"I would like very much to hear your story, if you could tell me," I said.

"'Old people and their stories,' that's what our young Kalmyks say when we try to tell them. They don't want to hear us talk. They can't believe us!

"Anyway, I was eleven years old. My family lived in the village of Kharba, on the steppe, where we raised cattle. Two of my brothers were off at the front at that time fighting the Germans.

All the young men, I should say, were at war. No one was left in Kalmykia but women and children and old folk. In my family we had a mother and father and two cousins, girls, with our blind aunt, their mother.

"The soldiers came at six in the morning that day in December, after the Germans had gone, and pounded on our door, waking us all up. These were Soviet soldiers. Papa answered. They told him to get his family together, that there was a meeting we had to attend at the village house. All of us, even me. I was sick with a fever at that time—they had to carry me out on a mattress. The soldiers didn't give us time to gather our things—we were only going to a meeting. They told us to lock up our cattle, and we not only did that, we locked up our blind aunt! We thought, Why take her to the meeting? To this very day, we have no idea what became of her. We left her locked inside the house.

"In Astrakhan they put us in cattle cars. It was cold, very cold. We Kalmyks eat *makhan,* a meat-and-bouillon dish, but they fed us borscht and rotten cabbage. This gave us diarrhea. Everyone in our car got it. We were so crowded there we could hardly turn around. We had to use a hole in the floor for a toilet.

"One morning, Mama tried to wake up one of our cousins. Our cousin was a little girl, you know, sick with diarrhea. Mama couldn't wake her. Mama tried to lift her from the floor, to pry her free, but she had frozen to it in her own diarrhea. She was dead. Mama had to hack at her with a trowel to break her free from her frozen mess.

"After fourteen days on the train, in this freezing cold, we arrived in Siberia, in Krasnoyarsk Krai, and were taken off the train at the village of Uyar. They kept us in the village house for two months. No one explained anything to us, and we were afraid to ask. After that, we were carted out into the taiga—the trees were so thick we couldn't see the sky—to a lumber station. That summer, I remember seeing swollen dead people there, starved people, lying around the forest floor by the mill, their blood sucked away by midges.

"Mama died from cold and hunger a couple of weeks after we arrived. You see, they were hardly giving us food, and we weren't able to adjust to the cold, being Kalmyks. Even in the city people were being rationed only two or three hundred grams of bread a day. All they gave us was borscht.

"I worked in the mill. We were not allowed to leave, of course. It was as good as prison. It was forced labor. A few years later . . . I am ashamed of this . . . Papa . . ." She paused and took a deep breath. "Papa . . . I came home and found him on the floor. All the lice were jumping off of him and crawling away. I stamped on the lice. I knew he was dead, but all I wanted to do was kill the lice! My papa! Even the lice didn't want him anymore. I was an orphan. By then, my other cousin had died, too.

"My brothers—I never heard from them again. Maybe they died at the front. Maybe they were exiled, too. Soldiers were supposed to be exiled, taken out of their battalions and sent into Siberia. But some ran away, some commanders wouldn't turn them in. I never found my brothers."

She gripped the edge of her desk with one hand.

"My cousin was a soldier at the front, too. A hero. He heard of the exile but ran away to Frunze and hid. Because he was a hero, the city gave him an apartment and treated him well. He found me, the only one left of our family, and got permission through his commandant to take me to Frunze to live with him. I refused. You know, I was quite a beauty and had a lot of boys after me. I was living in the dormitory then, an orphan. I wanted to get married. I wanted a family, you see. I married in 1953. He was a Kalmyk, of course.

"In 1958, Khrushchev rehabilitated us. What did that mean?! I was an orphan! Anyway, my husband and I came back to Kalmykia. I've never gone to my old village since the day we were removed. That seemed like a part of a different life.

"'You cannot escape fate,' isn't that what we say? I had so many men after me, and I picked my husband. He seemed strong. But he died in 1967, leaving me a widow, so even in my second life

I've had bad luck. I'm not angry with my fate, though. I have my three children: two daughters and a son. In my heart I'm a Buddhist, so I try to make peace with my life. But even now, what peace do I have? Our country is a mess, there's inflation—no peace." We sat in silence, the silence that descends when any words would only rattle feebly against the iron shroud of tragedy.

NINETEEN

Black Earth
under Cossack Boots

Volodya the taximan agreed to take me to Stavropol for twenty-five thousand rubles, though he had asked for forty at first. He had curly gray-brown hair and wore sandals and a red-and-white checked shirt that looked cut from a picnicker's tablecloth. As soon as I hopped inside, he dropped his foot to the gas and floored it. We spun out of the bus station lot, firing gravel in all directions, and shot around Elista onto the only road leading west. Once we passed the trees planted around the city, we hit open steppe.

The road ran dead-straight to the horizon, rippling in the fluid shimmers of morning heat. Russia humbled her children—and foreign visitors—with horizons like these, making them feel as helpless and puny as scurrying ants on a six-lane freeway. We drove and drove, never nearing anything, the horizon ever receding from us, the immensity of the flat land reducing us to a metallic fleck streaking through bleached grass. We did at least a hundred miles an hour on the open stretches. It was impossible to judge distance as we flew around and passed trucks; it seemed we were always on the verge of a head-on collision.

"Russia needs a strong hand to stop inflation and all this *spekulyatsia*," said Volodya. "We don't have a free market like you do. In America, things are ordered. People in business are honest. Here, we have the criminal element and *spekulyatsia*. We need a power, maybe a benevolent dictator, to set up a free market where things are fair and where prices conform to what people can pay. Like in America."

"Volodya, it's just not true that Americans can afford to buy so much, or that they are so honest in business. Maybe what Russians need to do is stop thinking that everyone who makes money at his business is a criminal. The market is not considered fair or secure in the West."

"I wouldn't mind a person making an honest living, but what we have here are people buying up everything from abroad and selling it here. These *spekulyanty* don't produce anything—they just resell foreign products. Why shouldn't they sell what our own country produces? It hurts me to see so much Chinese junk in our stores, it humiliates me. We were once as great a country as America, and now look at us—we buy Chinese junk from street traders. And most of us can barely afford that. Every year, I used to get a free vacation on the Black Sea, at a resort. Sun, sand. Maybe the service wasn't so good, but it was free."

I had seen Russia during the Soviet days and knew that where standard of living was concerned, the country then was more on a par with the Third World (in fact, a joke used to circulate among Soviets that the Soviet Union was "Upper Volta with missiles"). But there was no point in arguing this with Volodya—his pride was damaged enough.

We shot through a couple of Kalmyk towns sitting naked and sunbaked on the flatness, all forgettable shacks and concrete and Kalmyks with ragged net bags of potatoes.

"Kalmyks like the steppe, can you believe it? They only want to live on steppe. Who would choose this place? *All* of Kalmykia is steppe, useless land. They don't farm, they raise cattle. They refuse anything but this flat land."

We descended in a long smooth swoop into the heart of Stavropolye, which was markedly greener and more fertile than Kalmykia.

"Black earth," said Volodya. "This is it! It's the most fertile land in Russia. This earth could feed the world. If we had order."

Stavropol is built on jaunty wooded hills. Its lanes run up and down them, shaded by sprawling aged poplars. Traffic moved as crazily and unpredictably as in any Mediterranean town, and half of its citizens, as in the Mediterranean, paid no heed to it, darting in front of cars and provoking a continual chorus of horn honking and fist waving from drivers. It was a vital, lively place.

I took a room for the night at a hotel across from Nizhni market, and set out on a walking tour, beginning with the market. It was jumbled and dirty. Faces were coarse and rough-hewn, eyes beady and deep-set, cheekbones angular and raw and jutting through tight skin. Women wore sandals revealing scraggly toes going in all directions, and men had big bony noses and jaws. Gypsy children chased one another through the refuse heaps, and Azeri women in shawls rocked back and forth in boredom over candy bars, turnips, and tomatoes laid out on sheets of yellowed newspaper.

Stavropol did not appeal to me. It was too coarse, too gritty; it had nothing to do with the birch-forest-and-steppe Russia I loved. It was in any case to be an overnight stop and no more. I bought a ticket on the bus to Rostov for the next afternoon.

A dull oppressive heat weighed on Rostov, wilting faces into putty, withering hair into stringy mop strands. Russians call it *znoy,* and there seems to be no single-word equivalent in English for it. *Znoy* both radiated from the ground, creating numerous sweltering minimirages over parking lots, turning them into deserts of tar, and pressed down from the sky, carrying a tenacious grit from Rostov's factories that settled on skin and streaked brown in sweat.

The climate in this southern Russian outpost was Middle Eastern, and the city's history is entirely interwoven with Russia's five-hundred-year struggle with Ottoman Turkey and the various Tatar khanates that once dominated the region. The Don River bisecting Rostov once divided Russia from Ottoman Turkey, and the first order of the Cossacks who fought the Turks was founded upriver at Cherkassk.

"Cossack" comes from a Turkic word meaning "free men"; most were originally runaway serfs from central Russian lands or escaped prisoners. These renegades fled the oppressive Russian authoritarian center for the wild border regions of Siberia and the south, beginning in the fifteenth century. Almost every town I had passed through on my way west from Magadan had been founded by Cossacks, and I was eager to see their "capital," as it were.

The Cossacks formed paramilitary units, then regular army units, and were united in a desire to remain free of the czar's crushing tyranny but defend "Holy Russia" to the last, living by their wits and bravery in the borderlands. Eventually, this love of freedom put them at loggerheads with the Bolsheviks, who liquidated their orders after the revolution. An untold number of Cossacks and their families were repressed—exiled or executed— during the first twenty-five years of Soviet power, but with the collapse of the USSR, their descendants have staged a revival of sorts. The *stanitsa,* or Cossack settlement, of Cherkassk near Rostov was their original capital, and it had drawn me to Rostov.

The hydrofoil I took up the Don to Cherkassk was crowded with sinewy-armed villagers who dozed over their dusty satchels and schoolchildren who swatted at one another despite the heat. It pulled out of the station around nine in the morning into the steaming river haze, with the sun badgering us from behind, and roared onto its wings a dozen yards from the dock. The city dropped away, and we pulled out into pure Don flatland of reedy swamps and low spreading trees. The river breathed a musk rank with the scent of black mud and ripening crops of barley and wheat, and the villagers, mainly middle-aged men and women, looked fat and healthy, if streaked with sweat and picking at gritty fingernails.

Dragonflies by the hundreds, green and blue and broad-winged, darted and hovered over the marshes running astride the Don by Cherkassk when the hydrofoil pulled into the tiny pier and let me off with the villagers and the schoolchildren from Rostov. The children bounded ahead and I followed them. We passed by the white-washed Petropavlosk church of 1749 and on into the settlement.

Cherkassk was founded when the first order of Don Cossacks was established here on an island fortress in the mid-sixteenth century. The czars needed the Cossacks as much as the Cossacks wanted their freedom; they offered the Cossacks alluring salaries and payment in bread, and accorded the *stanitsa* the status of a duty-free trading zone. *Stanitsy* then sprung up all over the Don region and their populations grew and grew, as did the scope of their trade, which came to include the Caucuses and the Ottoman Empire, and even Venice and Marseilles. The Cossacks were not just traders, however; they were most famous as raiders and pillagers of Ottoman lands and conducted successful attacks on Turkish towns on the northern coast of the Black Sea.

Then as now, life in the *stanitsa* of Cherkassk derived from the fertility of the soil. The people living there today tend little plots just outside the settlement. Most of the houses looked like peasant *izby* with bright green or blue sides and flourishing flowering bushes and drooping willows everywhere.

The other reason I came to Rostov was to see the nearby city of Azov on the Sea of Azov. It, like Cherkassk, lay some forty kilometers from Rostov, but to the west down the Don River.

Another hydrofoil ride of an hour or so brought us to Azov through *znoy* so fierce it wilted the passengers like wildflowers uprooted and tossed into midday sun.

Azov glistened white and sea-green and turquoise, drenched in penetrating, bleaching light. Its Mediterranean colors reminded me of Greece, and this was no errant impression: Greeks founded Azov more than seventeen hundred years ago as a trading outpost through which they conducted commerce with Asia. The city, over the course of its history, was destroyed by the Huns, brought under Kievan Rus dominion, raided by the Golden Hordes, became a commercial center for the Genovese and Venetians, pillaged by Tamerlane and finally brought under Ottoman Turkish rule, where it languished until Don Cossacks freed it. But Russia proved too weak to hold on to Azov and it fell into Turkish hands repeatedly until 1783, when the Russians routed the Turks and khanates of the Crimea and took the city once and for all. Throughout all of these tribulations Cossack orders, such as the Cherkassk Don Cossack *voisko,* played key roles in fighting for Azov. But by the time they took and held it, Azov no longer was as strategically important as it was before. Finally, Soviet power decided that the city's future lay not in defense but in shipyards and fish canning plants, and it became a backwater town.

Azov sweltered, its maples and ash trees and acacias exhaling a pungent cloying musk into the *znoy.* The central square overlooking the sea was strewn with a jumble of tables topped with tomatoes and carrots and beets watched over by haggard women waving flyswatters, whose every wrinkle and wart and sweat stain was magnified by the white penetrating light. But Azov itself was not an ugly town; its main streets were lined with blue and white buildings and spreading elms.

But Azov, like every former Soviet city, had its dark past.

WE WILL DRIVE HUMANITY TO HAPPINESS WITH AN IRON HAND!

EXPERIENCED ENGINEER COMRADE STALIN IS AT THE HELM OF THE LOCOMOTIVE OF THE REVOLUTION LEADING THE TRAIN FROM THE STATION OF SOCIALISM TO THE STATION OF COMMUNISM!

These slogans covered red banners in the history room of the regional museum and initially shocked me. They were hung with a certain flourish suggesting pride, even grandeur. Could it really be that the citizens of Azov took such pride in the Soviet era that even *today* they littered their museum with its banners, and Stalin-era ones at that?

They did not. The exhibit chronicled a past that, though no longer officially taboo, remains a dark and frightening cellar of skeletons into which few wish to descend—Stalin's Great Purges of the 1930s, during which he exiled or executed his political opponents as well as millions of rank-and-file party members and workers and peasants (estimates on the number of victims range from Khrushchev's understated thousands to twenty-two million, which is probably accurate).

Their official justifications were stark and simple—massive plots of sabotage, economic "wrecking" or stabbing at the underbelly of the economy through poor production or unfulfilled quotas, espionage, "anti-Soviet agitation," and so forth. In fact, almost all of these charges were simply concocted to destroy anyone who did not owe his or her position to Stalin—he would tolerate no one who might enjoy a popularity he had not sanctioned or created. Purges *were* Soviet power and began with Lenin's Terror; they reflected the destructive, crushing essence of Soviet power. Their result was a people that did what it was told and largely thought what it was instructed to think. The purges atomized Soviet society, driving people into the personal burrows of their family and closest friends, shattering all class cohesiveness that might have at some point or another coalesced into resistance, and turning apathy into a trait necessary for survival. Russians often told me that the purges destroyed their nation's gene pool by eliminating the cultured and skilled and brilliant. Whether or not this is so, they broke the back of Russian society. It has not recovered to this day.

A collection of photographs and newspaper articles followed the fate of V. D. Dudarev, the Azov city Communist Party boss, from trusted apparatchik, surrounded in a photo from the early

1930s by the pride of Azov's female proletariat, to "enemy of the people" in 1937, when he was executed after a trial by a military tribunal during the worst of Stalin's purges. His spouse was also arrested (as the "wife of an enemy of the people") and a massive hunt for "Dudarevist Scum" was initiated ("We shall uproot the Dudarevist Scum!" shouted the headlines of an old front page from *Priazovskaya Pravda*), which turned up twenty-two "accomplices." The Dudarevist exhibit ends with the same photo doctored so that the "enemy" Dudarev disappeared, skillfully replaced by a flowing curtain.

More headlines from the local *Pravda* documented the purges as they swept through Azov's Communist Party elite. My eyes swam as I perused them: WE APPROVE OF AND WELCOME THE SENTENCE! THE HIGHEST MEASURE OF PUNISHMENT TO BETRAYERS OF THE MOTHERLAND! TRAITORS OF THE WORKING CLASS — TO EXECUTION! VIGILANCE, VIGILANCE, AND STILL MORE VIGILANCE! A DOG'S DEATH TO DOGS! LET US UNITE MORE FIRMLY AROUND THE PARTY AND OUR BELOVED COMRADE STALIN! Another, heading a full-page, multi-column diatribe in eye-splitting tiny script, read OUR TASKS IN THE STRUGGLE WITH TROTSKYITES, WRECKERS, DIVERSIONISTS, AND SPIES. Another declared: THE SENTENCE OF THE PEOPLE HAS BEEN CARRIED OUT, heading an article describing how a "vile criminal band of fascist no-accounts . . . wanted to destroy socialism, take factories away from the workers, rob [workers] of their free life, place around their necks the yoke of oppression and exploitation . . . and drown in blood all the achievements of the Soviet people, reestablishing the rule of the whip and cage."

Sunny Azov, wafted over by sea breezes, saw as many vicious, senseless purges as any grim, snowy Russian city to the north. This was hard to fathom and appreciate, and was, it seemed, alien to the slow-paced southern way of life of the people there, but in all the museums I had seen throughout Russia, I had seen not a single exhibit on the purges elsewhere. When I asked the museum staff about this in other places, I invariably got a guarded response such as "Purges? Oh, yes, there were purges. But that is past now, and we are no longer interested in them." The past cannot be past as long as former Communists still reign across Russia through an impenetrable bureaucracy and network of nepotism and Soviet-era connections.

TWENTY

Ukraine:
Unlawful Entry, Uncanny Exit

Flies were buzzing around the meat pies an old woman was selling on the station platform. Her face was gnarled, and her toes hung raggedly over the edges of her sandals. *"Chebureki!"* she called out, rattling her tray. *"Chebureki!"*

I was waiting for the train to Kiev. People began to stream out of the underpass onto the platform, dragging cardboard boxes they had bound with twine, carts loaded with burlap sacks, shoddy little wooden crates; some were towing children by the hand and even dogs on makeshift leashes. The sun baked, the heat whirred. A suspense built. Train arrivals in Russia always wreak havoc with your nerves; you try to guess where your car will stop, how many minutes it will stand at the platform, and whether you and your baggage will survive the crush and rush of boarding. After that follow ten or twelve hours, if not twenty-four hours or even two or three days, of sitting and languishing and drinking tea and looking out the window at flat land and mud roads and mist.

The intercom blared the arrival of the Adler-Kiev Express. Passengers crept up to the platform's edge as if it were a starting line. *"Chebureki! Chebureki!"* A fly sipped at my sweat. Then a resonant *honk* from the green-and-blue diesel emerging from around the bend of freight cars. Passengers shifted string bags and cart handles from hand to hand, edging toward the white line. The train pulled up screeching, straining, rattling to slow down, and, as it did, women and men with thinning gray hair and boxes and tattered suitcases and sticks of sausage were throwing themselves toward the metal steps under car doors. The *chebureki* woman got caught in the stampede and clutched her tray. She cried out and slapped at the jostling bodies. Passengers grabbed at moving door handles, and *chebureki* scattered to the concrete and got trampled. She stepped back and let the wave roll by, picked up her plastic bag, and waddled away.

I burst into my compartment ahead of all the others, carried aloft onto the train first by the torrent of passengers, a young man with permed hair and clear blue eyes washed up beside me. We both sighed with relief once we hit the dry ground of our compartment. A languid woman in her forties, with a sharp nose, peered in and asked if seat number three was with us; it was.

We introduced ourselves. Both Ray and Nastya were headed to Kiev. I sat back in my seat, content with my travelmates.

I took up my book, Ray rummaged in his bag for something, and Nastya tugged her legs up under herself and reclined on the seat arm. We smiled at each other.

A clinking of bottles, then a grunt and a throaty cough from the corridor.

"Hey, brother!" croaked a voice. "Be a sport and help me drag this bag into my compartment. I'm an invalid, got it?"

A shuffling sounded outside our compartment. Bottles rattled. The conductor, a slovenly fellow whose belly extended in a loop well past his belt, passed our door and shouted back at the voice.

"Help yourself! I'm working!"

In stumbled a wiry man reeking of sweat, with thick hands and a dull brow, pushing a three-foot-wide sack and trying to kick along beside himself two smaller cardboard boxes. He was all boxes and bottles and sweat and snorts. When he passed our threshold, he tossed a handful of gritty sunflower seeds onto the little table between Ray and me.

"Help yourselves! Ha ha!"

He belched once, held his breath suspensefully, raised his forefinger like a conductor's baton, and belched again.

"Ahh! So, who will help me put this sack of beer and vodka under the seat? I'm an invalid, got that?"

Ray, Nastya, and I glanced at each other. Twenty-four hours of reading, pleasant conversation, and watching Ukraine go by the window had evaporated in belches.

"I *said,* who will help me, an invalid from the Afghan war, put these bottles under the seat?!"

We sat still. The conductor dropped in, hearing the drunk's raised voice.

"Show me your ticket!"

"I'll be happy to, but there's a bottle of beer in it for you if you help me get settled here."

"Ah. Certainly."

The two took to shoving the sack this way and that until it was under the seat. They sat down next to me.

"I want your passport and your place of work and an address," said the conductor, wiping his brow with his sleeve. *This drunk is going to cause trouble,* the request for all this extra information meant. Ray and Nastya and I exchanged glances again.

"Ah, my passport? Don't have it, damn my luck. But here's my ticket. And one of these comrades here is going to have to switch places with me, 'cause I have an upper bunk, but 'cause I'm so drunk, I'll fall off of it during the night. I need this here lower bunk!" he said, thumping his fist on my seat.

"Can't help you there," said the conductor, after taking his ticket. "You arrange that with one of them. Where's that bottle of beer you promised?"

The drunk introduced himself as Sergei. His eyes were moist and veiny, his voice guttural from booze, his mustache studded with slivers of unidentifiable dried food. He wore stained blue jeans and a T-shirt and looked to be about forty, though his arms were muscled and his stomach tight.

"So," he said rubbing his hands together, "I've introduced myself. Let's hear from you all! Ha! If there's anything to tell!"

Ray stared at his book fervently, as did I mine. Nastya looked out the window. Sergei asked my name.

"Dzh . . . Dzh—what kind of name is that for a man?"

I studied my book.

"Let me call you by a real man's name, like Yuri or Sasha. Your name is not a name for a real *muzhik*."

Sergei jabbed Ray's knee with his forefinger and leaned into his face.

"You, what's your name?"

Ray winced.

"Ray."

"R . . . R . . . R—what? What the hell kind of name is that?"

Sergei stared at him and stealthily reached into his sack for a bottle of warm beer, as though he were drawing a weapon on a foe.

"Well, answer me!" he said, wiping the scum off his bottle with a flap of shirt.

"I'm Jewish," said Ray.

"Jeeewish?" he mocked, drawing the word out and taking a slug of beer. "*Now* I see. Now I see. And you, woman, what's your name?"

Nastya, in a heavy Ukrainian accent, said she would like to be left alone.

"Oh, just my luck! Riding all the way to Kiev with a Jew, a guy with a funny name, and a *khokhlushka* [slang for "Ukrainian woman"]!" He turned to me again. "I still want to know why you have such a funny name. Like I said, it's not a man's name. I—"

Ray cut in.

"Shut up."

"I . . . What? Oh, the Jew is telling me, a Volga German, to shut up? I like that!" He grabbed the strap hanging from the upper bunk and hoisted himself into the air, upended his beer and drained it with three or four spasmodic swallows, then tossed his empty into the hallway, and pulled another out of his sack. He popped it open with his teeth, squirting himself and Ray in the process. "I like that! Anyway, one of you is going to switch seats with me—you decide while I'm in the john."

He stumbled to the door and disappeared down the hall toward the bathroom. Ray looked at me; he had never asked me where I was from or even if I was foreign, but I took it that he understood and was too tactful to pry.

"Just ignore him. He'll go away," Ray said.

"Aren't you upset? He's attacked your religion, hasn't he?"

"I pay no attention to people like him. They don't deserve it. He's just a drunk. You know, before, when we had socialism, types like him would have been thrown off the train. There was a law against appearing in public in a state that 'insults human dignity' and they'd be arrested. Now, we have *bezvlastye* [anarchy, an absence of state power or authority]. You think it's just at the top with our rulers? No, it's everywhere, from the bottom up. This is typical for Russians. I'm Jewish. You know we are sensitive to this, because *bezvlastye* in Russia means anarchy, and anarchy means violence, and violence means pogroms. We go from totalitarianism to *bezvlastye* and back. It won't be different this time, I'm telling you. Russians are anarchists. They need force to restrain them, real power. This is all very, very sad."

Nastya looked at her feet.

"Don't make any concessions to him, Ray," she said. "It's so aggravating that drunks always end up running the show. I don't think we need an iron fist, we need to drink less."

We were coasting through lush wheat fields and deep, umbral forests, the last before the Russian-Ukrainian border. It was hot in the compartment, and the odor of Sergei's sweat and beer breath lingered around us and stuck to our skins.

An hour later, he returned in a jovial humor out of sync with the bad vibes he had left us with. He wanted something.

"So, you with the funny name—I'm switching with you, right? You've got the lower bunk?" He drew a vodka bottle from his bag and plunked it on the table.

"I'm staying where I am."

"Oh, we're going to be that way, are we? Here, let's drink this vodka. We can forget our troubles together."

"No, thanks. I'm staying where I am."

"Jew, make him switch!"

Ray kept his eyes on his book.

"Okay, let me tell you all my story," he said, waxing familiar, his eyes wandering this way and that over our faces, searching for a smidgen of interest. "I used to drift around Russia with Azeris and Chechens planting potatoes. Seasonal work. As if that didn't exist in the Soviet Union! Of course it did! Unofficially. I saw all of western Russia through freight car slats. And on our way out of town, the Chechens would knock over the local store. For spending money. Good guys, they were!"

He heaved the bottle to his lips and gurgled vodka.

"You're going to think I'm a crook," he slurred, addressing no one in particular. "But look, I'm the purest family man. I give all my money to the wife and my two daughters. I do it all for them. Principle and principle alone guides me."

He gurgled more booze and leaned on his knee, drawing his watery eyes into a critical squint.

"You, Jew, probably don't like Poles. Because of what they feel about your race. But this Polish guy I know gave me a shiny card—when you held it one way to the light, it showed a flower vase. When you turned it sideways, the flowers turned into a naked lady!" He laughed and took another swig of vodka. "You won't find those cards anywhere but in Poland, and I plan on going there soon. Poland's a country for men."

"Shut up," I said, putting down my book. I couldn't stand his idiotic ramblings another second.

"I'll do better than that! I'll find a bunk in another compartment! You're all abnormal! You're all psychotics!"

He threw himself into the hallway and slammed his shoulder into the curtain rod, snatched at it as it dropped to the floor, and stumbled away.

After a long, sweltering stop in Taganrog on the Sea of Azov, we arrived at the Ukrainian border town of Lisvaiska, pulling in to a platform where only hunchbacked Ukrainian grandmas stood in the heat with plastic sacks of *pirozhki*. I bought a couple and strolled about on the deck, wondering when the passport check would begin. Flower buds and moist foliage scented the air; we were on the threshold of fertile, black-earth Ukraine, one of Europe's breadbaskets.

Our diesel honked and drew the cars into motion. I jumped aboard. Would there be a passport check? There had been, said the conductor, but as he had no foreigners aboard he waved the guards through.

"What about me? I'm a foreigner!"

"You didn't tell me!"

"You saw my passport, didn't you?"

"Oh, that's right. You'll have a problem now. We're not supposed to allow non-Soviets across the border without visas. You're illegal."

"Thanks for reminding me. How can I get a visa now?"

"Probably you can't, since you're in the country already. This is a problem."

I fretted a moment then decided to forget about it until Kiev. There was nothing I could do until then.

At dawn we pulled into rainy Kiev. In the haze of sleep I grabbed my bag and stumbled down to the platform. Tall, navy blue-suited policemen were making the morning roundup of drunks, *bomzhy,* and wild-eyed derelicts, pushing them ahead with their batons and shouting "March!" I took the metro out to Darnitsa, then the bus the last couple of miles to Oleg and Valya's apartment. They were friends of mine from years ago—both had thought my idea of a trip across Russia was a bad one and told me so bluntly before I began in Moscow. Now, arriving at their apartment, I felt as if I'd come home safe and sound.

Valya opened the door and peeked through the chain.

It was seven in the morning. Valya was graceful in her black kimono, her blond hair flowing off its silken shoulders and down her back. Oleg sat up, still in his underwear on the couch. Ever ready to leap into a political discussion, before he had even wiped the sleep from his eyes, he scratched at his beard and shook my hand.

"It amazes me that you made it! Across all of Russia—the most criminal country on earth! Now you've seen enough to let the entire world know what the true meaning of communism and the 1917 revolution is."

Maybe I had, but the first thing I wanted to do was square away my visa problem. Oleg and Valya thought it best that I call on the good offices of the Peace Corps in Kiev. Yuri got dressed, preening before the mirror for some time, and said he'd go with me down to the office on Pushkinskaya Street. We jumped on the tram.

"A country worse than the Ukraine you will not find here in the former USSR. Every month prices double and our currency devalues. This is the one place on earth where people are happy to see Russian rubles. That's how bad off we are."

Ukraine's economy was in a free fall. Since the dissolution of the Soviet Union and Ukrainian independence, things had changed very little or gotten worse. If Russia was in the throes of a huge campaign to privatize state industries and Yeltsin was leading reforms, however falteringly, Ukraine would have nothing of it and even seemed to be slipping backward. Industry remained state-owned; agriculture was still in the grips of wheezing inefficient state collective farms (the same was true in Russia as well, but Yeltsin's camp had been trying to push through a decree that would make the sale of land legal). But none of these problems was discernible on the surface.

"Oleg, I have to tell you, this may all be true, but Kiev looks so well manicured in comparison with Russian cities. It's almost like Western Europe."

"I am Russian, but I'm not afraid to say it: Russians are terrible landlords. They let bums piss anywhere. They let drunks rule the streets. Here, you will see that the Ukrainians are good housekeepers. They take care of themselves and their land and city. But what difference does it make, really? Our economy is far worse off than Russia's. It's a struggle to survive. I was fired from my job in machine repair and can't find work. What could I find? I refuse to play the game. I won't compromise."

"In what way?"

"I'm talking about cooperating with the Mafia or keeping my mouth shut around Communists. You have seen how it is in Russia: the Bolsheviks still run everything in the provinces. In Ukraine, we still suffer the same cursed KGB thugs right here in the capital. They are running everything, and running us into the ground."

We disembarked on Kiev's main shopping street, Khreshchatik, and began walking up toward the Peace Corps office. Khreshchatik was orderly and busy, though the kiosks were scarce and ill stocked by comparison with those in Russia. Still, the avenue had a sleek European feel.

"I'm telling you, I wonder how we will get by. Things are getting so bad, soon even sausage will be a rarity on our table. And I'm not able to keep my mouth shut about it either, and never have been."

This was true. Oleg and I first met in 1985 during my tour of the western Soviet Union. He wore his hair long and hippie-style, drank a lot, got quite belligerent about Communists, and told me that if I had caught him on a good night I'd have seen him shouting antigovernment slogans out the window. In the late 1970s his sister and brother-in-law had emigrated from the Soviet Union to the States, but he and Valya, for whatever reasons, had not taken that step. He regretted it, but said he was now too old for the change.

"The KGB has a file on me this thick," he said as we turned up Pushkinskaya Street, holding apart his thumb and forefinger. "They tried to blackmail me and my mother, calling her down to the station and telling her they would arrest me if I didn't shut up. I said the hell with them. When this happened I decided to be even more vocal and critical. I wanted things public. They left me alone after that."

At the Peace Corps office, I explained to a man named Vlad that I needed a visa before heading for Lvov, my last stop before Poland.

Vlad's smile was steely, his eyes cold like those of a python. Instinct told me I should be on my guard.

"Visa problem? No, this cannot be, cannot be in our country! I'm sure you will have *nooo* problems whatsoever; just explain your problem to them."

Oleg and I exchanged glances. Vlad caught this and turned to Oleg.

"And you, if I may ask, are doing *what* here with this American?" His voice deepened, turning almost gravelly, his eyes wandered over Oleg like a predator sizing up his prey.

I explained that Oleg was a friend of mine. Vlad took my arm and led me away.

"Be careful of people here." He gave my arm a conspiratorial squeeze and dipped into a back room.

"He's KGB," said Oleg in a low tone.

Vlad emerged from his office and told me he had "set me up" in Lvov at a volunteer's apartment.

"There is no problem," he said. "I am a former employee of Intourist and I was also a border guard—I can tell you, you will simply arrive at the frontier and explain truthfully what has happened. They will smile and wave you through."

I didn't believe him. Nothing was ever so easy here.

That evening, while Oleg was off visiting friends, Valya cooked dinner for me.

Valya worked as a manager in a plant that supplied Ukrainian industries with piping. She was poised and well spoken, and didn't share Oleg's delight in political tirades.

I asked her if life was difficult.

"I try to remain above the humiliations life forces on us here. I refuse to wait in lines, for example. If I need something in a store with a line, I'll skip it. I don't want to complain, though life here has become unbearable since independence. I'm getting involved in business myself, doing some trading and dealing. This is my own perestroika. It will not be easy, but I will not sit around and gripe."

"How do you and Oleg make ends meet on your salary alone?"

"Oh, this is a problem. At times I don't eat breakfast. Other times I sacrifice in other ways. But this is typical of the men here— they ride on the backs of the women. Oleg will not look for a job. He's given up."

"How long has it been?"

"Give or take a month or two, he's been out of work four years now."

A look of shock must have registered on my face.

Rain splattered in puddles glinting with yellow from streetlamps and formed rivulets rushing through the cobblestones. Lvov was still asleep, drifting by my train window in a funereal hush. We drew into the station. Water dripped from car roofs and spattered in sonorous drops in the echoing, four-thirty-in-the-morning silence.

Inside the station, people huddled in long sullen lines around ticket windows, mothers snored over their children and scattered luggage in the pews, *bomzhy* loitered around the entrance. It took me the better part of an hour to find out that trains west to War-saw were tough to get tickets for and creaked along for an ago-nizing fifteen to twenty hours to cover a distance of only three hundred miles. It seemed better to leave the question of how I would get to Poland until the next day.

Nothing had been resolved with my visa while I was in Kiev, and without one, I knew it would be difficult to get a hotel room. So, after inquiring about train schedules, I caught a cab uptown in the drizzle to Naukova Street, where I was supposed to find a Peace Corps volunteer's empty apartment waiting for me. But the key, for whatever reason, would not fit in the lock. I walked out into the alley and thought about what I'd do next.

Not a taxi was in sight. But the rain had stopped, leaving be-hind a fog that felt like steam on my face. I wandered out to the main street past Naukova and saw a jumble of cement blocks and crooked glass that could only be a hotel.

"Well, a representative from Mr. President Boosh! We have a room for you that you will never want to leave!"

The wiry little man grabbed at my elbow and tried to jerk the bag out of my hand. I ignored him and walked over to the recep-tion. It was deserted.

"You would like a room, I take it?" he oozed, his smile stretch-ing in ear-to-ear unction.

I looked at him. Such parasitic shysters are to be found the world over in transit points and fleabag hotels. He was a doorman by trade, but his true profession was extracting their last tattered rubles from the unwary departing the former Soviet Union. And like his fellow hucksters, he dressed the part: his suit was too tight under the arms, his pants too high above his ankles; he looked disreputable. He fawned about me, picking lint off my shirt and standing too close, bathing me with his breath and drawing me into the pores on his nose.

"You want a room, of course. You are in the right place. We have rooms at the international standard and I will select the best, and only the best for you, Meester American! Hee-hee-heeee!"

"Where is the receptionist? Is there anyone here at all?" I said.

He straightened up and struck a mien of indignation, slapping the desk with his hand.

"Natasha! Natasha! Get out here at once! We have an important guest from the country of Boosh!"

He smiled and stood too close to me again. A woman with disheveled hair padded out of the back room in fluffy slippers and yawned at me.

"Assign the best room to this American from the U.S.A.!" he barked.

She looked at my passport and shook her head.

"You are here illegally. You have no Ukrainian visa. I can't give you a room."

She slapped my passport down in front of me and rubbed her eyes. The little man faded away from me as though I were a leper, frowning exaggeratedly and mumbling *nelegalno* [illegal] as though he were ashamed of me.

"Listen, it was a mistake," I said. "At the border, the guards didn't check my cabin. I only want to stay a few nights anyway."

"I'm sorry. You are illegal. I'd get into trouble if I gave you a room. You must go to the airport and apply for an emergency visa. Then I'll check you in."

The little man shouted to the other doorman on the couch, a drowsy old codger with a high crop of white hair.

"Get up, Leonid! Emergency! Emergency! We have to get this illegal American to the airport at once!"

He yanked at my sleeve and cast furtive glances in all directions, as though fearful for my safety. The old codger made a phone call and motioned to me to step outside. The little man grabbed at my bag.

"I'll carry it!" I said.

"Nonsense! Emergency! Emergency!"

He wrested it free of me and dragged it across the lot, raising a trail of dust and sending pebbles rolling all around.

A white Toyota Mark II with dark tinted windows skidded to a halt in front of the hotel, showering us with gravel. All these histrionics looked well thought out. I had a feeling I was going to be fleeced a hefty sum.

"Emergency! Emergency!" cried my escort as he struggled to hoist my bag into the trunk. The cabbie, a fat man with short greasy hair and a gold tooth, jumped out.

"Emergency man" extended his palm.

I handed him a dollar to be rid of him. He backed away, bowing and chortling. The cabbie and I set a price and were off.

Roman, as he was called, kept up a steady blather, waves of mixed Ukrainian and Russian spilling out of him in effusive babble. At my every response, he shouted *"pravilno!"* (correct) and thumped his forearm on the wheel.

"I want to keep my hide in one piece . . . this place is all Mafia . . . the racket is on every corner . . . all these transit businessmen . . . all these Poles and Czechs and Russians . . . I risk my life every day just going out my door . . . everyone is on the take and anything is for sale."

We shot through skeins of fog that parted only to disclose cement blocks and ghosts of cars, and screeched into the airport lot. Roman leapt out and opened the door for me, waving me inside and up the stairs to a room with a closed door marked KPP, in front of which stood twenty to twenty-five blank-faced sleepy people leaning on each other.

"They'll give you a visa," he winked. "I'll wait down here." He scurried away.

I got in line. Roman scuttled back to me, his white socks peeping from under his highwater trousers.

"Don't wait in line!" he whispered. "You're not one of them!"

He dragged me up the stairs, pushing people out of the way right and left. He pounded on the door and hurried away again, as though he were a little boy playing a prank on a neighbor, leaving me there alone.

The door opened. A guard in a green uniform.

"*Da?*"

"I need a visa. The Hotel Sputnik has called about me."

"Get in line," he said, and shut the door.

I did. Within seconds Roman was at my side again whispering.

"No, no, no! Go on back! You didn't offer him any money— of course he didn't listen!"

Roman tugged at me and dragged me up the stairs again, pounded on the door and ran away.

The same guard reappeared.

"*Da?* You again. What do you want?"

"Listen," I said, searching for words and trying to look slick. "I'm in urgent need of a visa. Urgent, if you know what I mean."

He looked at me for a moment and opened the door wide, stepping aside.

"I can't get a hotel room without a visa . . . a mistake at the border . . . will only be here a few days . . ." I recapped my story, adding, "I will pay you what you like, but I need a visa now."

"Have a seat. You will pay the official rate for your visa, no more," he said politely. "Please sit and wait for our boss. Only he can issue it."

I dozed in front of the television in their office. The Road Runner honked and raced over a cliff, hung motionless, and dropped to the canyon floor with a puff of dust. The border guards laughed, but remembered themselves in front of me and straightened up. At eight-thirty, the boss arrived and, with no ceremony, issued me an "emergency" visa for a fee of fifty dollars, which was not a bribe—he gave me a receipt. And so Vlad had been right. It was "no problem."

Roman was snoozing in the car, his head thrown back over the seat and his Adam's apple rising and falling. I tapped on the windshield and he coughed himself awake. We drove off toward the hotel.

"You still set on this hotel?"

"Where else is there?"

"My place. Real Ukrainian hospitality."

I didn't like the sound of that, for some reason.

"Of course, I'd take only five bucks a night, not fifteen, like the hotel. And of course, you could toss the wife another five or so for food."

"Thanks. I'll stick to the Sputnik."

"Pravilno!" he chanted back. "Why risk it? I'm honest, but you don't know me from Adam! Say, you on your way in or out of the Soviet Union?"

"Out."

"Pravilno! Who needs this rat hole! It's hell here. Do your business and get out. Nothing to hang around for. By train, plane?"

"I thought I might hitch. To the border, at least. From there I'll get a train or bus to Warsaw."

"Prrrravilno! Hitch! I provide that service!"

I laughed.

"How much will it cost me to ride to the border?"

We settled on twenty dollars, not a bad price considering it was an hour west of town.

"Once you cross over, there are fleets of buses and trains leaving around the clock for all of Europe! You'll be in Warsaw within an hour or two."

Doubtful, I thought, but it didn't matter. I had a couple of days ahead of me to enjoy Lvov.

Stalin chiseled Lvov off Poland right before World War II and quickly Sovietized it, sending away the Poles and attaching it to the Ukrainian Soviet Socialist Republic. It was, at various times throughout its long history, Polish, Russian, Austro-Hungarian, and Ukrainian. The current flavor happens to be Ukrainian—indeed, Lvov is a bastion of western Ukrainian nationalism. There was a lot going on in its streets—poets giving recitals, people shouting to crowds through microphones about Chernobyl, others mobilizing political parties, but it was all in Ukrainian and I understood little. When I spoke Russian to people, they frowned and responded in Ukrainian.

Lvov's old town is huge, dating from the sixteenth century, for the most part, and full of baroque mansions, Gothic towers, Renaissance houses, and Catholic churches, as well as Orthodox cathedrals for Russians, Greeks, and Armenian segments of its population. It looks as Polish as it does German, and as Ukrainian as it does Polish, and, more than any other place in the former Soviet Union, has retained its historical contours and fine patina of age—Stalin had no time to destroy all its churches, and it was not bombed to smithereens by the Nazis. Its traditional cafés and restaurants bear family names (instead of the usual city names or other bland appellations such as "Volga," "Russia," or "Victory"), and the whole place has a human, European feel, instead of the depersonalized Soviet overlay of grit and cement. At the town's museum, though, the old Soviet line on history is still thoroughly preserved, with the Ukrainian national figure, Bohdan Khmelnytsky, celebrated for uniting Ukraine with Russia in the 1650s, officially canonized as the national hero.

My alarm beeped and beeped and beeped. Roman was due in an hour. It was six in the morning, but the room was hot with the breaking day.

At seven, he inched up to the head of the lot, fearful lest the doorman should see him and demand a cut of what he was getting from me. But the doorman was asleep and I slipped out unnoticed.

I asked him about his Toyota and how he came by it.

"No, this car was not easy to come by, no, sir! I had to work ten years for it!"

It was right-hand drive. It could only have been imported through Vladivostok in the Far East, where Japanese cars were the rage.

"*Pravilno!* You guessed it! I earned ten thousand rubles—a fortune until the Soviet Union collapsed—working out east, in a place in Siberia you'd never know."

"Where?"

"Tynda. A real hellhole. Not even a road, and all gloomy larches and muck. They paid us extra on account of the muck. A real hellhole."

I remembered Tynda well and told him how I had been there and what I'd seen. He was ecstatic, grabbing me by the arm and asking all about it and how I happened to end up there. If it was a mucky hellhole, it was one he had learned to love. I summarized my trip for him.

"You don't say! No one has done that sort of thing. Not even us Soviets would do it. Well, like I was saying, I bought the car out east, then shipped it by rail here. You wouldn't catch me dead trying to cross this country of ours. It's too big, too dangerous."

We flew through rolling hills of lush green, forest and field and hill and dale, with Roman telling me of his years in Siberia. He'd been in the army then; he had a homeland; he wanted for nothing. At times he got so wrapped up in his story, he passed where he shouldn't have and nearly drove us head-on into approaching cars, but this didn't fluster me. It no longer mattered; nothing, it seemed could go wrong now. I was a few hours from Warsaw, from the end of an 8,325-mile odyssey. My spirit was light and frisky.

An hour on, a police checkpoint arose. Roman slowed. The two officers looked in and waved us through.

"Look," he said, dropping his voice to a low tone of some gravity, "these guys, these border patrol fellows, they're used to people with hefty wallets, you see. Once you're at the border, you're so close, yet so far. Got it?"

"What are you saying? That I have to bribe them?"

"Exactly! Or you'll be there for days!"

I didn't believe him. He was wrong before; he would be wrong again. He just loved to talk and paint vivid scenes of corruption only his intrigues could solve.

"So, you pass each one ten bucks, then you're through in ten minutes. Ten bucks—ten minutes. Remember."

We drew up to the border and slowed. It was a fenced-off complex of white buildings and swing gates. There were only four cars ahead of us. Roman jumped out.

"Any one of these cars will be happy to take you across."

He ran in quick ministeps to the first car, a Lada with two sleeping Ukrainians in it, and tapped on their window and asked them to take me. No. After looking at me and shrugging his shoulders, he walked down to the next vehicle, a station wagon crammed with luggage.

"Where would we put him?" they mimed through the glass, and shook their heads. No.

The third couple he approached seemed not to understand Ukrainian. Roman waved me over.

"They'll take you! Good-bye!"

We shook hands. Of course they hadn't agreed, but what was Roman going to do for me now? Maybe he was even repelling rides—the sight of this agitated man with a gold tooth and greasy hair would probably set everyone's nerves on edge at a border, a zone of dangers and murky intrigues and contraband.

Inside the third car was a young couple: a bearded, sandy-haired man and a striking young woman with brilliant blond hair and bronze skin. When I knocked and asked for a ride, the man, in thickly accented Russian, asked, "You are Russian?" He looked as though he were about to refuse.

"American."

The girl pulled on a sweater and hopped out and cleared me a space in the backseat. Her Russian was native.

"Welcome! Have a seat!"

Tomasz was from a town just inside Poland, but lived and

worked in Odessa with his beautiful wife, Oksana. As soon as we finished introductions, the guards ahead of us waved at us with their batons. We drove into the border complex and pulled up to the inspection booth, which sat under an overhanging roof and looked like a gas station.

Tomasz and Oksana began smiling nervously, but I was done with nervousness. These guards had a lot of power, but within minutes I would be free of it, and safely across the border into Poland.

A guard took their passports and leered at Oksana.

"This your wife?"

"Yes, sir. My wife," answered Tomasz.

"Not according to your passport. You have different last names!"

A haw-haw from all three. Tomasz stroked his beard and shrugged; Oksana smiled sweetly to no one in particular. The guard said *ladno,* stamped their passports, and motioned them to get back in the car.

I handed him mine. He took it and flicked at the loosened plastic lamination around my picture, and looked up at me and back again at the passport.

"State your name."

With as much of an American accent as I could muster, I did. He called over his partner, and they drew shut the little window.

He and the partner picked at the lamination and gently peeled it back, trying to see if, in fact, I had tampered with it and replaced the photo inside, if I weren't someone else. The partner asked me my name and I repeated it.

"Sign this!" he said, shoving a little paper at me through the window. Tomasz and Oksana looked at me from the car. What was wrong?

I signed and handed them the paper, and they compared it to the signature on my passport. With a heavy metallic *thud-clink,* they stamped my passport and waved me through.

I was out of Ukraine, with more than eight thousand miles on the road across the former Soviet Union behind me. It was hard to comprehend; at first, I dared not believe it, or think about it. My trip was over, and with it, an era of anguish and discovery and fascination I felt I could never relive or equal.

We hugged the white line, ascending and descending the manicured hills of southern Poland until we hit Ivanicz Zdruj, Tomasz's hometown. There we had lunch. Alas, as I had suspected, there were no taxis or buses at the border; there was no transportation at all, in fact. Tomasz and Oksana showed me Ivanicz Zdruj for the afternoon, then drove me to Sanok and put me on the all-night train to Warsaw. We just made it, and our good-bye was brief but warm by the sleeping car.

The train was cold and plush. I was alone in my compartment. The conductor checked my ticket and grinned, and brought me a cola, in that very polite style the Poles have of doing almost anything.

"Prosze bardzo!" she said, and retreated, drawing my door shut for the night.

The rails clacked rhythmically. Drifting by my window were tailored fields, Polish village houses with their manicured facades and gardens, and the sky of Europe, no longer threatening to swoop down on those below as in Russia, but sheltering, even nurturing, bringing rain for crops and softening the sun. I felt at home. I closed my eyes and fell into a deep, dreamless sleep.

TWENTY-ONE

Return to Moscow

In Russia, church domes are covered with pure gold
So that God might notice them more often.

VLADIMIR VYSOTSKY, RUSSIAN BARD

"Yeltsin has just imposed a state of emergency," said Betsy, taking my coat in her doorway. It was October 3, 1993. I had been back in Moscow since the end of July. "You should see what's going on down by the Parliament. Watch it on CNN with Marla while I make dinner."

I walked into the TV room and sat down next to Marla, a young lawyer from Colorado working in Kiev. She had stopped in Moscow to visit and ended up riveted to the television watching a revolution.

"The Khasbulatov and Rutskoi forces have broken through the police barriers around the White House and are marching on the

Russian state television station. This is incredible! I wish I could go see it! We're so close!"

I thought about this. Sasha walked in, wringing his hands and shaking his head. He looked all charged up.

"Jeff," he said, "try to convince her not to go. She's been saying that all afternoon. Tell her she's crazy. I've been in Afghanistan and can tell you what a stray bullet can do."

I turned to Marla.

"What do you think? Do you really want to go down there?"

Betsy came in.

"Don't even think of it, at least not until you've eaten. Dinner's on."

Within an hour, we were riding the metro into the center of the revolt.

At Pushkin Square, where we emerged from the underground, not only was there no fighting, Muscovites were strolling around as though the uprising were happening in some distant land, not a few blocks away at their own Parliament. A few paces farther up, on Tverskaya Street, a certain electricity charged the air; there, people were stepping briskly, chattering in animated tones, and even laughing. Still, there was no hint of danger.

We walked down Tverskaya toward the Kremlin, all redbrick ramparts and citadel grandeur rising above traffic on the busy street like a floodlit backdrop on a huge stage. The air was bracing, sirens wailed in distant quarters of the city. At the Moscow City Council building a crowd had gathered, obstructing traffic where it spilled into the street.

"Citizens, we call on you to remain calm and maintain order!" shouted a man perched on a lamppost through a microphone. "The mutineers are forming an armed brigade to take the Moscow City Council. We call on all those who want to save democracy to stay here and defend it. Remain calm, please, and maintain order!"

No one appeared to be on the verge of breaking into a panic or inclined to sow disorder. Those gathered there looked cheerful; a few had Russian flags; others were unfolding pro-Yeltsin banners.

"They are so young!" said Marla. "Look at their faces!"

They *were* young—most must have been under forty. In contrast, the "defenders of the Parliament" that I had seen on the barricades were, on average, some fifteen to twenty years older. The uprising had a generational aspect that had everything to do with upbringing: those who were sixty had lived through the Stalin era and were inculcated with its ideals (as much as they may have later renounced them). Those who were thirty grew up during the stagnation under Brezhnev, reaching maturity with Gorbachev and glastnost and perestroika.

Red Square was dark and quiet. We had expected to see troops there setting up to defend the Kremlin (Khasbulatov had earlier declared he would storm it), but there were none, although soldiers with automatic rifles lurked high above on the citadel walls. By the main entrance to the Kremlin on the square, an argument was raging amidst a crowd of people. We walked up to see what it was about.

"How can you say that?" shouted one man in a ski cap to another, his arms spread wide in indignation. "Are you a patriot or not?"

"I'm as patriotic as you are. But I have every right to distribute these Catholic Bibles here if I want to!"

"You forget that Russia is Orthodox! We have our own translation of the Bible! That is what you should be giving people if you believe in your country!"

Across the square, by the entrance to the department store, GUM, on Nikolskaya Street, flashlight beams darted in the darkness and there was shouting and a dragging of metallic debris, as well as the hiss of wooden boards being hauled across asphalt. Some fifteen young Russians were throwing up a barricade.

"Defend Yeltsin! Defend the Kremlin!" shouted one man to

himself. Ahead of us, down Nikolskaya, youths ran about, some with beer bottles in hand, looking for junk to add to the pile. "Where is the army? Where are our troops?" shouted another.

We hopped back on the metro and headed over to Smolensk station, the closest stop to the Parliament.

Shards of glass littered the pavement on Smolensk Square. There was a faint smell of ash in the air, as of fires extinguished hours ago. Unlike Pushkin Square, this area was deserted, except for a few drunks and an occasional hurried citizen, rushing home holding his hat and staring at the ground ahead of him.

We walked on. Toward the American embassy, the street lights diminished, then disappeared. No cars, no people. Only a resonating darkness and the broad deserted avenue and a scent of ash.

At the head of Devyatinsky Street, where the embassy is located and which abuts the besieged Parliament, two policemen in heavy gray overcoats glanced at us as we approached the corner and turned away. We walked on.

Down dark Devyatinsky. A drunk lurched at us, mumbling threats to himself, and veered away toward the wall. Marla took my arm. At the street's base, where Yeltsin's forces had once sealed off the Parliament and been overrun, stood three or four grizzled, middle-aged men with bulky automatic weapons and metallic shields wrested earlier in the day from policemen. They loitered by a barricade of trash and sheet metal and strands of wire.

One stepped into our path as we approached.

"State your purpose!"

I hadn't thought of one, so I said the first thing that came to mind.

"We have none. Our way home leads through here. That's all."

"Let them pass," said another.

"Pass!"

Beyond, across the empty lots and streets in front of and around the Parliament, little fires burned—tires, scraps of wood, paper—over which stood sentry ragtag clusters of men and women, nearly all over fifty, most dirty and dejected and wearing

Soviet-issue synthetic suits and formless shoes and bleak overcoats. They huddled and murmured to themselves, and vodka
bottles flashed between them. Above us, the Parliament loomed
eyeless, a dark stone monster. A man in a green parka gathered up
vodka bottles from the street and deposited them in neat piles by
a burned-out taxi, presumably to use in making incendiary de-
vices if need be. Applause resounded from one corner of the lot as
a captured militia car was driven up and added to the Parliamen-
tarians' rolling stock, which consisted of wrecked buses and a
couple of armored personnel carriers.

We walked around to the square in front of the Parliament.
There the air was thick with smoke from the fires, and a woman
burned incense as she prayed in silence under an array of icons.
Banners for the Communist Party along with Soviet flags stood
propped by the lampposts.

As we walked around the front of the building a man emerged
from the Parliament front door.

"Comrades! I have in my hands the keys to all the offices of the
mayor's building! It is ours now!"

A few applauded. Most stared. Some gulped vodka and wiped
their lips.

Farther down, a man shouted into a microphone, walking
about in semicircles with his arm raised.

"Comrades, President Rutskoi has authorized me to form an
armed unit to march on the Moscow City Council. We need
brigades of ten men apiece. Everyone who wants to take part in
this operation step forward."

He began shoving dazed-looking proletarians this way and
that, ordering "loafers" out of his zone of authority, repeating over
and over again that he was Rutskoi's deputy. Lines of ten formed.
They did not look like the rabid, vengeful fanatics we had seen
hours before on CNN. Some were not even sober; most shuffled
and dawdled in line, unsure of themselves and maybe about what
they were being asked to do.

We walked on, passing out into the street through barricades of burned-out buses and smashed trucks and barbed wire, loosely guarded by men with rifles and vodka bottles.

Where were the foreign journalists and CNN? we asked ourselves. And more important, what was Yeltsin going to do? How had this group of derelicts and drunks been able to do so much damage?

Early the next morning, tanks and troops arrived at the Parliament. I followed them down there a couple of hours later. It was a spectator's uprising, and thousands had shown up to crowd around the banks of the Moscow River in front of the Parliament building to watch the battle. Rounds of machine gun fire rattled continuously from all sides, but seemingly without ill result to the bystanders, though people raced this way and that when the gunfire seemed directed at them, and white-robed medics with stretchers rushed about picking up the wounded. Soldiers below, by the tanks, crouched and occasionally ran from one to another. The tanks themselves opened fire around nine-thirty, rending the air with concussive blasts and sending chunks of Parliament flying into space.

Around midday, a tank column roared down Smolensk Square and veered onto Novy Arbat Street. All of us in the crowd stopped and gawked. Another column trundled by, followed by armored personnel carriers and jeeps. The roar of the tanks deafened, and their passage stirred up thick dust. Yet on top of them sat teenagers swathed in puffy camouflage gear looking like Siberian schoolchildren bundled against the cold, red-cheeked and smiling. I stood watching them and tried to comprehend that some were sure to die by the end of the day. This thought grabbed me and dulled my perception of what was going on around me.

But not for long. From high above, on the Novy Arbat Street-Smolensk Square intersection, machine gun fire broke loose in rapid, sustained rounds. From the top two floors of the twenty-five-story office building, two gun barrels scanned the ground below, firing incessantly. Everyone around me dove to the ground, and several teenage girls thumped into me, knocking me into the wall. One laughed and shrieked in hysterics; another whimpered, "My God! My God! My God!"

We stayed crouched and huddled together for several minutes, feeling the reverberations of the weapon fire and occasionally being dusted with chips of concrete flying from the wall above us as bullets struck it. I thought of nothing: the gunfire paralyzed my mind and shot down my thoughts. In an eerie state of tranquillity, ready for anything, I waited for the shooting to stop.

Several minutes later, it did. We disentangled ourselves and began sprinting down the avenue, but a new round began and once again everyone hit the concrete. Within a minute, though, a massive barrage of army machine gun fire from below cut it short, and glass and concrete flew in shards from the windows on the top floors until they resembled cavities in a skull. When this exchange ended, Smolensk Square and Novy Arbat were quiet. I dusted myself off and walked back to the Moscow River to await the end of the siege. Dusk was coming on.

Epilogue

Five years have passed since I took that frigid Aeroflot flight to Magadan to start my journey across Russia. Since then, I have lived in Moscow. The changes that have taken place here have affected me personally. On the whole, life in the capital has become easier, and the streetfight passions evoked by the tumult of the early nineties have waned. It is now possible to enjoy being here without having to live on hopes of reform or reserves of love for Russian literature and history, and one may appreciate the charms of a great northern city, a city of lingering summer dusks and long winter nights, of Kremlin cathedrals and radiant central boulevards.

This is progress, but it has disconnected me from the Moscow I knew: the city of 1993, with its tension and dangers, has been built up, ordered, and glamorized by development projects, capital investment, and a settling in of the political forces.

Disconnections, in fact, have permeated my life since my return to Moscow and have extended to the friendships I began during my trip: Galina of Tomsk visited me twice, but eventually, differences arose between us (I resisted when she pressed me about converting to the evangelical brand of Christianity she had adopted). The flame between us dwindled and died; we have not seen each other since April 1994. Betsy and her children have returned to the States. Alexander of Magadan never replied to the letter of thanks I mailed to him. Sasha and Sergei of the Kolyma Route and Stal of Yakutsk did not give me addresses, and I now regret that I didn't ask them to do so; I don't know what became of them. Nevertheless, these people remain luminous in my memory and light up my inner life still.

There were other ruptures. In 1994–95, I comanaged a Russian-American security company with a Russian friend, one of the cleverest and most talented people I have ever known. He spent hours talking with me about my journey across his country (of which he had never seen more than a few western cities) and helped me to assimilate it. In 1996, he was killed in a car accident.

The only exceptions to the ruptures have been Oleg and Valya of Kiev; they have stayed close friends and I travel regularly to Ukraine to see them. After Oleg almost died of acute appendicitis in 1996, he found work as a technician; Valya left her state-enterprise job, retrained herself as a trader in natural gas, and is doing well. They have provided me with continuity and mature perspective, and I hope to know them the rest of my life, no matter where I am.

And I do not know where I will be, for sure, next year or any other, and I relish this lack of certainty: unsure of the future, I try to live in the present, I try to follow the inscription on Kazantzakis's grave as much now as before. This is one reason I have remained in Russia: although Moscow has developed, the country seems ever to be teetering on the brink. We are all teetering on the brink, whether we admit it or not, and one day we will fall. Russia never lets me forget this; it conflates geography with this hard truth.

Still, I may move on. I have been abroad for the better part of sixteen years now, and don't expect to settle down, either in Russia or anywhere else. The sense of movement, of wedding time and space through travel, continues to excite me. The Russia I have known I carry with me in the friendships made before and after the journey, as well as in the works of Tolstoy and Nabokov, Turgenev and Chekhov, and the bard Vladimir Vysotsky. Despite all the time I have spent here, despite my fascination with the country, I have not "become Russian" (*"ty obrusel!"* my Russian friends like to say, but they are wrong). Although I have spent six years speaking Russian and writing English, to the point that at times I stumble for words in my native tongue, it now and again occurs to me that there are other horizons to set out for, that where I live has fundamentally little to do with my identity.

I hope that this book, a personal tribute not only to my passion for Russia but also to the people I met during my passage across it, will illuminate for them the grandeur of the land that will remain the love of my life, wherever I am.

Moscow, August 1, 1998